Happy Birthday to
Shelia.
Agnes Scheel Kivett
2007

The Strength
To Persevere

The Autobiography
Of Erna Kluge Scheel

Erna Kluge Scheel

Fairway Press, Lima, Ohio

THE STRENGTH TO PERSEVERE

REPRINT 2007

FIRST EDITION
Copyright © 1998 by
Erna Kluge Scheel

ISBN 0-7880-1430-7

TABLE OF CONTENTS

FOREWORD   3

CHAPTER ONE: My Father   5
  Tientsin (Heavenly Ford)   7
  1907 - A Time For Decision   8

CHAPTER TWO: The German Bride   13
  1908 - Married Life in Tientsin   14
  1909 - Year Of My Birth   16
  1913 - Mother Takes Me To Germany   19

CHAPTER THREE: Back In China With Papa   33
  Being Raised Without A Mother   36

CHAPTER FOUR: My Childhood In Tientsin   43

CHAPTER FIVE: My Troubled Youth   51
  1919 - Our First Repatriation   52
  1921 - Return To China   57
  My Animal Friends   68
  Alcohol And Abuse   70
  Back To The House Where I Was Born   72

CHAPTER SIX: My Gain, My Loss   84

CHAPTER SEVEN: On My Own   98

CHAPTER EIGHT: Married Life   112
  1931 - The Japanese in Manchuria   118
  1932 - Our First Child   119
  1934 - We Start Over In Nanking   122
  1937 - Our Second Child   124
  1937 - The Rape of Nanking   125
  1937 - Escape to Kuling   127

Evacuation to Hankow   130
We Flee to Hong Kong   134
On To Shanghai   136

CHAPTER NINE: We Begin Again In Shanghai   145
Family Health Problems   146
1940 - The Vacation In Germany   152
The Growing Business in Shanghai   166
Kiessiling and Bader - Shanghai   170
Herr Zaudig's Concern For The Children   173
Every Day Life In Shanghai   175
My Joy - The Children   180
1942 - The American Presence In China   184
The Long Arm Of Hitler   185
An Old Friend Needs Help   186
Germany Loses The War - We Lose Our Business   188

CHAPTER TEN: China Exodus   197
1945 - Our Home And Business Are Confiscated   198
1946 - A New Arrival Provides A Delayed Departure   208
1947 - Our Year Of Grace Is Over   217
The Voyage To Germany On The GENERAL BLACK   219

CHAPTER ELEVEN: Life In Post-War Germany   229
The Refugee Camps   230
Probstried - Rural Life In The Mountains   233
Shopping With Ration Cards   236
The School House Apartment   237
Protestants In A Catholic Community   238
Christmas In Germany   240
Away To School   241
The Candy Business   243
Our Refugee Vegetable Garden   244
Wild Berry Picking   245
Gathering Firewood   247
Laundry Day   249
Other New Experiences   250

A Visit From Mother   251
The Little Farmhouse   252
We Move To Munich   257
Tante Liete   264
Meager Times And Welfare   267
1951 - The Voyage To America   276

CHAPTER TWELVE: The United States - A New Beginning   281
1951 - In Cleveland With Relatives   284
1952 - New Orleans, Louisiana   292
The New Orleans Bakery - "Quality First"   298
The Christmas Rush   300
Our German Christmas Traditions Continue   301
"Success" - With A Price   304
1957 - The Separation and Divorce   316
1964 - A Brief Vacation In Germany   321
1964 To 1968 - The Healing Years   322
1968 - Brownsville Texas   324

CHAPTER THIRTEEN: The Joyful Years   328

Epilogue   335

Acknowledgments   337

The
Strength
To
Persevere

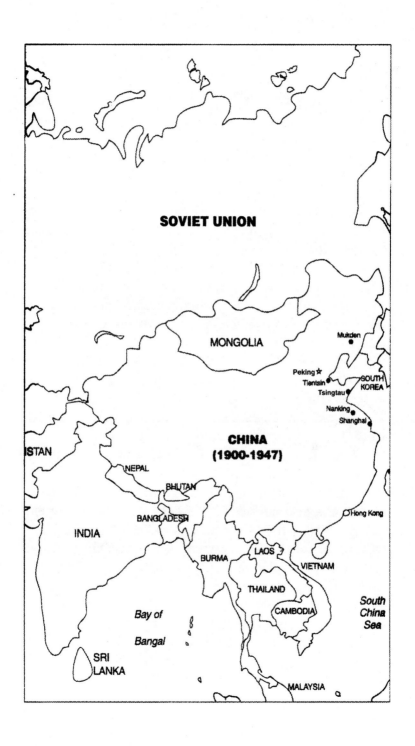

SOVIET UNION

MONGOLIA

Mukden ●

Peking ☆
Tientsin ●
Tsingtau ●

SOUTH
KOREA

Nanking ●
Shanghai ●

CHINA
(1900-1947)

ISTAN

NEPAL

BHUTAN

BANGLADESH

Hong Kong

INDIA

BURMA

LAOS

VIETNAM

THAILAND

Bay of

Bangal

CAMBODIA

South
China
Sea

SRI
LANKA

MALAYSIA

FOREWORD

The year was 1900. The Boxer Uprising was underway. It was in that year that my father, Karl Heinrich Kluge, went as a soldier to China. The German government sent troops to China to protect its interests, its people and their properties, and young Heinrich was among the troops.

The Boxers were a band of disorderly militia which had first formed in the northern provinces of China. They were in resistance to the reform movement of Emperor Kuang Hsu. The Emperor's movement was designed to transform China into a monarchy and to update the economy. The Emperor's program was in direct opposition to the power of the Dowager Empress Tz'u-hsi and her appointed Manchu officials. The Empress supported the secret society of the Boxers and upheld their rebellion.

The Boxer militia units from the north called themselves "I-ho Ch'uan," or "Righteous Harmony Fists." This name resulted in the label "Boxers" in the foreign press. They were actually anti-foreign extremists trying to get the foreigners out of the country once and for all. Their slogan was; "Save the country; destroy the foreigners!" They called any foreigner "White Devil."

Earlier, in the autumn of 1898, the Boxers had started persecuting a great number of Chinese Christians. And on December 31, 1899 they had even murdered an English missionary.

By the following June more and more Chinese Christians, who were called "Secondary Foreign Devils," were attacked. All foreigners were in imminent danger of the Boxers. On June 17, 1900, the foreign military forces seized the Taku forts to gain access to the Pei Ho River, which would open the way to Tientsin and Peking for them.

The Chinese Empress Dowager, against the advice of her counselors, wanted all foreigners killed. Mr. Von Ketteler, the German minister was murdered. This further enraged the

German government. Many other foreign ministers, their staff, missionaries, and hundreds of Chinese Christians were besieged in the Legation Quarters. Thousands of Chinese Christians, scores of Protestants and Catholic missionaries were killed. The foreign powers declared that they simply wanted to rescue their nationals, protect their interests, and ultimately suppress the Boxers.

After the period of violent reaction had swept the country, the suppression finally came. Heinrich Kluge and the other German troops fought valiantly. The Western expeditionary forces defeated the Boxers at Peking. Gradually the Chinese people calmed down. And in 1902 the Manchu government began making plans to establish a somewhat constitutional government, a welcomed improvement for the Chinese residents.

Erna Kluge Scheel in Southport, North Carolina. 1998.

CHAPTER ONE
My Father

Heinrich Kluge was a handsome man, perhaps five feet seven inches tall and powerfully built. He was slightly on the heavy side. He parted his dark blond hair on the left side. His eyes were steel gray, his nose shaped like a hawk's beak, and his moustache was full and turned up at the ends much like Kaiser Wilhelm's. Heinrich was altogether striking in his appearance.

After serving his four years and fighting in different parts of China, he was going back home to Germany. He had already telegraphed his family of his return and boarded a merchant marine transport when he sent the message. Heinrich, with his friend Otto, was leaning against the railing watching the huge cranes hoisting large bails of cotton onto the loading deck.

Coming up on the wooden plank to the lower deck they saw a stream of coolies carrying baskets of shiny black coal on their backs. A sweat band tied about their heads kept the perspiration from getting into their eyes. Their blue, sweat-drenched shirts clung to their stringy bodies. They hummed a monotonous tune, "Hee Ie Ho An," as they walked up one plank, where they disposed of their load into the coal chute and then ran swiftly down another plank.

"Poor devils!," said Otto. "I would not like to have their job."

"Neither would I," said Heinrich. "The Chinese are hard working people. I like them. These four years have opened my eyes about these folks."

"They get so little pay for their work," said Otto. "The poor get poorer and the rich get richer. Have you noticed, Heinrich?"

They were interrupted by a loud voice, "Heinrich Kluge, come immediately to the Captain's cabin." "I wonder what he wants of me?" thought Heinrich, as he adjusted his cap and walked toward the Captain's cabin. It was just a few meters away from where they were standing. Heinrich knocked at the door and a rough voice answered, "The door is open. Come in." He entered and reported, "Heinrich Kluge. You called me?"

The Captain remained seated at his desk. "Yes, there is a telegram for you from Tientsin, I think."

"May I open it here?" asked Heinrich.

"Of course. Sit down."

The Captain leaned back in his comfortable chair and lit his Meerschaum pipe. He wore a navy blue Captain's uniform. With his full beard and serious expression, he looked like a Captain. Heinrich took his pen knife from his pocket and slit the envelope carefully. The Chief Mess Sergeant of the French Arsenal in Tientsin was offering him a good job as their head butcher. Heinrich rose from his chair, ran his fingers through his sparse blonde hair and went to the porthole. He thought of his job he had left just recently where he was familiar with the people and the working conditions.

"Well, Kluge?" the Captain interrupted his thoughts. "Good news?"

Heinrich handed him the telegram with a smile.

"This sounds like a good offer," said the Captain. "Will you accept it?"

"I don't know," Heinrich sighed, "I have already telegraphed home that I was coming. They will be disappointed if I don't return."

"You can save money and go home in a few years. You are still young. The boat won't leave until morning, with the tide. This will give you ample time to get your belongings and be on your way to the Arsenal. Stop and send another telegram."

6

"Thank you, Captain. I do think this is a good chance for me."

"Good luck, Kluge."

Otto was still standing at the railing. "What was this all about?" he asked. Heinrich told him.

"You can go home and open your own butchery in Landeshut in a few years. Now, let us go and get your luggage."

They called two rickshaws — one for Heinrich and the other for his belongings.

Heinrich turned and waved to Otto and his friends and shouted, "Grüsst mir die Heimat" (Greet my Homeland.)

They answered, "Alles Gute, Heinrich."

His first stop was the telegraph office. He had tears in his eyes when he sent the message, "I am not coming home. Will write." It was quite late when Heinrich arrived at the Arsenal. The sentry at the gate recognized Heinrich and greeted him "Bon soir, Monsieur Kluge."

Heinrich answered, "Bon soir, Pierre. Have you a place for me to stay the night? I don't want to disturb Monsieur Le Sergeant this late."

"Yes, I was notified of your possible arrival."

It was 1904 when my father, Heinrich Kluge, decided to stay in Tientsin, China, to work at the French Arsenal as head butcher. China would be my birth place.

Tientsin (Heavenly Ford)

Tientsin became the third largest city in China, after Shanghai and Peking. It is located east of Hopeh province about 96 kilometers south of Central Peking and 35 kilometers inland from the Bo Hai Gulf, a shallow inlet of the Yellow Sea.

Tientsin had been an important transport and trading center since the Yuan (Mongol) Dynasty of 1206 to 1308. It was the leading port in North China, a city noted for its woven handicraft products, terra cotta figurines, painted wood block prints and very expensive seafood cuisine.

The Hai Ho river flowed through Tientsin eastward into the Port of Tang Ku. The climate averages 39 degrees Fahrenheit (4° C) in winter and 84 degrees (29° C) in summer. Severe winter storms were common but typhoons seldom occurred. The city stands at an elevation of less than fifteen feet or five meters above sea level.

When the western powers tried to get a foothold in Tientsin in 1858, designating it a treaty port, China refused. Then, the British and French governments signed treaties establishing their concessions from China. Later, between 1898 and 1902, concessions were granted Japan, Russia, Austria-Hungary, Italy, Belgium and Germany. Western style buildings were constructed and electric trams were installed, port facilities improved, and textile industries expanded. By 1900 Tientsin became an important shipping center in China.

Trade with European countries was booming. Railroads were being constructed and mining companies sold the latest mining equipment. The Kailan Mining Company was one of the largest German mining enterprises. The Chinese government and its people had gained confidence in foreigners. The German community grew immensely in Tientsin and so did the communities of the other nations.

1907 - A Time For Decision

Heinrich was appreciated by the soldiers of the French Arsenal as a "Meister" of his trade for he knew the specialities of the French palate; Boudin Blanche and Boudin Rouge, the tastiest sausages ever. (Boudin Blanche was made of liver and bacon which went through the meat grinder three times. Bread and spices gave it that special taste. Boudin Rouge was made of finely ground meat, blood, spices and bread. Both the size of Knackwurst, they were served fried with steamed peeled potatoes and braised apples). Another specialty was Pate' de fois Gras, a goose liver sausage. There was no doubt that Heinrich could have continued to work at the arsenal permanently. But he was ambitious and became increasingly restless.

In 1907, after three years at the arsenal, Heinrich wondered if he should go back to Germany or establish his future in Tientsin. He soon found himself in the German Consul's office seeking advice. "After my experience at the French Arsenal as their butcher, I am thinking of operating my own Schlächterei (Butchery), Herr Konsul. I have saved some money."

"Excellent!" the Consul replied. "There is room for a good German Schlächterei and I know of a good location across from La Banqü de L'indochine that is vacant at this time."

A bell rang and the Consul asked to be excused. His German secretary explained, "Herr Konsul will be busy now, but he wants you to see Herr Wiehert in charge of the Chamber of Commerce. He can supply you with names of firms in Germany where you can order machines and utensils for your business." She showed him the way. On the way home Heinrich stopped at the vacant house. Heinrich told the Rickshaw Coolie, "Den Yi Don" (Wait a little). Heinrich knocked at the door and shortly a distinguished looking elderly man appeared. He wore a white silk ishang (robe) making him appear taller than he actually was. A thick plaited cue hung down his back and a small cap like a beanie adorned with buttons covered the top of his head. He looked at Heinrich through small, metal rimmed spectacles and bowed. "My name is Liang Chang. What can I do for you?" Chang spoke some English, while Heinrich spoke a little Chinese and English, so they managed to communicate.

Heinrich introduced himself..., "this house is for rent, isn't it?"

"Yes, it will be available in a few months," Chang answered. "Come inside. We can talk and have some tea."

9

Heinrich's host opened a door to a spacious back room of the building. It had a large oval shaped gray carpet with a floral design of blue, red, brown and green around its border. Heinrich noted a richly carved teak wood table with straight backed chairs placed beneath the window. Two evergreen plants in blue and white china containers , along with the fine silk scrolls hanging on the walls, gave the room an oriental look.

"What kind of business is yours, Mr. Kluge?" Chang asked as he poured the tea.

"I'm a butcher."

"This location would be good for a butchery. Would you like to see the house?"

"Yes, I am very interested," Heinrich told him.

When they finished their tea, Chang said he would show the ground floor store first. The house itself was larger than it had looked from in front of the bank across the street. It was a two story, modern gray brick building of European architecture.

The store had two large display windows facing the bank. It was used to display carpets. A stairway led to the upper floor with a large room, two smaller ones, and a bath with the unusual facilities of both hot and cold running water.

In the back was a house with four small rooms for servant quarters. A large main floor room was used to weave carpets.

Heinrich and Chang returned through the back yard and had more tea. Chang asked, "Are you married, Mr. Kluge?"

"No, I'm not married yet, but I hope to find a German wife."

They agreed upon the amount of rent and Heinrich told Chang he worked for the French Arsenal.

"I will come in eight or ten days to bring you the key-money if that is alright with you," he told Chang.

"When do you think you will open your butchery?"

"It will be a year because I have to order machines and utensils from Germany."

This pleased Liang Chang since he wanted to liquidate the carpet business and move it to the Russian concession across the river. They shook hands. It was as good as in writing.

On his way to the Arsenal, Heinrich thought of all the things he had to do. He was glad the house was taken care of, and he was not going to quit his job yet. First, he needed to get in touch with the Alexander Werke in Germany, a company specializing in outfitting butcher shops. Once he knew the machines and utensils were on board the ship, he would give notice. The Sergeant was not going to be happy because he would be hard to replace.

After several trips to town, the Deutsch-Asiatische Bank gave him a loan without any difficulties. The restaurant and seven rooms had to be furnished. He thought it was a considerable loan to make.

Heinrich told the Sergeant of his intentions.

"Didn't we treat you right?" he asked.

"That's not it, but I want to have my own business. I could furnish the Arsenal with the meat and sausages you need. I will give you a special discount."

"We can get to some agreement, I am sure," the Sergeant replied.

Heinrich thought to himself it would be a good income for a start. The businessman in him came out. The months were passing quickly and there was much to do. Heinrich wanted to find a wife. He knew he could not find one in Tientsin. The daughter of a doctor, diplomat or wealthy businessman would not want to be a butcher's wife. Standing behind the counter selling sausage and cutting meat, bacon and ham all day long was hard work. Heinrich had no other choice. He decided to put an advertisement in *The Berliner Tage Blatt* newspaper in Germany. His ad read:

11

Wife Wanted

Young German woman needed as a helpmate for nice looking 26-year old man. Help in prospering butcher business; willing to relocate in China. Photograph requested. Train fare will be forwarded immediately upon acceptance. Contact: Karl Heinrich Kluge, 204 Rü de France, Tientsin, China.

Heinrich waited, hoping for a positive response to his advertisement. Daily he checked the mail, anxious to learn if someone suitable might respond. He so hoped someone like himself might be in a similar situation. He had little hope of ever finding a suitable German girl to marry in Tientsin. Daily he visited the room upstairs which he had picked out for himself and his new bride. He had purchased new furniture and a beautiful carpet for the floor as well as pictures for the wall.

CHAPTER TWO
The German Bride

Else Louise Marta Frieda Hellene Voss was her full name. She sat with her mother at the kitchen table in the dim light looking at the newspaper. It was a dreary morning, but Else's infant son, Walter, cooed on his tiny feather Pallet on the floor. "It's a good opportunity, Mutter. You and Vater forbade me to marry Wilhelm. It would mean a new life for me."

"Hush, Else! No more talk about your Walter Wilhelm Kleman. Your Vater and I will not allow you to marry that happy-go-lucky fellow. He may be well-to-do but he is not your sort. He shouldn't have gotten a girl like you pregnant in the first place."

"But Mutter, we are in love."

"No more about it, Else."

"Then I shall answer this advertisement and have a photograph made and send it to China as soon as possible."

"Else!"

"I have no trade, Mutter. Shall I live here in Schwerin, Mecklenburg all my life with you and Vater? Does not little Walter need a chance? This advertisement says; "prospering butcher business." Perhaps I could send money for Walter, Mutter."

"Ach! Else, must it come to this?"

"Ja, Mutter. I must get away. Far away. China would be far enough away. I could start a new life, away from the townspeople, away from my Wilhelm."

"You are a wise one, my teure Else. You are right of course. Drink your sweet chocolate now and we will talk about it with your Vater this evening."

After supper Else approached her father. "Vater, I would like to talk to you."

"What is it my child?"

Else showed him the ad in the newspaper. "I have decided to accept this," she said.

It became very quiet in the kitchen. Her father took the newspaper and laid it aside. He looked at his daughter for a while, then said in a firm voice, "I think this is the right thing for you to do."

Else jumped up and hugged her father. " Thank you so much, Vater! I'm glad you have agreed with my decision. Tomorrow, after I have my picture taken, I shall go to the town hall and get all the information I need."

In China, Heinrich's heart swelled as he got the news saying out loud, "My bride is coming!"

Else made the long journey to Tientsin on the Trans-Siberian Railroad. She had left her heart and her son in Germany. Her mother and father promised to raise little Walter.

1908 - Married Life in Tientsin

It was September 1908 when Heinrich and Else married in a quiet ceremony and went on a short honeymoon. Afterwards she wrote:

Dearest Mutter and Vater,

Yesterday Heinrich and I returned from our honeymoon to Pei-Tai-Ho, a beach resort. Heinrich had made reservations for a comfortable room in a German boarding house. We could stay only a few days because of the business, but it gave us some time to get to know one another. Heinrich's butchery is going very well along with his restaurant and boarding house. He is proud of it and I feel he is also proud to have a German wife. Most of the time I am selling in the butcher shop, especially when Heinrich is in the workshop butchering or making sausages. He has Chinese helpers who followed him from the Arsenal. When business is slow in the shop I stay in the restaurant. There is always someone

there, either one of the boarders or a traveling sales-
man, perhaps even a sailor. Most are Germans but,
some are Frenchmen.

Life is so different here. I don't do any cook-
ing or cleaning. We have servants for that. One of
them speaks a little German. I communicate through
him to the others. They are all good and hard work-
ers. I mostly supervise and sell in the store. I like
that.

How is my little Walter? I miss him. I am not
telling Heinrich yet that Walter is my son, and not
my nephew, and I feel I need to know Heinrich bet-
ter. I miss my family and Walter.

Love, Else

Else found it hard to adjust to her new life. Heinrich was
from Landeshut, Silesia, a textile town. Most of the town's
inhabitants worked at these textile mills. Heinrich's father
was a weaver. They were poor. Heinrich had to quit school at
an early age and worked to help support the family. First he
worked in a bakery but he did not like that. He always wanted
to be a butcher and so his father found a vacancy as an apprentice at the a butchery. And so, Heinrich had started in this
trade. He never learned to read and write well, but, he helped
support his parents and his two older sisters.

Else's life had been very different. She was born in
Schwerin, Mecklenburg, located in the northeastern part of
Germany which was founded by Henry the Lion in 1161.
Destructive fires and hardships from the Thirty Years War
destroyed many of the old palaces and ancient houses. One
very conspicuous building was still standing. It was the former
Ducal Palace which had been built in 1844 in the French
Renaissance style. In Else's time, the Duke and his family
lived in the palace. Else's father was his Lordship's Taylor,

and Else often accompanied him to the palace and played with the Duke's children.

Else told Heinrich that she had a nephew in Germany and wished to send him a little money now and then. "Very well," Heinrich agreed, "A few dollars occasionally will be alright." Else was pleased and was determined to be a good helpmate. She always dressed nicely, wearing a starched white apron over her dress when she worked in the butcher shop. The customers liked Heinrich's pretty young wife. Heinrich worked hard and the business grew. He raised his own hogs, slaughtered his own calves and oxen. He also cured hams and bacon. He made delicious sausages — both fine and coarse liver sausages. His calf liver and truffle liver sausages were the most asked for by his customers.

"Ah, Herr Kluge," they said, "This is the most delicious sausage in all of Tientsin." They also liked his frankfurters, especially when they had just come out of the smoke house. Also, he canned several kinds of sausages, sauerkraut, cheese and marinated herring.

Heinrich's homemade cheeses were the size of English muffins and he called them "Harzer Handkäse." He ripened them on a board in a warm place, then he stacked them in an earthen vessel and covered them with beer for several days. They were delicious. The smell of the cheese was strong but the customers loved it. Heinrich could never make enough of them.

1909 - Year Of My Birth

I was born on December 26, 1909, the daughter of Heinrich and Else Kluge. They named me Erna Dorothea Else. My mother was very proud of me. She had a photograph taken of herself and me. She sat in a carved wooden armchair holding me on her lap. She wore a pretty, dark, taffeta dress trimmed with fine ivory colored lace around her neck. Her auburn hair was puffed out softly around her face and gathered into a bun on top of her head. There was no smile on her face. She sat erect, and although her face was stern, it wore a somewhat sad expression. She had dressed me in a long white dress trimmed with lace.

Even with a new baby my parent's marriage was not happy. Mother and Father were too different; they both were too strong-willed. Another year slowly passed for them. Mother dressed very "up-to-date." She bought her clothes at a fashionable dress shop. She had my dresses made by a Chinese Taylor who came to the house and took measurements. The following week he would return with a well made dress.

The clothing that Mother and I wore was quite expensive. Father was not pleased and started to check the cash box more closely.

He was suspicious and on one occasion intercepted a letter from Mother's parents. Near the end of the letter it read;

> *"Your little Walter is doing fine. He is growing so round and can say a few words now. Don't worry about him, Teure. The money you send is sufficient for his food and for a little clothing.*
>
> *Two weeks ago, however, I took him to the doctor. He had a little croup. So everything costs money. We miss you, Else. Take care of yourself. We are loving Walter for you. Your son looks like his mother.*
>
> *Love, Mutti"*

Heinrich reread the letter. At first he was stunned. Then he grew angry. He took the letter and thrust it into Mother's face. "Liar!" he yelled. "You led me to believe I was marrying an innocent German girl! You had a bastard!" Mother's diary revealed that he grabbed her, shook her, then slapped her in the face. She tried to get free of him and run but he held her fiercely. Mother was pregnant again and reminded

17

Heinrich of the fact. She feared she might lose the baby. Still, he would not let her go.

"And whose baby might I believe you are carrying now?" he spat at her, "answer me!!!"

"You know the baby is yours, Heinrich!!! I have always been faithful to you. How could I be otherwise? I am always in the butcher shop!!!"

After this the marriage got worse. Father did not trust Mother anymore. He became immensely jealous of other men and he took to drinking a lot. When he had too much to drink he mistreated Mother verbally and physically. My little brother, Erwin, was born soon after but lived only six months. Father even accused Mother of not taking good care of his son and allowing him to die. Mother was hurt and the marriage continued to worsen. She knew this marriage could not last and wished for someone to help her. Mother had to be careful that the servants and boarders did not suspect her intentions of leaving. She decided to confide in Frau Goldau, her next-door neighbor, whom she believed she could trust. She had visited Frau Goldau in the past. So, one afternoon, Mother took me over to see her. Frau Goldau noticed right away that something was troubling Mother and inquired.

"Oh, Heinrich is drinking heavily and is impossible to live with," Mother told our neighbor. Frau Goldau gave me some cookies and sent me out to the back yard to be with her husband. "Tell him to give these to the dogs." Then she asked Mother if I could have a sugar cookie. Mother agreed and I skipped happily out the door.

"Onkel Goldau!" I called, "I have some cookies for Fritz and Max!" (their two Irish Setters) I ran into Onkel Goldau's open arms. He caught me and set me on his shoulders like he always did. We went to the dog pen where Onkel sat me down and I told the dogs to "Whuff" for their cookies. I also got a cookie for Wolf, our German Police dog and Schnapps, our hunting dog. After a while Mother called and we went home.

Secretly, Mother had begun saving money. She hid it behind a loose board in the bookcase in our parlor. With Tante Goldau's help she applied for her travel papers and train tickets. The four years Mother spent in Tientsin were very difficult for her. The life-style was different, language a problem, and Papa's attitude was unbearable. Not a day went by without a quarrel, abusive words and insulting language — in front of customers. Her only thought was to get away. But how?

Little by little Mother gathered clothing and the necessary items for the ten day train trip to Germany. She kept them at Tante Goldau's house for safekeeping. Then one day as Papa went to the slaughter house we gathered the last few necessary items and went to Tante Goldau's house to pick up our belongings. Onkel Goldau took us to a friend's house which was not far from the train station. The train left the following day for Manchuria where we made connections with the Trans-Siberian train.

Mother left this note for Papa:

"Heinrich:

I am taking Erna and going home to my parents. I cannot bear to continue to live this way. I hope you will understand.

Else"

I was three and one half years old at that time.

1913 - Mother Takes Me To Germany
From Mother's diary:

"The Trans-Siberian train departs Manchuria every fortnight. Never had I imagined such a bitter ending to our marriage. I am returning to Vater and Mutter and am bringing back another little child. How is this all going to work out? Lord, my God, help me."

19

A loud screeching noise woke me up. The dim light was hardly enough for me to recognize where I was. The monotonous "click-de-clack, click-de-clack" made me realize that I was on the train. At that moment the light went on and Mother came into the cabin. She took me in her arms, soothing me, "don't cry Mausi, the train had to stop for a bridge." She carried me to the window to see the river the train was crossing. "Where are we going? I want my Papa," I cried. Mother held me tightly. "Kleines, (little one)" she whispered, "Papa is not with us." She explained that we were going to my grandparents. I wanted to know why but Mother did not answer. She just held me close and wrote in her diary.

"Let us see if the porter has made some fresh tea in the samovar and if we can get some warm milk for you in the dining car." After Mother had tea, we walked two cars to the rear of the train to the dining car. It was dimly lit as it was not dinner time. The tables were covered with white tablecloths and in the center stood a vase with fresh flowers. Mother ordered a cup of warm milk for me and we returned to our cabin.

At the next station a Russian lady and her seven year old daughter Katja joined us. The lady spoke some German. Katja and I enjoyed playing games. In Moscow we said good-by. We stayed in a hotel in Moscow until we made connections with the train to Schwerin where my grandparents lived.

My Grandfather and my half brother Walter were at the station. Walter looked handsome in his navy blue sailor suit. Grandfather took me in his arms saying, "komm, Kleines" (come, little one). After getting our luggage we went to the horse and buggy which was waiting for us. We drove to the apartment where my Grandmother was waiting for us with a warm meal. After supper Walter showed me the apartment. There were two bedrooms, a living room, kitchen and a small room which Walter would share with me. When bedtime came I had to go to bed in a strange room. It was Walter's bedroom which was already small and cramped without me. Grandmother brought a narrow cot for me to sleep on. She and Mother tucked me in, covering me with a thick feather comforter. Mother kissed me and said, "gute Nacht, Mausi" (goodnight my little mouse). They went out and closed the door. I buried my head in the feather pillow and cried. I missed my room at home in China and longed for my Papa. I did not hear Walter get out of his bed and come to his newly discovered sister. But I soon felt his small hands stroking my hair. "Don't cry, Sissy," he said, "It will be all right." The soothing little man's voice hushed me and I soon fell asleep. It took but a few days for me to get used to the surroundings and relatives. The only thing I liked about my new home at first, was my "big brother," Walter. The apartment and all my strange relatives were new to me. I felt afraid and clung to my mother. One morning after breakfast Grandmother said, "you have been wanting to go to the park. Today is such a nice day, Walter can take you when he comes home from school at 1:00. Would you like that?"

"Yes Oma!!" I replied, joyously.

She had saved some stale bread for the ducks. I was so happy. It is fun to have a big brother, I thought. After Walter had a snack, we left. I wanted to know why he was taking an empty can along. "We are looking for earth worms to feed the ducks," he said.

"Earth worms?" I asked, and wrinkled my nose.

"Come, I will show you," he said.

We soon came to a bridge. Just a few steps down were some rocks with grass growing in between. As he lifted a rock he called to me, "come look, Erna. See the worms crawling there?" He lifted one with his fingers and held it up to me with a funny smile.

"Yuck! I don't want to touch it, Walter."

"They don't bite. You are acting silly," he said, but he could not persuade me.

"What are you going to do with them?" I asked.

"Feed the ducks," he replied, "They like them."

Walter took my hand and we walked a short distance to the Stadt Park. There were many big trees. Walter said they were mostly oak and maple trees. He picked up two leaves and showed me the difference between the long shaped oak leaf and the broader maple leaf. But I wanted to see the ducks. "We are on our way to the pond," he said. He only wanted to show me the different leaves and flowers. "All these flowers are roses," he said.

"I know what roses look like. We have roses in Tientsin too," I answered sheepishly. We could see the pond already and I soon heard the ducks.

A little to our right was the playground. I could hear the children. But we turned left to the big pond. It was very large. Many ducks were swimming around and a little further to the center of the pond were a number of white swans. "Let me throw some bread to them, Walter!," I pleaded. The ducks drew closer but the swans would not come. I could not throw the bread far enough to reach them. They spread their wings and swam to fetch the bread. It did not take long before we were out of bread.

"Let us go to the playground," said Walter. But the swings were all filled with other children, so we went home. It was a fun afternoon.

After supper we usually spent the evening in the kitchen which was a cozy place. The radio transmitted German folk music. While Grandfather read the Tages Zeitung (Daily News), Grandmother finished the supper dishes. Walter did his homework, working on his "figures." I knew because he was chewing on his upper lip. He looked so funny when he did that. He got angry when I teased him about it so I kept still and continued working on my puzzle.

Grandmother hung her apron on a hook behind the door and approached the table. Grandfather handed her a section of the newspaper. She looked at the date and then to the calendar on the wall. "Oh, I forgot to change the date," I heard her say. "Today is June 28, not the June 27," The year was 1914. "Come and sit down," Grandfather said, " Let Walter change the date."

Except for the music and the ticking of the clock it was quiet in the kitchen for a while. Suddenly the music stopped and the announcer said, "latest news!" We looked up and listened. I heard the word "assassinate" and asked what it meant. "Hush!,." said Grandfather, "I'll tell you later."

During the next few days my grandparents spoke a lot about war. Even Walter related that the older boys in school were talking about the war too.

"We will see what the next few weeks bring us," Grandfather said.

Walter told me that war meant fighting. I did not understand what was going on. My grandparents discussed what was happening. The Austrian Archduke, Francis Ferdinand, had been assassinated. I learned then that "assassinated" meant murdered.

With her experience in Papa's business Mother soon found work in a nearby town at a well established butchery. This meant that she would only be home on weekends. She liked her job but I missed her very much. The next week when she left, I held on to her skirt and cried, "Mutti, take me with you please."

"Mausi, I can't take you now. I will soon find an apartment near my work. It should not be long. She knelt down and whispered, "Now, Mausi, be a good little girl. I love you. I will be back in a few days."

Weeks went by and Mother had not found an apartment. It was getting too much for Grandmother to take care of both Walter and me. Also, Grandfather was not feeling too well at that time. When Mother returned from her work I heard her saying to Grandmother, "Yes, I can understand that. Let me

23

talk to Cousin Karla and see if she can take Erna until I find something. Magdeburg is only 150 kilometers from here. The train stops there and I could get off and see Erna."

Having to adjust to another move frightened me. I told Grandmother that I would help her. I did not want to go to Aunt Karla. I begged her to let me stay with her.

"Erna," she said, "You know Tante Karla was here the other day and brought you that cute doll. You will like her and it will only be for a short while." She hugged me and lifted me to her lap.

The following weekend Mother took me to Uncle and Aunt Georges. They lived on the ground floor of an apartment building. The windows were tall and reminded me of my bedroom in Tientsin. I could sit for hours at the windows watching the people walk by. And when the rain splashed on the sidewalk I thought of Papa and my dog, Wolf. Wolf loved the rain, except lightening and thunder brought him into the house where he would hide under the table.

Tears came.

"Why are you crying, Mausi?" Aunt Georges asked. I did not answer. I just hid my head in her lap.

"Tante" Karla Georges was a kind person. She wore glasses resembling Oma's and she smelled so good like the roses in the park. I loved to sit on her lap and cuddle my head on her soft bosom and listen to the fairy tales she read to me. Her voice was very soft and I especially enjoyed the story of the Seven Little Goats.

One day "Onkel Georges" (I called him by his last name) showed me a photograph of himself in a military uniform.

"You look so handsome," I said, "and your moustache was bigger than it is now. I like that uniform too. It looks so good on you."

"Your Papa wore the same uniform," he said." We were in the war together in China."

24

When he mentioned Papa I wanted to know if Mother and I would go back to Papa soon. I told Uncle Georges, "I have not seen Papa for such a long time." I started crying, "I want to see my Papa."

Uncle Georges did not say a word. He just patted my cheek and rocked me. Just then Aunt Georges entered the room.

"Look, Mausi, what I have for you," and she handed me a small brown paper bag. I opened it and cheered. "Look, Onkel Georges, a new storybook!" "Thank you, Tante," I said. Then I asked if she would read me a story before I went to bed.

"Sure, Mausi," she said.

Aunt Georges read a story to me every night.

Mother came every week-end. I was always thrilled to see her. On her last visit she said, "Mausi, next week I will take you with me. I have found an apartment for us."

I jumped around the kitchen for joy.

Saturday we had a fun day at the zoo. Mother brought a sack of snacks to feed the animals. The monkeys were so funny when they reached through the cage for the nuts. The brown bears stood on their hind legs begging for a snack. I also remember the elephants reaching with their long trunks for snacks. Aunt Georges had lunch ready for us when we got home.

It was raining slightly as Mother left that Sunday afternoon. I watched her from the window. She wore an olive green suit with a soft light yellow scarf draped around her pretty face. In one hand she carried her umbrella and in the other a suitcase. The strong wind blew her pleated skirt to one side. Little did I realize that this was the last time I would see my mother in many years.

On the Monday after that weekend Aunt Georges was ironing in the kitchen and I was looking at a storybook when the doorbell rang. She was expecting the caller. "Stay here,

Erna," she said and went to open the door. She let the caller into the Gute Stube (good room). After a while Aunt Georges called, "Erna, come in here. This is Fräulein Gertraut." I curtsied and gave her my hand. She was a pretty blond woman with big brown eyes and rosy cheeks.

"Come and sit with us a while," Aunt Karla said. Fräulein Gertraut asked, "How old are you, Erna?"

I answered, "four and a little more," and raised four fingers.

"She will be five in December," Aunt Karla added.

"Fräulein Gertraut lives in Tientsin," Aunt Karla said. "She is here to buy her trousseau because she is getting married next month."

When I asked if she knew my Papa, she said, "yes. I have been to his butcher shop several times. I am going back to where your Papa lives. I want to take you with me to see him. Would you like that?"

"Oh yes. I want to see my Papa. When can we go? And Mutti can come too!"

I had no way of knowing that my father had filed for divorce and had obtained custody of me. In those days the divorce laws were severe. He had only to say that Mother had deserted him and kidnaped his daughter. Through the German Consulate he was able to arrange for a young German lady, who was going to Germany to buy her trousseau, to bring me back to Tientsin. This young lady was Gertraut.

"Your Mutti is working and can't come right now. She can come later," said Gertraut.

After a few days Gertraut came again to pick me up. Tante Karla had packed a small suitcase containing my clothing.

When my Mother returned on the weekend to take me to the new apartment that she had rented I was gone. What a shock this must have been for her. I don't know to this day what Aunt Karla said to Mother or why she let Gertraut take me without Mother knowing. Even years later when Aunt Karla wanted to see me I refused because I had not forgiven her.

Gertraut and I traveled for eight days on the Trans-Siberian train. This was the very last train leaving for China as the war in Europe broke out in 1914. Mother's hands were tied. There was nothing she could do as all connections to China were cut off.

The cabin in the train had two lower and two upper beds. Gertraut and I occupied the lower one and two English ladies the upper one. Gertraut tucked me in bed and asked if I wanted to say my goodnight prayers. I asked, "prayer?" She lifted me on her lap and showed me how to fold my hands. I remember to this day the German prayer she taught me. Translated it said:

"I am small. My heart is clean.

Nobody shall live in it but Jesus alone."

Gertraut had planted a seed in my heart. We prayed every evening and she read to me many stories about Jesus and his angels.

I was almost five and was fascinated by the things that we saw while passing through Manchuria. I saw some strange looking animals. "Oh, look," I cried to my guardian. "What are those strange looking things with the humps on their backs?"

Gertraut laughed. "Those are camels. They have humps on their backs so they won't get thirsty when they are in the desert and there is no water available for them" she explained. "Oh," I nodded wisely. I stared at the animals and they stared back as they trotted along side the train tracks. I listened to the click-clacking of the train wheels as we rode along. The rhythmic clicking reminded me of the trip to Oma. I scooted closer to Gertraut. She put her arms around me and smiled. I nestled my head in the warm curve of her firm young arm and was soon fast asleep.

Heinrich and Else Kluge on their honeymoon trip to Pei-Tai-Ho
China. 1908.

Ducal Palace in Mecklenburg, Germany where Else often played
with the Duke's children. 1844.

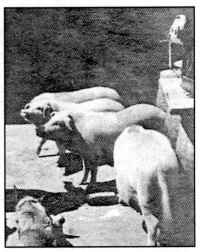

Pigs at Heinrich Kluge's butcher shop in Tientsin, China. 1908.

The fate of pigs that went to Heinrich Kluge's butcher shop in Tientsin, China. 1908.

Else Kluge holding infant Erna in Tientsin, China. 1910.

Child Erna with mother on picnic during Chinese New Year.
Tientsin, China. 1912.

Erna at age 3 ° years.
Tientsin, China. 1914.

"Aunt" Karla Georges in Magdeburg, Germany. 1914.

"Uncle" Georges in German military uniform during the Boxer Rebellion in China. 1902.

"Uncle" Georges in Magdeburg, Germany. 1914.

CHAPTER THREE
Back In China With Papa

The next thing I remembered we were at the station in Tientsin and there stood my father waiting for me. He was standing on the platform wearing a furry winter coat. Next to him stood an elderly Chinese man, wearing an ishang and a little cap on his head. He was holding a blue enameled teapot. They made a funny pair I thought.

My Father gathered me up into his arms and I saw tears rolling down his cheeks.

"Don't cry, Papa, it will be alright," I said. I cuddled my head in the soft warm fur of his coat and clasped my arms around his neck.

Papa greeted Gertraut and I heard him say,"I hope you had a good trip and Erna was not too much of a burden."

"No, Herr Kluge, Erna was looking forward to seeing her Papa." She looked up. "Here is my fiancé and my mother coming. Auf Wiedersehen, Herr Kluge. I'll see you in a few days." She hugged me and rushed to see her family and fiancé.

I was back in China. But Papa needed a housekeeper or someone to care for me. Since the Goldaus had helped Mother when she and I left for Germany, Papa would not let me go to them. A young German couple, Herr (Mr.) and Frau (Mrs.) Corinth (who knew my parents and the situation my Father was in) offered to take me into their home until they had children of their own. They knew Father had no one to look after me while attending to his business. Herr and Frau Corinth were very kind to me. As I became closer to the couple I started to call them "Onkel" (Uncle) and "Tante" (Aunt) and regarded them as family.

Tante Corinth had brown eyes like the ones of a deer. Her auburn hair was pulled back in a chignon and her round face always seemed to be a little flushed. Tante Corinth's husband was a prosperous interior decorator and architect. Almost all the furnishings for bank offices in the area were made in his workshop.

One of my first remembrances at the Corinth's was not pleasant because of something that I did. They had just had the banister painted in white enamel and it was still wet when I went up the steps. All the way up, with my fingernails, I scratched all kinds of designs into each banister post. It was such fun! But Frau Corinth did not think it was fun. She was not happy when she saw my art work. She took me by the hand and went up a few steps with me and said, "Now, Erna, you know better than that. To scratch up all these posts was very naughty. For shame! Don't you ever do that again!"

I was frightened and ashamed. It was all I could do to hold back my tears.

"The painters will have to paint them again tomorrow." She ended her speech by spanking my little rear end until it was hot. I didn't realize at the time how much I deserved it.

A few mornings later I was playing in the garden with a water hose. As the water was not purified, we could only drink the water after it had been boiled. We learned that we could not drink water from the faucet at an early age. I decided to be bold and drink the water anyway. Frau Corinth saw me from the kitchen window drinking from the hose. The water was running down my clean play dress. She called me into the kitchen and asked, "Mausi, did you drink from the hose?"

"Oh, no!" I lied. I looked at my dress which was proof of my guilt. Then I looked at Frau Corinth. I could see that I had disappointed her again. I felt bad and said, "Don't be angry. I'm sorry." I was prepared for another spanking but she surprised me.

"It's all right Erna, but don't forget, unboiled water could make you very, very sick. And you must always tell the truth." I soon cheered up and went to the yard to play.

One sunny afternoon Tante Corinth and I went for a walk. I could hear chirping. "What is that noise, Tante Corinth?" I asked. "I think it comes from that big straw basket. Let's go and see," she said. "Look, they are little ducklings and baby chicks. May I hold one?" I asked. The vendor gave me one of the ducklings.

Tante said, "Coming Sunday is Palm Sunday and the following Sunday is Easter. Why don't we buy a few?" We have a fenced-in area in the back yard where we can keep them." I was so happy. Every day I went outdoors to play with them. They followed me wherever I went. One afternoon I finished playing with them and was going home. One duckling followed me and, as I stepped through the gate, it snapped shut so quickly that the little duckling was caught and crushed to death. I burst out crying and called for Tante.

She came running and saw the accident. Kneeling beside me she hugged me and said, "Don't cry, Mausi, you could not help it. Come, we will bury it under the lilac bush." I was upset for a quite a while.

Onkel Corinth came home for lunch. He seemed excited and disturbed. "What is bothering you?" Tante Corinth asked her husband. He said, "War has broken out in Europe and all connections with Germany have been broken off."

"Heinrich surely will be glad that Erna is here," Tante Corinth said.

"Does this mean that Mutti can't come?" I asked.

"Not for a while," Onkel Corinth replied. After that Mother was very seldom mentioned. I began thinking less and less about her.

The Corinth's had a cook, a house boy, and a gardener. Although Tante Corinth would cook a special dish, the cook did most of the regular cooking. The house boy did all the cleaning but their bedroom. Tante would not let him go in there. Why, I did not know. One day Tante told me why. She told me that after they had returned from their honeymoon, she saw the Chinese barber go into the bedroom to shave her husband. She had him out of there in a jiffy because she believed he was not clean enough. From that day on, Onkel had to do his own shaving. I thought that was funny. Papa had a barber that came every morning to shave him and every few weeks a man came to pedicure his feet. Before entering he always knocked on a hollow bamboo box rather than knock on the door. "clack —, clack, clack."

Tante Corinth and I went often to see Papa. Wolf, our German Shepherd, always came running when he saw me. He licked my hands and followed me wherever I went. Papa always asked, "Mausi, have you been a good girl? Did you listen to Tante Corinth?" (He had been really upset when he heard about the bannister artwork and my lying about the water). On one trip, while I played with Wolf (and the new kitten Papa had found in the gutter almost drowned after a heavy rain), I heard Tante Corinth tell Papa, "Herr Kluge, I am expecting a baby. You will have to find someone for Erna to stay with."

Papa told Tante he was happy for her.

Being Raised Without A Mother

Between the Amah (the Chinese maid) who came in the morning and the Russian traveling saleslady, Ludnilla Resnikoff, who stayed in our boarding house, I was somewhat taken care of for a while. No housekeeper would stay long with us because Papa became too friendly with them. I asked our last housekeeper about this and she said, "Your Papa likes to touch me after he has some beer and I don't like that." I didn't quite understand and decided to ask Tante Corinth but I don't think I ever did. I was looking forward to these days when she would come, especially since she brought little Bernhard along. Every time she would remind me, "Wash your hands before you play with the baby." I always forgot. He smiled and could sit up now. The last time Tante came she

36

said, "Erna, we have been talking about school for some time now. The time has arrived for you to go."

"Do I have to go to that convent?" I asked.

Papa joined us after hearing my last words and said, "Mausi, you will surely like it there. You remember when we went last month the nuns were so friendly and you saw all the girls?"

I remembered and I didn't want to go.

Papa continued, "You will come home every Saturday and Sunday. Next week Tante Corinth will go with you to buy your new uniforms (white blouse and blue jumper). Erna, you will also need new shoes, underwear, sweater and winter coat. Winter will be here in a few weeks."

In September 1915 Papa entered me in the Pensionat Saint Joseph Franciscans Missionaries DeMarie. I did not want to go to the convent, and once there, I did not like it. I was not even six years of age when Papa took me there. Ludmilla, and one of the servants who placed the suitcase in one of the rickshaws, saw me off. I sat on Papa's lap in the other rickshaw. I hid my face in Papa's shoulder. I did not want them to see me cry. Papa told the rickshaw coolie the direction. It was not far. The coolie stopped at the big iron gate. Across the top of the gate it said in cast iron letters, "PENSIONAT SAINT JOSEPH FRANCISCANS MISSIONARIES DEMARIE." Papa paid the coolie and rang the iron bell. A young nun, wearing a black habit and white shawl, approached us and introduced herself as Sister Agatha. She showed us the way to the office where Mother Superior and her secretary greeted us. Mother Superior turned to me and said, "Erna, Agatha will take you now to the dormitory. You must say goodbye to your father. Papa hugged me and said, "Be a good girl. I will see you Saturday."

I was brave and did not cry.

I was the youngest girl in the dormitory, not yet six years old. The fourteen- and fifteen-year-old girls looked after me and helped me dress. It was so crowded. Fifteen or twenty girls slept in one large room. I cried a lot. I also missed my dog, Wolf. Was I ever happy when Saturday morning came and I saw Papa and Wolf standing at the big gate.

I was so happy to see them, I did not know whom to hug first — Papa or Wolf. Papa took my hand and let me hold Wolf's leash with my other hand. "Well, Mausi, how was the first week and how do you like the girls? Are they nice to you?"

"Renee helps me to dress and comb my hair and sometimes Suzanne gives me a hand with making my bed," I told him.

"How is the food?" Papa asked.

"I like the food at home much better," I said.

"What classes are you taking?"

"English, French, arithmetic, writing and sewing. We also have music and sing songs and some girls play instruments," I answered.

Wolf started pulling at the leash when we neared home. "Let me have him now," Papa said. "Just one more street and we are home." I went and said hello to the boarders. Some were still having breakfast. The cook came from the kitchen and said, "Nee How Ma, Guniang?" which meant, "Are you well, girl?" Then he asked what I wanted for breakfast. He knew what I liked — a slice of ham, a fried egg, a slice of toast with honey and a cup of sweet hot chocolate. Within minutes the tasty food was placed on the table before me.

How good it was to see so many friendly faces and to sleep in my own bed again.

It was not a happy time for me at the convent. Some mornings we had to get up at 4 or 5 a.m. to go to chapel for prayer. I usually sat in the first or second pew where I could be easily seen by Mother Superior. Nothing escaped her sharp eyes. I fell asleep a few times. This disqualified me from going home the following weekend. One cold morning I needed to go to the toilet. I was not allowed to go, had an accident, and again lost my week-end at home. Mother Superior was so cruel, I thought, and I cried.

I missed my dog, Wolf. I was happy when Papa told me that Wolf missed me too. Papa said Wolf knew the day when it was time to pick me up. As soon as Papa put on his good clothes Wolf sensed it was the day to pick me up. His collar and leash always hung on a special hook. Wolf would sit beneath it and wait for Papa to put it on him. When they were close to the convent Papa would let him go. He was a big, husky German Shepherd. He had thick gray fur with black on his back and matching black paws. He was always so happy to see me he would almost push me down. I was happy to see him too. When I was not at the gate waiting they had to turn back. Those were sad days for Papa, Wolf and me.

My only happy remembrance of the convent was one of the nuns, Sister Mary Josephine. She was very pretty in her black habit and white shawl that framed her kind face and flowed over her shoulders. She spoke German and taught me to play the violin. At the Christmas program I played a song, "Eine kleine Geige möcht' ich haben" (A little violin I would like to have). The melody sounded so sweet. Papa came to the program and I could see that he was proud of me. I felt so grown up. I was finally six years old and enjoyed playing the violin. But I did not like the practicing of the scales.

After I had been at the convent for about one year I became ill one day. Papa was notified that I had scarlet fever and asked to take me home. He picked me up and called our doctor who examined me and found nothing wrong. I heard the doctor say to Papa, "Herr Kluge, there is nothing wrong with Erna. What she needs is some good nourishing food. Give her a plate of ham and eggs and a glass of milk. They were not feeding her well."

Papa certainly saw to it that I was properly fed. Being back home with Papa's good cooking, my strength soon returned. I never returned to the convent. I was not permitted to. Papa said, "Perhaps the war is the reason they do not want you back. It is a French school and you were the only German child."

In June of 1916 I was back home again with no particular person to look after me. Papa and I moved from the big front room in which I was born to the room adjacent to the bathroom and the staircase leading to the ground floor. The bathroom had a big white bathtub with both hot and cold running water just like Tante Corinth's. Not all houses were equipped with the luxury of hot and cold running water. On one wall was a wash basin and the commode was on the other wall. Papa said it was more convenient to have our bedroom next to the bathroom.

Ludmilla Resnikoff, a Russian lady in her forties, was living in one of the front rooms. She offered to take care of me whenever she was in town. She had very black hair, quite a big nose and wore heavy make-up, but she had the kindest brown eyes and a good heart. We had great fun together. She taught me Russian songs and poems. She called me "Malinkaya," which meant "Little One," and said that I could call her by her first name.

Like always, Tante Corinth came often to check on me and to see if I needed any clothes or shoes. She wanted to make sure that all was well with me.

My Amah took me often to Victoria Park in the British Concession. It was a place where most foreign children gathered to play where they could hear primarily the English language being spoken. Across from the front of the park was the well known Astor House Hotel. On the street corner stood a full-bearded Indian policeman, tall, broad-shouldered, with a turban matching his khaki uniform. These policemen kept order in the British Concession.

Adjacent to the park was the majestic Gordon Hall, a British government building with a huge clock in its tall tower. Everybody set their time by this clock. One day it stopped, which it never had done before. The cause, it was said, was that a Scotchman had overpaid a rickshaw coolie by one cent!

Once, after Ludmilla Resnikoff returned from a trip she told me that she would be in town for two weeks, and that she would take me to the park in the Russian Concession, on the other side of the Hai Ho River.

"Oh, that will be nice," I said. "I have not been there for a long time." I looked forward to this outing as we would have to take a boat to cross the river. It was not so bad to stay with Papa after all.

I had no playmates, only animals and my dolls. But I liked animals better. Wolf and Shuan, my Pekingese, were my best friends. One day I took my doll carriage out and walked up and down the sidewalk in front of the butchery. A lady stopped and looked into the carriage and exclaimed, "It's a dog! I thought you had a doll in there." I smiled and answered, "I like dogs better" and explained that her name was Shuan. I told her I had a big dog at home whose name was Wolf.

"What is your name?" she asked.

"Erna Kluge. I live in that big stone house. Papa makes good sausages."

"I have been to the butchery," she said. "Yes, he makes the best. I did not know Herr Kluge had a little girl. I am going to the shop now. Auf Wiedersehen, Erna."

Farther down the street was a French apothecary. It was quite a modern store with a counter that ran from one side of the store to the other with shiny glass shelves. Different kinds of instruments and white enamel basins were displayed. On the shelves were jars and glasses where medicines were exhibited. Sometimes I visited there to speak with the friendly, French saleslady. She usually had something for my sweet tooth. Across from the apothecary was a Grecian bakery. Karatzas was the name of it. They had Grecian honey cookies, and bread, and they roasted their own coffee beans. When

41

Ho, our cook, went to buy coffee for the restaurant, he took me along. Mrs. Karatzas always gave me a cookie and one for Papa.

Herr Ecke, a German, was a captain of a British merchant marine ship. He was one of our regular visitors and customers. His ship stopped at different ports along the coast between Tientsin and Foochow. He always stayed several days in Tientsin. "Onkel" Ecke was a bachelor in his fifties. He was tall and slender with graying hair at his temples. His moustache was full like Papa's. He spoke the dialect of the people of northern Germany-Hamburg and Bremen. When he came to town he always brought a nice toy or a box of candy for me. One Easter Sunday he happened to be in town and hid some chocolate eggs and bunnies in his room for me. "Erna, come and look in my room for what the Easter Bunny left for you!" he said. Excited, I began looking everywhere. I found all but one nest. No luck for that nest. I gave up. "Onkel Ecke, I can't find the other nest. I looked everywhere. Please, help me look for it!" I begged. He took my hand and led me to his bed and said, "Now, Mausie, did you look under the pillow?" I quickly crawled into the high bed and under the pillow was a big nest filled with two bunnies and eggs.

"The Easter Bunny brought so much," I said as I looked up into Herr Ecke's smiling eyes.

I enjoyed sitting on one of Papa's work benches observing him as he made sausages or mixed meat for the sausages. I even watched him butcher hogs and calves. It did not bother me at all. I thought it was exciting. Growing up in that environment I was soon used to it. Papa had his Chinese helpers do the dirty work of cleaning up. They also tended the smoke house. I spent my days mostly watching Papa and playing with the animals. Time went by pleasantly but things were about to change. Soon I would have to start school.

CHAPTER FOUR
My Childhood In Tientsin

Tientsin had a very good German school, the Deutsche Schule. But when Papa decided to enroll me, we found they would not accept me. "She's not baptized," the Head Master explained. Papa looked furious but said nothing. We walked away.

How very strange! Children of various nationalities and faiths were admitted to the school. The Lutheran children were instructed by a Lutheran minister, the Catholics by a priest and the Jewish children by a Rabbi. If they were of a Christian religion they had to be baptized. Papa was determined that I attend that German school so on December 28, 1916 I was baptized into the Lutheran faith at seven years of age. For a reason unknown to me, the baptism took place in our restaurant. Uncle Ecke was my witness or Godfather. Just think! I was a little heathen until then.

We had an hour of religion in school every day. How lucky for me as I surely did not get it at home. Gertraut had planted the seed. Praise the Lord. But I remember so well that I prayed at night in bed by myself, asking the Lord to give me a mother. I thought she was dead because Papa never mentioned her. When I saw a mother cuddling her child I wanted to cry. I just longed so much for a mother and to be loved. Papa was good to me, took me on his lap, and let me stand on his feet, and tossed me up in the air. But he was not a mother. No one ever mentioned "Mutti."

Tientsin, an industrial and commercial city, is situated on the Pei-Ho river (now named Hai Ho River). Most foreign settlements were located downstream on the right bend of the river. Papa's business was located in the French concession. In 1917, because of the First World War involvement of France and Germany, all German nationals had to leave the

French concession. Papa found a much smaller house on Taku Road, in the German concession. He was not able to take all of his machines and furniture and had to sell them at a big loss. Also, the electricity in the German concession was supplied at 110 volts, while the French concession had 220 voltage. Papa could not have used all of his machines anyway. The machines he did take had to be rewired.

The German concession was like a small city in itself. It had a German school, church, bakery, and confectionery, two butcheries, a printer, tailor, photographer, and many other merchants. They all did well.

At our new house we had rooms to rent to boarders. Uncle Ecke rented a room from us. He had lost his job because he was German and was employed by a British firm. He helped Papa take care of me. He even washed my hair every week. We spent much time together and he took hours teaching me to play the zither. Since I already knew how to play the violin, it wasn't too difficult to learn another stringed instrument.

Uncle Ecke and I often went on outings. Before we went he made sure I had finished my homework. He sometimes took me to Kiessling and Bader, a German cafe and pastry shop, where I ate delicacies until I almost popped. When the weather was nice we went to Victoria Park in the British concession. There were both small and big swings on the park's playground and he pushed me high into the air while I squealed with delight. I loved the slides and the merry-go-round best. I hated to leave the park when it was time to return home.

Once in a while Uncle Ecke went on a drinking spree. When he was most happy he stood up and sang "Letzte Rose," (Last Rose). Later he would go to his room, then appear again three days later, all washed, shaved and neatly dressed as if nothing had happened.

In the back of our house stood a row of small houses. One of these was occupied by a petite French lady, Mademoiselle Dujon. She was a small, thin person and had a sort of mousy look. Her English had a strong French accent. She used to buy her meat and sausage from us. She saw me playing in the alley and we became acquainted. Sometimes she took me to her house for a cup of tea and cookies. After a while I began going to her house often. She insisted on speaking French with me. When I was at the convent school I had to speak French so I did not mind. It was easy to speak more than one language in China. By then I was speaking German with Papa and our friends and customers, Chinese with the servants, English with children in the park, and Russian with the Russian people who stayed with us. But my knowing four or five languages was not unusual. Many people there were multi-lingual.

As in the French concession, we had dogs at our new home. We now had a new mixed breed hunting dog, as well as Wolf, our shepherd. The two dogs were quite different. The coloring of the hunting dog was white with black spots. He was a friendly dog. His tail was always wagging. Wolf was not everybody's friend, however, and we had to keep him on a chain. The new dog's name was "Schnapps." We were told that someone had given him some beer to drink when he was a puppy which made him tipsy. So his name became Schnapps. He was very protective of me. If he was alone in a room with me and someone entered, he would not let the person leave the room. He held on to their heel until Papa or one of the servants came.

The following incident illustrates that Schnapps and Wolf had a special kind of friendship going.

In our kitchen was a cabinet specially built to store eggs, a dozen or so, on a shelf. Papa had noticed that some eggs were missing, usually during the early afternoon when there was a siesta time. He asked the kitchen helpers, "Do you know anything about the strange disappearance of our eggs?"

They all replied, "No, Master."

Papa thought to himself, "I am going to find the thief." He knew that he could observe the kitchen from the butcher shop without being seen himself. So he stood there and watched. Before long old Schnapps came along and very cautiously opened the kitchen door so it would not slam, and went straight to the egg cabinet. He opened it with his snout and took out one egg, backed out very carefully, and took it to where Wolf was chained. Wolf ate the egg, shell and all. The two dogs left no evidence of their egg-stealing. Schnapps went back for another egg, but Papa was at the door and had caught Schnapps in the act. But lucky for Wolf, from that day on, Papa gave him a raw egg every day.

The year that we moved, a terrible flood struck our area. Tientsin was situated on the lower coastal plain. Just west of the city six small rivers came together which made the town subject to flooding. Papa and I went on a special boat ride one Sunday afternoon to view the flood. Here and there we could see the roof of a house or the tip of a utility pole. Almost everything was covered by the muddy water. "This is awful," I said.

"Devastating!" said Papa in a depressed voice. "Nothing but mud and debris." Holding my nose, I said, "It stinks terribly."

Our own road, the Taku Road, was six or seven feet under water in some areas. We could get to our house in a small boat. Papa took me to school in the boat. The school was located on the side of town which was elevated, so the flood waters did not reach that part of the city. Many people had to be evacuated to that part of town. The flood made business good for the peddlers. They went by boat everywhere selling vegetables, rice, and other foods.

Sanitary conditions were terrible for a long time. Human waste, dead animals, plants, and pieces of furniture floated down the streets. The stench of the polluted water was nauseating. We had to boil the water for several minutes, and we had to eat only cooked foods. The flood lasted seven long weeks.

Having to wade in the flood waters at times aggravated Papa's rheumatism. He had rheumatism for many years, but in the fall of that year he suffered from a terrible attack. The servants had to wash him and feed him because he could hardly move his rigid body. During that period I spent many days at Mademoiselle Dujon's house. We had our usual "tea parties."

Uncle Ecke supervised the servants and took care of money matters for Papa. Business was slow during that time anyhow. The servants, who had been with us so many years, did the best they could. After a few weeks of agony, Papa was able to work again.

Erna at age 7 years in Tientsin, China. 1916.

Erna's Certificate from French Convent in Tientsin China. 1915.

Deutsche Schule
in Tientsin.

Zeugniſſe

für

Erna Kluge,

geboren den *26. Dezember* 1909

aufgenommen den *5. September* 1921.

Abſtufung der Zeugniſſe: ſehr gut 1

gut 2

genügend 3

ungenügend 4

Front page of Erna's report card from German School in Tientsin
China. 1921.

50

CHAPTER FIVE
My Troubled Youth

The war in Europe had gone on and on. It seemed far away to me, though. After all, life had not changed much for us. Finally, in November of 1918, World War I ended. I remember well the night after it was announced that Germany had lost the war. Papa, our boarders, the servants, and I sat around a coal-burning stove. All the lights were out and the shutters of the windows firmly closed. A slight glimmer of coals was the only light we had. Crowds in the street were yelling and screaming. Now and then someone shouted, "Down with the Germans!" Foul words filled the night air.

I was scared and cried, "I am afraid, Papa. I want to sit with you."

"Komm Mausi," Papa said. And he took me on his lap and held me and spoke soothingly to me until I calmed down. He had not called me Mausi for a long time.

Papa wanted to know what was happening in the German neighborhood where the stores were located. "Will you take care of Erna for me, Ecke?" he asked suddenly.

"No! Don't leave me," I cried.

"Don't go, Heinrich," said Uncle Ecke.

But Papa insisted on going. Our pleading was in vain. Turning up the fur collar of his coat, and pulling his hat over his eyes, he left the house through the back door like a thief. I watched as he faded into the thick night darkness.

I sat stone still and silent on Uncle Ecke's lap while Papa was gone. After some time he returned.

"The war is over in Europe," he said painfully. "But our troubles might be just beginning." He began to tell us of the things he saw.

"The streets of the German concession are crowded with foreigners and Chinese people. They are throwing bricks and rocks into the businesses and houses, and looting everywhere. Roaring and shouting masses of people on every street and alley." Then his voice changed to an almost awesome tone as he added, "How vicious people have turned from one day to the next."

A grand monument had stood only hours past in front of the German consulate, "The Roland of Hruodland." I had heard the "Roland" legend. Roland was a hero. In 778 A.D. he was a nephew of Charles the Great. He had fought and fell during the battle against the French in the Pyrenees. "The monument is torn down, hammered into small pieces," Papa said. I began to cry.

Papa continued. As he had walked through the streets, he had run into a Frenchman, an old friend. He said they both stopped, looked at one another and shook hands. The Frenchman said to Papa, "Monsieur Kluge, it does not matter what goes on here and that Germany lost the war. We will remain friends." Then each had gone his own separate way. Papa spoke in a low and somber voice as he told us about this encounter.

After a few days matters settled down. Everybody tried to make the best of the situation. Windows were soon repaired and businesses opened their doors again.

1919 - Our First Repatriation

The year 1919 came along. Rumors were spreading that the Germans would be repatriated. Papa and I would be going back to Germany, Papa's mother country. I tried to prepare myself.

I had grown close to a girl named Maria Kandulsky. Like me, she grew up without a mother, but she did have one brother. We were about the same age. We met on the way to school, and we took our swimming lessons together. We hoped to be on the same boat when time came for our departure.

Soon rumors became reality. The first people called were the single men. I cried when Uncle Ecke had to leave. "Don't cry, Mausi," he said. "We will meet again." Later, Papa and I heard that he had made it to Hamburg, then we lost all connections with him.

Our turn came to leave. We were notified to be ready in three days to board the ship. But not all Germans had to leave. People over sixty, pregnant women and their husbands and children, and the sick had permission to stay.

Mademoiselle Dujon offered to help Papa. She suggested that he write the business over to her. She said that she and the employees who had been with him for so long would keep it going. But Papa would not hear of it. He was too proud. He simply told her, "I will sell the business." His business was worth 55,000 Chinese silver dollars. All he could get for it was 1,000 yuan from the buyer, Mr. Shang. Mr. Shang had sold Papa the sausage casings for our sausages for many years.

We were allowed to take only our personal clothing. I could not take my zither which Onkel Ecke had given me and taught me to play. Neither could we take our dogs. It was very painful for me to leave our dogs behind. I hugged the dogs and did not want to let go of them. Friends brought Wolf, our shepherd, to an English friend. Our employees took Schnapps and Lumpi. Lumpi had been our newest addition to the household.

Lumpi, with his shiny, long black coat, shy brown eyes and cute goatee had won Papa's heart some time back. From behind the counter in the butcher shop Papa had noticed the dog passing the store every morning. He stopped in front of the door, sniffed the air, waited and went on his way. One day Papa decided to give him a piece of meat. Every day the dog came back for more. He came a little closer day by day until one day he ate out of Papa's hand. A few more times of this interaction and the dog followed Papa into the house and stayed. I named him Lumpi. Schnapps and Wolf willingly accepted him. Of course he became another friend and play-mate for me.

For the trip, Papa had the marvelous foresight to pack some sausages, a few slabs of bacon and some cans of cocoa. These items kept our bellies filled on the thirty-day long freighter journey.

Happily, my friend Maria, her father, and brother were on the same boat. The women and children were separated from the men, so Maria and I were very glad to be together.

The boat was a freighter reconstructed to transport the Germans. Roughly built, wooden bunks were installed in the hold. They were so close together one could hardly pass without touching other people. I had an upper bunk bed, and I always thought I was about to roll off. Our mattresses were sacks filled with straw. We were given one hard, grey horse blanket. It was musty smelling and thin. I was cold and uncomfortable.

The food was awful. Meat and potatoes in the skin were cooked together. This was when the sausage, bacon and cocoa came in handy. Papa shared these with others.

I was used to taking nice daily baths, but I had this luxury no more. We took baths in warm salty sea water and the soap wouldn't foam. My skin felt strange somehow, rather slimy. I did not feel clean after such a bath.

Maria and I were together daily. One day we experienced a frightening event as we sat playing cards. We heard over the loudspeaker, "All passengers put on your life jackets and go on decks two and three immediately!" Maria and I hurriedly went on deck. We soon found out that a drifting live water mine had been spotted and one of the engineers was trying to detonate it. All the passengers, young and old, men, women and children, were standing close together. Husbands were looking for their wives and children and women were looking for their men. Papa found me and I held on tightly to him. After several unsuccessful attempts, the engineer finally hit the mine. I heard people praising God and crying with joy. Every one was hugging and clinging to their loved ones. The explosion was far enough away that our ship was not damaged.

After some thirty days, we arrived in Rotterdam, Holland. The Red Cross was there when we landed and served us piping hot pea soup. All the children received a bar of chocolate. I held my candy bar up to Papa and said, "look Papa, Schokolade."

He said, "Ja, but first, you eat your soup."

I can still see the big hall with the long lines of tables and the many people crowded in. I remember smelling the wonderful aroma of hot pea soup. It had tasted just as good as it smelled.

At the port we were separated from Maria and her family. We never saw them again. I missed my friend terribly.

We stayed in schools for a few days, then went by train to Berlin where we were housed in barracks for about a week. Then we took a train to Landeshut, my father's birthplace. We arrived on a Sunday morning. Papa was trying to locate his sister, Berta. He did not know her address. After asking several people, we finally found her apartment. We rang her doorbell. She opened the door, looked at Papa and me, and asked, "Whom are you looking for?"

"Berta, it is Heinrich your brother."

Immediately Tante Berta recognized Papa. They hugged and cried for joy. She had not heard from Papa in years. She did not know that he had a little girl.

We entered her one-room apartment. Her husband Karl, who had been sitting on the sofa reading, joined us and exclaimed, "Welcome! Welcome!" He took me in his arms and said, "So you are Heinrich's little girl. Let me look at you." I felt at ease at once with these nice relatives, such warm and friendly people.

After taking off our coats and bringing in the suitcases, (Papa had deposited the trunks at the station), we sat on the sofa and talked with Onkel Karl while Tante Berta tended to her cooking. Soon she served us a typical Sunday dinner, Silesian style. We ate roast pork, potato dumplings, and sauerkraut. We enjoyed such a delicious meal after so many weeks of poor food.

My aunt and uncle were poor people. In one room they lived, cooked, and slept. I stayed with them until Papa could find a place for us to live. Then, for a while, I stayed with another sister of Papa's. She had a handicapped daughter and her living quarters were also very small. Finally, a cousin of Papa's and his wife took me in. These relatives were comfortably situated. Their apartment was nice. I had to help quite a bit in the household. In the mornings before going to school, I had to cook breakfast and after school I had to help with household chores. But, all in all, they were good to me.

Papa found a small room for himself. All that time, he was looking for work. There was nothing. All that he really wanted was to go back to China.

My father did not like it in Germany. His only goal was ... back to China. As soon as the Germans were allowed to enter China again he bought the necessary machines and tools he needed for his trade, purchased tickets for us with almost his last money, and informed me that we were ready to sail back to China.

Shortly before we left Germany Tante Berta became very sick and was not expected to live. Papa and I visited her. She looked so pale and thin. Her face was so small embedded in the big feather pillow. Papa lifted me up to her so I could kiss her. "Auf Wiedersehen, Tante Berta. Be well soon," I said.

Onkel Karl bent down to me, hugged me and said, "Erna, you be a good girl, and have a safe voyage to China."

Then Papa bent and whispered something to his sister. A slight smile crossed her lips and her mouth formed the word

"Heinrich." Then Papa moved from his sister's bed, stood erect, and shook hands with Onkel Karl. The pastor came then and gave Tante Berta the last rites and Holy Communion. This was a sad memory to take on our journey.

1921 - Return To China

Our train for Triest, Italy was to leave the following day. We had been in Germany for only fifteen months, from the end of 1919 to March of 1921. I was eleven years old when we left Germany. We went by train to Italy. There we boarded the boat which was named for the north Italian city *"Aquilea"* owned by the Lloyd Triestino Company. The original name of the boat was *"Innsbruck"*, and it belonged to a company in Austria-Hungary until 1918. This boat would take us back to China. With the small amount of money Papa had left, we could only afford a place in the hold. We were given two mattresses and a few sheets. To have some privacy, Papa hung up a sheet for us. Most of the crew on the boat spoke German. There were a few German missionaries, another German butcher, and other business people on board who were also returning to China to resume their trades.

On the way we stopped in Venice. We stayed a few days and were able to do some sightseeing. At the St. Markus Plaza we fed the pigeons. There were hundreds of them and they were very tame. I loved it when they ate out of my hand. But other things attracted me too — like the colorful gondolas gliding across the canal. I watched as the oarsmen guided the boat while the gondolier played his guitar and sang a romantic Italian song. There were three or four people in each gondola. "Papa," I pleaded, "Let us take a ride." "Nein, Erna, nein! We need the money for other things." Disappointed, I turned my eyes away from the gondolas.

Our journey continued down the boot of Italy in the Adriatic Sea to Spoleto, well known for its good wine. Papa, the butcher which we had met and I went for a walk and

57

stopped at a "Botica" where they served wine. The men ordered wine while I had some water with just a little wine to give it some taste. It started to rain and we stayed longer than we had intended. So the men ordered more wine. When they did not look I nipped from their glasses, just a little at a time. "Well," I thought, " the men are having more than they should too."

The rain did not stop but we had to get on board the ship. So, off we went in the rain through muddy streets. They each took me by one hand. I was crying and trying to walk along. I did not like walking in the rain. The men were not too steady on their feet.

In this state we approached the ship. Everyone, including some missionary ladies, were waiting for us. When the ladies saw us coming, they exclaimed, "Now just look at that poor child with those drunken men!"

Papa said, "We are not drunk. My daughter is. She drank wine while we were not looking." Papa seemed quite angry with me.

The kind women cleaned me up and put me to bed. I felt sick and dizzy. Drunk at eleven years of age.

I awoke the next day feeling not too well, but I was soon better. Our voyage continued. We sailed across the Mediterranean Sea to Port Said and through the Suez Canal, entering the Red Sea. That took us to the Gulf of Aden and across the Indian Ocean. We passed through the Strait of Malacca and stopped in Singapore. From there we went to Hong Kong.

One day an officer on board was watching me. He came over and asked in German, "What is your name?"

"Erna," I said simply.

"Whom are you traveling with?"

"I am with my Papa."

"Well, now, where do you come from and where are you going?" he asked, just as the lunch bell was ringing. Before I could answer him Papa came for me.

"Good day, Sir," the officer said to Papa.

"Good day, Captain," Papa said with a nod.

"May your daughter eat with us today, Sir? I think she might like that."

To my surprise Papa said, "Yes, she may, and thank you Captain."

To me Papa said, "behave, and eat properly."

The officer took me by the hand and led me to the mess hall. Most of the men were already sitting at the long table. They were talking in German to each other. Only officers and engineers were eating there. The Captain announced, "This is Erna; she will eat with us."

In one voice the men replied, "guten Tag (Good day), Erna."

I felt rather shy at first eating with all those men, but they were friendly to me and I ate. I ate the delicious beef and cabbage, the fried potatoes, and the German chocolate cake as I halfheartedly listened to the gentlemen conversing. I am a real lady, I thought, and these are all the knights of my court. This is a banquet my servants have prepared especially to honor me. The men—my knights—were also very honored to eat with me, as we all feasted on the banquet.

The meal was over too soon. After we had finished eating a server brought a full plate for me to take to my Papa. I excitedly took the plate of food to Papa, but he wouldn't take it. "Take it back, Erna. I do not want them to think I let my daughter eat with them so that she would bring food back to me."

"Please eat it Papa. The food in the hold for us passengers is not good at all."

"No. Take it back."

I reluctantly took the plate of food back, then I went on deck. Going on deck would make me feel better about Papa's not eating. My special friend, the ship's carpenter, was there. He gave me some leftover pieces of wood and some string to play with while he worked. I built myself a little boat and threw it overboard to let it ride on the Waves. I spent hours doing this. The sea was calm. I let my boat float and watched the flying fish and dolphins following our ship.

I even enjoyed myself when the sea was rough. I never seemed to get seasick. When the ship's bow was in the water I would run that way, and back to the stern when it went the other way.

One day, though, I did get seasick. We had pineapple for dessert and I did like pineapple. The men let me eat all I wanted. And I had just one helping too many. When I later went on deck, the sea was pretty rough and my stomach could not take it. I had to run to the rail and vomit into the sea. I didn't tell Papa. I was afraid if I told him he might stop buying pineapple for me. And he always bought fresh fruit— because I loved it so—when we stopped at different ports.

On the last night of our trip, a strange thing happened. Papa woke me and asked, "Did you call me?"

"No, Papa," I answered, "why?"

"I heard a knock and someone was calling me by name," Papa answered.

"Papa, I never call you by your first name."

"I wonder if something has happened to Tante Berta. Let us remember the date and time."

Our trip from Trieste to Hongkong was so far, it had lasted thirty-three days. We arrived in Hongkong at night. What a beautiful sight the city was by night. I stood on deck and stared out across the water. The city looked like a huge Christmas tree to me. Different colored lights twinkled all over the mountains, and between those lights I could see the moving lights of streetcars, just like tiny toy cars moving in and out of the streets and houses.

We entered the harbor in Hong Kong where we had to wait quite some time. The next morning we continued our voyage to Shanghai. Here our luggage was inspected by the customs officials. I had just one small suitcase which contained all my belongings. When the customs officials came to where we were waiting, my suitcase was gone. After a long search we found the suitcase in a restroom. It was empty. Knowing father's wallet was nearly depleted, I wondered what I was to do.

In Shanghai we stayed for eight days with a German family who had a butchery. Father had known them for many years. They did not leave China in 1919 when we left. There was sickness in their family, so they were able to keep their business.

It was the year 1921.

I was glad to stay the eight days with the family. They shared their home and made us feel welcome. They had two daughters, a little older than I. They gave me some of their clothes, which they altered a little. But they were still too big for me. I knew I looked a sight. I was just glad that I had clothes to wear. We seldom went on land on our voyage and the short stay in a real home was a welcomed event to me.

From Shanghai we went by train to Tientsin, back to the city where I was born. We were happy to discover that Mademoiselle Dujon was still there. We went to see her first thing. She grabbed me into her arms and exclaimed, "Ma petite Erna, how you have grown! You are almost as tall as I am."

After getting re-acquainted, she suggested helping us look for a room. We could not afford much. We found and rented an empty room with just one mattress on the floor.

The first night in our new room was a very restless one. I tried to sleep, but I felt something biting me. I woke up and called, "Papa, I'm itching!" Papa turned on the light. We looked at our arms and legs. Bedbugs were crowded on our skin, glutting on the taste of our blood. We jumped up and began shaking off the bugs. We killed all that we found. I felt nauseated. After that, sleeping was impossible that night.

The next morning we went to buy some insect powder. When we returned to our room, we made a little wall about a centimeter wide all around the mattress. We began looking forward to a good night's sleep.

That night, however, we had not been in bed long when the itching started. I woke up scratching and screaming.

"Papa," I called, "the bedbugs are back."

Papa got up and turned on the light. The bugs had turned away from the poison Papa had sprinkled around the outside of the mattress. When we looked up we saw the ceiling was speckled with bedbugs. To our amazement, the beastly bedbugs had crawled up the wall to the ceiling and dropped down upon us. Papa scraped the ceiling with a broom. As the bugs landed on the mattress, I swept them to the floor and stomped them. It was a dreadful experience.

I went to sleep at night with the terrible dread that they would attack us again. And they did. Papa said we had no choice but to endure the bedbugs until we found a suitable house. (At that time bedbugs were common in China. They came into the house unseen with the laundry and other items which we brought in. Later when we slept in beds Papa went so far as to fill an iron frying pan with kerosene which he lighted and maneuvered around the frame of the bed. The heat from the flames would kill the eggs. This is the reason why most people had iron bed frames. This was dangerous but effective. Still, there were always a few that got in.)

I entered the same "Deutsche Schule" which I had attended before we were repatriated. As I had lost my suitcase aboard ship in Shanghai, I had very few clothes and only one pair of shoes. The ones I did have were given to me and did not fit properly. They were much too big and I felt most uncomfortable wearing them. Eventually Papa took me to a German neighbor and asked her to help me buy some new clothes for school. It was wonderful having nice clothes that fit.

While we were still looking for a house and waiting for the machines to arrive from Germany, we often visited friends who had returned on the same boat we did. One day we went to see the people who had bought "Wolf", our German Shepherd. I was so eager to see him, but to my amazement he did not recognize Papa nor me. He did allow us to pet him. As I ran my fingers through his thick coat I recalled memories of Wolf and me running through the fields. He was always by my side and for so many years I considered him my best friend. I felt dejected as we walked away.

Going down Taku Road, where we used to live before we were repatriated, we saw Lumpi, our stray dog. A Chinese officer had him on a leash. He looked well fed and groomed. I wanted to call to him but Papa would not let me. "Nein, Erna. He looks good. So let it be." I was hurt and it was the last time I saw Lumpi.

Several days later we saw our old dog, "Schnapps." Again, Papa would not allow me to call him as we had no place to keep him. Schnapps looked so pitiful. I feared I would never see him again.

Within a week we found a house about a block away from the main street. It was big enough for a butchery, restaurant, boarders and a bedroom each for Papa and me. It also had a good-sized kitchen and work room for Papa to make his sausages. I liked our new home and seldom saw a bedbug.

Not long after our move, I was walking home from school one day when I spied "Schnapps." He was in front of me, not far from our new home. I was excited and called, "Schnapps!" He stopped, turned, and then went on. I called again, "Schnapps, Schnapps, come here!" He turned around, sniffed the air and ran towards me almost knocking me down. I hugged him and he licked my face. He just wouldn't stop. Of course, he followed me home. When I entered our house I called, "Papa, Papa, look whom I brought home." Were they ever happy to see each other. Papa had tears in his eyes and Schnapps whimpered. Old Schnapps was once again a part of the family.

Business was slow. Papa could hardly meet his expenses. I heard him say, "If I had all the money people owe me, I would be a rich man." Papa was a person who could not refuse anybody food or lodging. "You pay me when you can," he would say. When the order for repatriation had come, we had only three days to get ready. There was no way Papa could collect his outstanding debts.

Papa was able to borrow 100 dollars from Mr. Shang, the Chinese man that had bought our business, and that did help for a while. Papa contacted several of the people who had returned to Tientsin, owing him money. One particular night, after we had gone to bed, the doorbell rang. Papa got up mumbling, "I wonder who that could be at this hour." When Papa opened the door, a mailman handed him an express letter. Papa thanked him but had no change to give the man a tip. The letter contained a 200 dollar check from a customer who paid his long over-due debt. Papa was dumbfounded. He turned to me. "There is no money at all in our cash box," he said. "I was wondering how we would manage tomorrow." Papa and I hugged each other, laughed, and cried. The Lord was good.

In the next two years more and more German families returned to Tientsin. The Corinth family was among them. I was so happy to see Tante Corinth again. She often invited me for Sunday dinner which always was a treat for me. It had been over three years since we had seen each other.

Little by little customers were beginning to pay their over-due debts. We felt things were looking up. But our luck was short-lived. One bad thing after another began to happen. Our small fortune didn't last long. On the second floor of our house, there was a large room which American soldiers used as a private club. They would eat, drink, and have a good time, mostly on credit. They paid their bills on the first of the month. Papa felt this extra income would help establish him again. This worked well for a while, but soon the soldiers became less and less prompt with their payments. Papa went to their superiors who urged them to pay. But more and more of them were being transferred. Some left for the United States and there was no way Papa could collect from them. Papa was losing too much money. We had to close the club.

Still, Papa trusted people. Customers would bring their hogs to Papa to be slaughtered, cured, smoked and made into sausage. They promised to pay upon delivery. Our customers' hams, bacon, and sausages, along with our own, filled our smokehouse. Many of the meats were ready to be picked up when someone broke in one night and cleaned out the smokehouse. Our two dogs, Schnapps and a new German shepherd, "Terra" never even barked. Papa and I felt sure it must have been one of our own employees who robbed us. That was a financial loss, as well as the letdown we felt because of Papa's unfaithful employee(s).

Papa bought a big sow to slaughter to try to regain some of his loss. When he slaughtered her, though, he saw that she had "little ones"—twelve of them. Papa did not notice that the sow was pregnant when she was brought in. She had been tied up on a cart and Papa had slaughtered her right away. The pork from the hog could not be used. "Will my troubles never end?" Papa asked.

In the summer of 1922 I became very ill. Papa sent for the doctor who came to our house to examine me. Papa was leaning over my bed when the doctor rose from examining me. "Well, Doctor?" Papa asked anxiously.

"I'm afraid she is very ill. She has amoebic dysentery. We will have to be very careful with her."

"How did she get that?," Papa asked.

"Any of a number of ways. Impure water. Undercooked pork. The germs of the disease spread somewhat like typhoid. The important thing is nourishing her back to health. She must have plenty of bed rest and as many fluids as she can take. I have a drug for her, but it is not foolproof. We must be very careful."

I was very ill, and their voices droned on as if I were in a dream. My stomach hurt constantly, my head throbbed, I was hot, and from alternating diarrhea and vomiting I thought I would surely die. I was sick for three long months.

Dear Tante Corinth came every day and brought me special dietary foods. While I was very ill, the doctor came two times a day. During that critical period, people had to walk softly in my room because the slightest tremble of the floor gave me horrible pain. To help me get better, Tante Corinth cooked nourishing meals for me. The doctor had prescribed a little red wine every day to build up my blood.

One morning Tante Corinth asked me, "What would you like to eat tomorrow?"

"Ah," I said, "please make me some tapioca pudding cooked with a little red wine. Top it with some whipped and sweetened egg whites." That was the only thing I wanted... She brought it that same evening. But, I did not like it. I felt great shame for putting her to all that trouble of making the pudding. But, I could not swallow it.

"It's all right, my dear," said Frau Corinth. "Do not eat it if you do not feel like it."

Frau Corinth did not have a car. She either had to walk or take a rickshaw everywhere she went. She came often to see me anyway. I created a pet name for her. "Vice Mother," I called her. She was closer than a second mother to me.

Finally, I got better and was able to walk about a little, but still I was in bed most of the time. One day a sudden fire broke out in the room where the staircase was. It spread awfully fast, and I was terribly scared. Papa came and was able to get me past the fire and down the stairs.

Papa took me to a Chinese family who lived close by where I stayed all day. In the evening an elderly German couple, Frau and Herr Krippendorf, who lived just a block away, took me to their house, because Papa had to have someone look after me while he worked in the butchery. Their house was very nice, large, and with a big garden. They had two German Shepard dogs and two cats. The animals were my playmates and friends. Another friend was their Chinese cook. He was elderly and quite hefty. He spoiled me and did his best to get some flesh back on my thin body. Until I was quite well again and able to go back to school, he served me breakfast in bed.

My Chinese name was "Liu Guniang." Guniang meant girl and Liu was an abbreviation from Kluge, my surname. He would bring me a big plate of porridge with butter and a raw egg stirred into it and say, "Liu Guniang jetzt schon alles aufessen —," meaning; "now eat everything up."

After several weeks I was well enough to go back to school. I found that I had a lot of catching up to do. Herr Krippendorf would help me with my homework, but I was not a very good student. Living with Papa and having to work in the restaurant, in the kitchen, and also in the butcher shop did not leave me much time to do homework. Often I did it in the bathroom. My grades were poor. I tried hard to make them better. While I was staying with the Krippendorfs, my grades did begin to go up. My teachers seemed really pleased with this improvement.

I had such a good time living with the Krippendorfs. They were very good to me. But our house was finally repaired and I had to go back home. I cried. I had lived with them for three whole months. I knew that Papa had found my sickness and the fire very trying, and that he had begun drinking heavily. I did not want to go back.

But I had to return. Back with Papa I resumed most of my normal activities. But I still had to be very careful of what

I ate. My stomach could no longer tolerate melons, tomatoes, and lettuce—foods that I loved.

Papa waited and waited for the doctor's bill. Several weeks had passed since the doctor's last visit to me. The bill never came. One day the doctor and his wife came to the butchery. Papa said, "I have not yet received my bill, Doctor."

The doctor replied," I will check, Herr Kluge."

Still, the bill never came. Papa was grateful. He made up a big basket filled with sausages, bacon, and a ham and had me take it to the doctor's house in a rickshaw. "Why, thank you, little Erna," the doctor said when he opened the door and saw me and the gift. He was very surprised. "And tell Herr Kluge thank you for me." His round face was beaming.

The following summer a German family took me to Pei-Tai-Ho. That was a very nice resort town by the sea. Most foreigners and rich Chinese spent their summers there. It was the same resort where my parents had spent their honeymoon. Pei-Tai-Ho was located north of Tientsin, between Changli and Shanghaikwan. It was about three hours by train from Tientsin. I had a wonderful summer there and didn't want it to end. The sea, the sunshine, and the good food restored me to good health again. But I had to go back home.

When I went home Papa hired a lady, Frau Ludwig, to come every day to help me with the household chores, and to help in the business. She looked after me also. She was a kind person, and we got along well. She made life a little easier for me.

My Animal Friends

Papa bought a female German Shepherd from a friend and we named her Terra. Terra had her sleeping place under the staircase. There she had new puppies. I was the only one who could go into her den when she had the puppies. I would crawl under the staircase and lie there with her and her family. Terra accepted my company.

Terra knew exactly the time when I came home from school. She would jump on a chair by the window and look for me. When she saw me coming, she barked and someone would let her out. She would come running toward me, almost pushing me down. I really had to watch out for her. I would give her my pencil box, which she would carry home. Soon any new pencil box was covered with all kinds of tooth marks.

She was trained by Papa to always carry a stick in her mouth-an eight inch broomstick—when she went for a walk with anyone. The stick prevented her from biting people or fighting with other dogs. Papa told me, "Always talk to her while you walk. This makes a good relationship between a dog and its master."

Terra and I always hung around together. When we were walking one afternoon, Terra suddenly became interested in a tree and dropped her stick. "Come, Terra," I called. She came running, but without her stick. "Go back and look for your stick." She sniffed and looked around. Then she saw a man walking in front of us with a rolled up newspaper in his hand. She ran up to him and snatched the paper away, bringing it back to me. The man did not know what was happening. I had a hard time getting the paper away from Terra. It was also difficult to explain to the man how Papa had trained Terra. Then Terra and I had to go back and look for the stick. Terra found it and came running toward me with her tail wagging rapidly.

Her eyes sparkled as she jumped up at me. She seemed to be saying, "See, I found it."

Terra liked to go shopping with me. She carried a small wicker basket. I filled it with a few items and let her carry it. She took it with her head held high. She was very gentle with our cat. The cat cuddled up to Terra when it was cold. When

Kitty was gone and did not come when we called, we only had to say "Terra, such Kätzchen." (Search Kitty). Off she went, and usually returned with Kitty in her mouth, carrying her by the back of her neck. Sometimes I put the cat in a basket and Terra carried her as the three of us went for a walk. Terra was my best friend.

Schnapps was getting old and quite sick. He had water retention in his legs, his paws, and his whole body. Only his head was still the normal size. Poor dog. So, with a heavy heart, Papa decided to have him put to sleep. We missed our old faithful "hound," and for comfort I grew even closer to Terra.

Alcohol And Abuse

I was not dressed as nicely as the other children around me were. I always felt a little out of place. The kids in school made fun of me because my clothes smelled of sausage and smoke. Having to help Papa in the butchery made the smell penetrate into my clothing. I did not change as often as I should and my clothes were not washed as often as they should have been.

But I did have some friends. Besides the Corinths, there were two other families nearby who had children my age. These families took a special interest in me. They would have me over for a Sunday dinner sometimes. Or, they would have my birthday party for me at their home. Papa did not have parties for me. I was born on December 26, not a good day for a birthday party, Papa must have thought. Somehow I usually got my birthday party. The kindness of these families took away some of the sting of wearing my poor clothing and being made fun of.

I was fourteen years old, and my figure was quite developed. Tante Corinth told me I was becoming quite the young lady. But the older I got the stricter Papa was with me. I couldn't quite understand his changing attitude. We rented rooms to single persons as well as to couples. There were always men around. Papa became very strict and mistrusting of the men and me. He was always watching me. When I went to visit Tante Corinth, she had to give me a slip of paper on which she wrote down what time I left her house. He knew how long it took a rickshaw coolie to take me home. Papa was afraid I would become a girl of the streets like so many girls in Tientsin.

Papa was drinking very heavily. Often he could not remember the next day what he did or said when he had too much to drink. He was like two different men.

At school we were studying about the French Revolution. A related film was being shown in one of the town movie theaters and my teacher encouraged all of us students to go and see it. Papa would not allow me to go. I told this to my teacher. He said, "Tell your father I will pick you up and bring you back home again." So Papa let me go. It was a very long movie. The evening weather was nice and instead of taking a rickshaw, we walked home. The walk home put us home about half an hour later than we had told Papa we would arrive back. My teacher took me to the door of my home and went on his way.

Papa was waiting for me with a cane in his hand. "Where have you been so long?" he demanded.

"Papa, it was a long movie and we walked." I could see that he was drunk. He did not believe me and started hitting me blindly, shouting, "tell me the truth. Where were you all this time?"

"Papa," I cried, "I am telling you the truth. Don't beat me any more, please, Papa." He continued striking me for what seemed like a long time. He stopped only when he had nothing but the cane handle in his hand. I fell to the floor. He began hitting my face now with his open hand. I covered my face with my arms. As he backed away I got up and ran to my room locking the door behind me. I knelt by the side of my bed and pleaded, "oh, Lord, keep Papa away from me. Don't let him ever do this to me again. You know I did no wrong. Lord, hear my prayer."

The following morning my arms and back were bruised. My side ached and I felt sick to my stomach. I didn't want to see anyone or have to explain what had happened to me. I put on a long sleeved blouse for school. Papa was up when I went downstairs. He asked, "Why are you wearing a blouse with long sleeves? It's going to be hot today." He acted as though he remembered nothing of the argument between us or the beating. He looked at my eyes, which were red and swollen. "What happened?" he asked.

"Papa, don't you remember? I rolled up one sleeve and showed him my arm. "You did that to me last night." When I told him what happened, Papa looked away and poured himself a cup of coffee.

At school that morning, several of the girls asked, "Erna, what happened to you? Your eye is swollen and your face is all red." They gathered around me sensing that something was wrong. "Why are you holding your arm?" one of the girls asked. When I pulled back, she jerked up my sleeve and pointed to the long black mark on my arm. I was too ashamed to tell them the truth. "I bumped into a door and fell," I said. Then I walked away. I don't think they believed me.

Tante Corinth knew of Papa's drinking problem. She told me many times, "Erna, you can come to me any time, day or night, whenever you need me." After school I wanted to go to Tante Corinth but Papa said no.

I spent the evening in my room alone.

Back To The House Where I Was Born

In 1923 Papa received his first of three compensation checks from the German government for the loss he suffered when we were repatriated in 1919. We learned that the house in the Rü de France, the house where I was born, was now

72

vacant. Papa decided to move back. With the government money he was able to re-establish himself. Once again we had a butchery, restaurant and boarding house. The day we moved in I raced up the stairs and into the room where I was born. It was a large room with tall windows, so different from the place we had moved from. But this would not be my room. My room was one of the four smaller bedrooms in the back next to Papa's. It was still much larger than my previous bedroom. I loved having so much space all to myself and pictured in my mind how it would look when it was furnished. I was curious as to who might be moving into the room on the other side. I would soon find out.

I worked long hours after school, mostly in the butcher shop, and serving food in the restaurant. I enjoyed being with people but was usually very tired when I went to bed at night.

We kept a few pigs in the back yard. There were always leftovers from the restaurant and butchery which we fed them. Ours were the cleanest pigs I had ever seen. They were white pigs. In China mostly we saw black ones. Their "sleeping quarters" were under the back staircase. It was cemented and built on a slant. At the elevated place, we had straw for them to sleep on. It was always clean and fresh. On the lower side was a place for them to "do their business." It was cleaned with a hose every day. The pigs came into the yard to get exercise. But there was no smell at all. We could not have kept boarders otherwise. I especially liked one pig, "Snoocky." She was English bred and had ears that stood out at the side of her head like wings. She came grunting when I called. I usually had some tidbit for her. The pigs and Terra got along famously.

We had one sow who was going to have piglets. When her time came, I sat with her. After every little piglet was born I gave her an apple as a reward. She grunted as if to say, "Thank you, Erna." I stayed up with her until five o'clock in the morning.

73

When the piglets were eight or ten days old, the mother sow suddenly fell over and died. We raised the little ones by putting milk in a rubber glove and letting them drink out of each finger. Every one of them lived. When they were big enough, father butchered them and sold them as suckling pigs. Sucklings were in big demand. I disliked it when Papa had to do that to the pigs, but we really could not keep them. There was no room for so many grown hogs.

I was never allowed to be idle. If I was not helping here or there, I was mending or doing embroidery work. An elderly couple lived in one of our rooms. The lady taught me all kinds of needle craft. Her handicraft was exquisite, and soon she was praising my work.

Our living room was the restaurant. It was there that I did my homework, mending and the needle work. One afternoon I was sitting doing some mending when Papa came in and sat in his chair. He accidentally sat on a needle which was stuck in the chair with the point upward. "Erna! you put that needle here on purpose, didn't you?"

"No, Papa, I never knew it was there."

Papa came toward me, yelling and fussing. I thought for sure he was going to begin beating me, but to my surprise he did not. That time he only verbally abused me.

I left the room to get away from Papa. So he wouldn't think I only wanted to leave to be idle, I went to the kitchen to help there. Even though we had a cook and a helper, there were still things I was expected to do. The whole place needed my help—the kitchen, the restaurant, and the rooms.

Although I sometimes helped with the cooking, I was not such a good cook. Two of our boarders were a Russian couple. One day the Russian lady called me to her room. She was not feeling well and she said, "Erna, please make some pigeon soup for me tomorrow."

"How do you make it?" I wanted to know.

She explained how to prepare it. The next day I cooked the soup and took it to her room. I had tasted it beforehand. I

74

thought it had a terrible bitter taste and I didn't like its greenish color. But I had never eaten pigeon soup and I thought that was how it was supposed to taste and look. I left the soup with the lady and went back downstairs.

Soon I was called back to her room. " Erna," she said, "what did you do to this soup?"

I looked at her with surprise and said, "I thought I did what you told me to do."

"Well, Erna, I believe you did not take out the entrails."

"Oh, no," I wailed. "I am so sorry. Please, please excuse me."

"That is all right, dear. Everyone makes mistakes now and then. You can make me some more soup later." I made fresh pigeon soup the next day and took it to her. She laughed and said the soup was much improved.

Besides the Russian couple, we had all kinds of different people staying with us. But very few were steady boarders. I became especially fond of one elderly gentlemen by the name of Mr. Grohe. He was the Captain of a merchant ship, like Onkel Ecke had been. He traveled up the Chifigli coast to Fuchou, the city famous for its raw silk, and back to Tientsin. Mr. Grohe's parents were German but he had been born in the United States; therefore, he was an American citizen. He had not lost his job during World War I because he was an American citizen. When his ship was in town, he usually stayed a few days with us. He liked to come to our place because there was always plenty of good food available. I liked Captain Grohe's beard, which had a touch of gray. I thought it made him look that much more like a Captain.

On his return trips to us, he always brought something for me, a piece of silk, or even, once a pair of shoes. "How did he know my size?" I wondered. I asked the servants if they had given him my shoe size. "No," they answered, "but he slipped to your room secretly and measured the size of your shoes with a bamboo sliver."

Captain Grohe often took me to the German bakery, Kiessling and Bader, where Onkel Ecke and I used to go. Captain Grohe let me choose whatever I wanted. He would also take me to a German or other foreign movie.

But Captain Grohe went out one day on a southern route and he never returned again to our place. Papa and I didn't hear from him again, just like we had never heard from Onkel Ecke again.

Papa did his share of work in the butcher shop and around the place, too—when he was sober. He was a hard working man who liked to get ahead. But once he had his first beer, he would stop whatever he was doing and forget all about the sausage he had started to make or the pig he had started to butcher. The Chinese helpers and I would try to finish up, but we could not do it as well as Papa.

Once Papa started to drink, he could not stop at all. His business began to suffer. I was in school during the day and could only help when I came home in the evening. There was always a reason for drinking, according to Papa. If he was not angry, which called for drinking, he would drink with his friends. "Well, look who stopped in, Erna," he would announce. "This calls for a drink. Let's bring out the bottle."

When Papa had his drinking spells, he would sit all by himself after everybody left and drink one bottle after the other, until he finally lost all control of himself. Then he would call me out of my room at night and make me sit with him. He would often say, "You are a whore just like your mother was." I could not quite understand what he meant. I would just sit and cry.

"You are a whore just like your mother used to be," he said one night.

"Papa, but I did not do anything wrong today," I cried.

"Be still," he shouted. He left his chair and began hitting me in the face and ears. I wore my long thick braids coiled over my ears. He hit me with his fists over and over.

"Stop it, Papa, you are hurting my ears. Stop!" I wanted to run out of the room, but he made me sit down again. This went on until he finally fell asleep. I sneaked out and ran quickly to my room, packed a few things in a sheet and took a rickshaw at the corner. I gave the rickshaw coolie Tante Corinth's address. Onkel Corinth came to the door to let me in, his wife right behind him. She took me into her arms and said, "Was it bad again, Erna?"

"Ja, Tante Corinth, I don't want to go back to Papa."

Onkel Corinth had gone to pay the rickshaw coolie. When he returned he said, "It is almost one thirty in the morning. Let us go to bed and talk about it after we have had some sleep."

Tante Corinth took me to the spare bedroom. She helped me take the hairpins out of my braids. My ears were still red. She caressed me tenderly and said an evening prayer. I hugged her, it was so good to feel her arms around me. I loved her so and wished that she was my mama. She tucked me in and turned out the light.

Going to Tante Corinth's didn't help much. I had to return home the next day. Staying with father really became unbearable.

Evidently the Corinths spoke to the German Council about the abuse. The German Council wanted to take me away from Papa, but they didn't because I had no relatives in China. Then one of my Papa's nieces and her husband moved to Tientsin. The German Council made arrangements for me to stay with this niece. They did not have any children and were very nice to me. I liked living with them. I stayed there for several months. Father wanted me back, though. He would not pay for my board and lodging, and also did not let me have my clothes. I had to go back home.

My old friend Sister Mary Josephine and I met on the street one day. We were so happy to see each other again. I told her all about my time in Germany and brought her up to date on what my life was like now. "Are you still playing the violin?" she asked me.

"No, I do not have one now."

"Well, if you would like to start playing again, I will lend you one."

"Oh, thank you, Sister," I said.

Papa agreed to the violin, so I started to take lessons with her. It did not last long. Papa said, "I cannot stand all that fiddling." I had to give up my lessons.

Not long after that someone gave me a mandolin. I played it by ear. I really enjoyed it. But, this it did not last long either. Papa became very angry one day, snatched the mandolin out of my hand, and smashed it on the corner of the dining room table. I ran from the room crying. Will I ever be able to enjoy my music, I wondered.

In contrast to his abuse of me, Papa got along well with his customers. Papa was in the restaurant one day when a German sailor walked in. The sailor had a big meal and a drink, and he and Papa conversed. The sailor said to Papa, "I have an Asian myna bird that can talk. Would you like to buy it?"

"I don't know," said Papa. "Bring it in tomorrow and let me see it."

The next day the sailor brought the bird in a big cage.

I thought the bird was very beautiful. It was about nine inches high and reminded me of an oriole. It had shiny black feathers and an orange bill. The sailor instructed the bird to say several sentences in German and some in English. The bird was hungry and he said, "Poor little Jimmy chow chow," in English. Then he said in German, "Mein kleiner Jimmy hast du garnichts zu fressen?", which meant, "My poor Jimmy has nothing to eat."

Some people came into the restaurant and the bird said, "son of a bitch, son of a bitch," so fast we could hardly understand it. I was embarrassed and hoped the people did not understand it.

78

Papa liked the bird immensely and bought him.

We hung the bird cage outside in the yard in the day-time. We could still hear the bird clearly when he talked. We had a gentleman who walked with crutches staying in one of the rooms at that time. In the morning the man would call the Chinese house boy to come up to his room to help him dress. "Boy!" he would call, and the servant would run up the stairs to his room to help him. Soon Jimmy was imitating the man's voice. "Boy!" Jimmy would call anytime he wanted to. It was next to impossible to distinguish who was calling, the man or Jimmy. Jimmy was annoying to the house boy. We only had Jimmy for a few months. He died. We thought he died of pneumonia.

The man was still there though. He was very grouchy, and Terra, our dog, did not like him. When the man would come home at night Terra would bark at him and he would hit her with his crutch. Terra tried to spite the man by showing him that she did not like him. At the dinner table at night Terra went from person to person and put her head on their laps and looked up at them. Everyone liked this and was glad that Terra liked them. Terra never went to the man; she deliberately passed him up.

I was confirmed when I was fifteen. Tante Corinth had a white voile dress with lace made for me. Girls wore white dresses, boys white suits. Confirmation was a time of changing from a child to an adult. Before I was confirmed, I had worn my hair in braids, after confirmation, I wore it up in a big bun, which showed that I was an adult. I began taking pride in my appearance.

I received several gifts on this occasion. Among the gifts were a black Bible, a lovely cross necklace, and a small heavy vase of muted colors. Flowers were embossed on the vase; it was one of my favorite presents.

Shortly after I was confirmed, I had to quit school very unexpectedly. Father had just bought a bulldog named Chubby from an American soldier who was going back to the States. We did not have him very long when, too late, we found out that he could not stand the smell of alcohol. His former master had mistreated him when he had too much to drink. One evening father and some friends were sitting around a table drinking, drinking pretty heavily, especially Papa. (I was already in bed.) Papa called Chubby to sit on a chair next to him, petted him and put his face next to the dog's. When the dog smelled the alcohol, he growled and snapped and nearly bit off Papa's nose. One of Papa's drinking friends rushed Papa to the German-American Hospital where his nose was sewed on again. Chubby had often growled at other men who had been drinking, but he had never bit anyone.

The next morning when I came downstairs and saw Papa, I was shocked to see his nose covered by a large white bandage. He told me, with great pain, what had happened. Papa's nose healed fast. The doctors did an excellent job sewing up a nose that had been left hanging on by the skin. When they removed his bandage and stitches, only a small scar was left across the bridge of his nose.

The French Police came and ordered us to remove Chubby from the French Concession. Papa and I figured a customer must have reported the incident.

We gave Chubby to a Russian family with three children. I hugged Chubby good-bye. As the dog was taken away Papa said, "I shouldn't have hugged Chubby with alcohol on my breath." The family told me that he was such a good dog; he played with their children and never growled or became angry. I visited them one day, to convince myself that Chubby was in good hands. Chubby was so excited to see me and did not leave my side until I left. I could see that he had a good home, they loved him, and he was happy there.

Papa was not able to be in the butchery for a while after that, so I had to stay home and that was the end of my school years. I really began doing the work of an adult. At six o'clock in the morning, I went to the market with our cook. We bought what was needed for that day's cooking. I had to account to Papa for every cent we spent. Papa did not give me any spending money. If I needed stockings, toothpaste, or other personal items he always fussed. I wore the cheapest of cheap stockings, black cotton ones. I mended them often, but there came a day when I could mend them no more and needed a new pair.

And when I needed toothpaste, Papa would say, "I never used toothpaste all of my life. What do you need toothpaste for?" Yet, Papa had the healthiest, strongest teeth despite never having been to the dentist until he was fifty-six years old. For necessary personal items I had to squeeze out some of the market money. I began to up the price of potatoes and other vegetables a cent here and a cent there. In that way I could save in a week or so for a new pair of stockings or a tube of toothpaste. I did not dare take money out of the cash register.

Karl Heinrich Kluge in Landeshut, Germany. 1921.

Erna's "Best Friend" Terra at the Tientsin, China butcher shop. 1925.

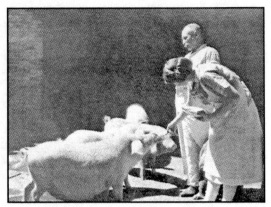

Erna, Heinrich and "Snoocky" the pig at the
Tientsin, China butcher shop. 1925.

"Chubby" the Bull Dog.
1925.

Erna at age 15 years in her
confirmation dress in
Tientsin, China. 1924.

CHAPTER SIX
My Gain, My Loss

In 1926 Father received his second compensation check from the German government, which really came in the time of need. Business was not going well. Because of Papa's drinking, he lost his sense of taste. Soon customers began complaining that the sausages were too highly seasoned. The Kiessling and Bader Confectionery was one of our best customers but soon, they too canceled their standing order because of the overly seasoned sausages. Father realized that his drinking was affecting his business and made an effort to stop but the damage was already done. Neither did he stop drinking entirely. His judgment was affected and he accumulated many debts. Even with the compensation check from the German Government he was unable to keep up his large business. He had to search for another smaller house in the German concession. He found one, and again, we had a butchery, a small restaurant and two or three rooms to rent.

Business soon began picking up. Our old customers came back and the German community patronized us, too. Also, the German consulate sent us a boarder now and then. Many Germans were returning to Tientsin and resuming their trades. Once again, Papa rented the large room on the first floor to American troops who opened a club there. Soldiers frequented the club both day and night and ordered meals from us. The added income was most helpful and enabled Papa to meet our monthly bills.

The German Consulate sent any jobless person, any drifter, or anyone with a bad reputation back to Germany. Such practice was to uphold the good reputation of the foreigners in China. In 1921 and 1922 several of these doubtful characters had re-emerged. They had disappeared into the interior of China when repatriation began after the war. As these drifters had no money, no jobs, and no places to stay, they looked for assistance to the German Consulate. If they could not find work, they were given a one-way ticket to Germany. Papa and I met some strange characters among them. One woman, Frau M., who was once a respectable lady, was one such person. She was a widow. One day, she suddenly re-appeared in Tientsin in a terrible condition. She had been sleeping in stables, had nothing to eat and was completely run down. Someone found her and took her to the German Consulate. They sent her to us. Papa knew her from way back before the war, back when her husband was still living and she was one of our good customers in the French concession.

Papa immediately ordered the servants to prepare a bath for her. (There was no running hot water on the second floor in our house. Water was bought in a shop on the street and then delivered to the house in buckets and poured into a galvanized bathtub right in each person's room).

After the boy had prepared the bath for Frau M. , Papa knocked at her door and asked, "is everything all right? Do you need anything else?"

"No I don't!!" she answered in an odd tone of voice.

Later when she reported to the German Consul, they asked, "are you satisfied with staying here?"

"Yes, Mr. Kluge even came up and asked if there was anything else I needed." It sounded as if she was insinuating that Papa needed a bed partner. Papa became very upset when he heard about what she had said. He did not like her insinuating something that was not there.

After a few weeks, she was also sent to Germany.

Life went on. On my sixteenth birthday Tante Corinth gave me a boy doll, about eight inches tall. She had knitted a blue suit and cap for him. The doll was adorable and I played with it that afternoon. Papa did not like that and he said, "Put that doll away; you are too big to play with dolls."

I snapped back, "I want to play with it. Tante Corinth gave it to me." Papa could not stand back-talk. Before I knew what was happening he smacked me across my face.

I grabbed the doll and ran to my room. Surprisingly, Papa let me keep the doll.

Some days were worse than others. Once more the German Consul was going to take me away from Papa. The Consulate knew my situation and wanted to help me when people reported Papa and his abuse toward me.

A German couple took me to a May Day festival at the German Club and I stayed at their house overnight. I came home the next morning.

Papa was waiting for me with a pistol in his hand. He had been drinking again and had forgotten that I was going to spend the night with them. "Where have you been all night?"

"I was with Herr and Frau Schuster, Papa. I told you last night I was spending the night with them." Papa struck my face once and I put my arm up to protect my face from the next blow. I was wearing a watch and when Papa hit me again, the watch cut my face and I began to bleed. Papa began shouting at me again and I was terribly afraid of his great anger. I fled from the house, running out into the street. I ran as fast as I could back to the Schuster's apartment.

"What happened, Erna?" Frau Schuster asked in alarm, when she saw my bleeding face.

"Please," I begged, "come and explain that I have been with you all night! Papa is terribly angry."

They went back to our house with me and explained the situation to Papa. Papa then calmed down. The next day Papa was summoned to the German Consulate for questioning. But, I stayed on with Papa, now with a new small scar on my face.

Terra was still with us, and her pup, Nelly. Nelly was a little smaller than her mother and was a shy dog; she did not make friends easily. She was Papa's special dog.

When I was not helping Papa I would take long walks with Terra. But Terra and I did not always walk alone.

I had fallen in love with an American soldier, Andrew, who had been coming to the restaurant. We met secretly for long walks. I would take Terra out, hoping that Papa wouldn't notice anything different.

Andrew was about ten years older than I. He was blond, tall, and slender. Not handsome, but kind and tender to me. I knew that he loved me. I was hungry for love and kindness and Andrew gave me the love and affection that I craved.

One day as we walked through the fields, Andrew drew me behind a tall haystack and began kissing me. We sat on the ground while Terra ran and frisked about in the field.

"I love you very much, Erna."

"And I, you," I said, laying my head on his shoulder.

"I want to take care of you and love you. I want to take you away from your father and be good to you. Please let me take care of you."

"That sounds wonderful, Andrew. Could it be possible?"

"I will rent a small house for us. We will be together every day, just like husband and wife. Will you come live with me, Erna?"

I looked into Andrew's eyes and saw the love and tenderness written there and I said, "Yes."

I began looking forward to going away with Andrew. I wanted to be away from my terrible life with Papa. I could hardly wait to move into the house with Andrew. Then, suddenly, Andrew said to me on one of our walks, "Erna, always remember that I love you. I am being transferred back to the States. My company is leaving immediately."

"No, Andrew! It can't happen. I love you too much." I threw my arms around his neck and held on to him, sobs jerking my whole body. I felt as if my world was coming to an end.

"We will write, Sweetheart, we will write. I will be back for you someday."

Andrew and I exchanged letters for a while. I had his letters sent to a post office box so Papa wouldn't find out about him. I was very sad for a long time. I knew deep down that I had lost Andrew.

I also lost my Terra. She had puppies again and had gotten hold of some chicken bones, which she could not digest. We had to have her put to sleep. I missed Terra so much. I began taking Nelly for walks now.

I was seventeen years old. Papa never mentioned my mother when he was sober, but, when he drank, he had nothing good to say about her; he called her such nasty names. I thought Mother was dead. Neither Tante Corinth, nor Frau Behrend (formerly Frau Goldau. Herr Goldau had died and she had remarried) who helped Mother and me run away to Germany, ever mentioned my mother to me.

One day the mailman brought a postcard from Germany addressed to me. All the address said was: Erna Kluge, Tientsin, China. I was surprised a card addressed so vaguely could ever reach me. On the card were the words; "Liebes Schwesterlein, viele Grüsse aus Deutschland sendet Dir Dein Bruder Walter Kleman"; "Dear sister, your brother Walter Kleman sends many greetings from Germany." I was astonished! I did not know I had a brother. His surname was Kleman, mine is Kluge.

I rushed with the postcard to Papa. "Look, Papa!" I exclaimed. "I found this postcard in the mail. Who is this? I did not know I had a brother. We don't have the same surname. Do you think Mama is alive? Tell me Papa!"

Surprisingly, Papa was not angry. "Go to Tante Corinth," is all that he said.

I went to her and showed her the card. I asked her all the same questions that I had asked Papa. "Erna," she said, "this is all I can tell you. Your mother took you away to Germany, but you were returned to your papa. Walter is your half-brother. Go to Frau Behrend. She knows more about what happened."

I met with Frau Behrend who explained what had happened when Mother and I had left for Germany. She had not been in touch with Mother over the years. She suggested, "Why don't you write to Walter and ask about your mother?"

I took Frau Behrend's advice and wrote immediately. Papa did not object. The next letter that came from Germany was from my mother. I opened it and read:

Dear Erna,

When I came home one week-end you were gone. Someone had come and taken you back to China. I could not believe it! They took my little girl away. Only a mother who has lost her child can understand my anguish. Until today I cannot understand why my cousin, with whom you were staying let this happen to me and you.

I was beside myself. To whom should I turn? After a day or two I decided to write to the German Consul in Tientsin. Because war had started, all communications were broken off with China. The letter came back. I was very unhappy because all my efforts were in vain. Later that year I met Walter's father again, William Kleman. We married that same year.

When the war was over, we heard that all Germans were repatriated to Germany. I thought you might be somewhere here, but where? All those years I longed for my little girl.

One recent Sunday afternoon, we were sitting at the coffee table, looking at some old pictures from China and wondering where you could be. Then Walter said, "Let us send her a postcard, perhaps she is still in Tientsin." I'm so glad you are alive, my Erna."

Love,
Your Mutti

I read mother's letter over and over again, hardly able to believe the words written on the paper. Mother and I began corresponding regularly after that. I had found my mother at last.

Meanwhile, Papa's drinking got worse. Instead of buying meat for the shop, he would buy beer, and, once he started drinking, there was no stopping. Everything was neglected and the business suffered. There were days when there was no meat or sausage in the store and nothing to sell in the restaurant. Some days we just had tea to drink and dry bread to eat. I wanted to look for a job, but Papa would not let me. "My daughter is not going to work for other people," he said. I went to see Tante Corinth secretly and told her about our situation and asked her to please try and find work for me. She found a job for me at the well known German pastry shop, Kiessling and Bader.

Herr Albert Kiessling, the owner of the bakery, learned his trade—baker and confectioner — in Dresden, Germany, before the turn of the century. He had traveled the world's oceans as a cook from 1901 to 1904. Then he had quit seafaring and stayed in Hong Kong three years. Through the German Consul there, he learned there was a growing German community in Tientsin, North China. He went there to try his luck and found a job at a Greek bakery, "Karatzas," but he soon started his own business. In 1908 he opened his shop in the French concession under the name "Kiessling, Confectioner and Baker." In 1913 Herr Friedrich Bader joined the firm. He also had traveled throughout many countries. He learned his trade, like Herr Kiessling, in Germany, then traveled to Scotland, London, America and finally, China.

At their bakery, I started my first job as a salesgirl. I was excited about working for such hard working, honest craftsmen and businessmen. I was very proud to work for them. Papa was angry at first, but he was glad when I brought home the money. I kept back pocket money for toothpaste and stockings.

In the beginning, Papa bought supplies with my money and started to make sausages again, and he also bought food for the restaurant. But that did not last long. Alcohol had the upper hand. He started drinking again and the money I brought home went for beer. We quarreled a great deal. I started withholding more of my salary, which made him very angry.

After several months I received a raise. I then made enough money that I could have rented a small Chinese house (they were cheap), and hired a house-boy to do the cooking and cleaning. Papa would not have had to work. I suggested these things to Papa but he would not hear of it. So I continued to give him just part of my salary, which infuriated him more and more. We just did not get along at all. This went on for months. We quarreled almost every evening. The weekends were the worst when I was home all day. He did not abuse me physically, but his words were harsh and insulting. I talked back. I did not want to take his insults and abuses. This made matters worse.

One evening during a big argument, Papa said bitterly, "Erna, take your things and get out of here." I was glad to leave. I threw a few clothes into a small suitcase and had a rickshaw coolie drive me to Tante Corinth's.

Onkel Corinth went to see Papa the next day and told him that I was staying with them until I could find a room. Frau Behrend had a boardinghouse. I rented a small attic room from her. I had my meals with her, too.

After a few weeks I went to see Papa. I was eager to know how he was doing. Tante Corinth went with me.

It seemed that Papa was happy to see me and I asked him, "How are you, Papa, how is business?"

"I'm all right, business could be better, though." I had noticed as I came in through the butchery that there was not much meat or sausage in the store.

Tante Corinth asked Papa, "Herr Kluge, is there anything I can do for you?"

"Ach nein, thank you," he answered.

As we were leaving I said, "Papa, I will come and see you every Wednesday evening after work." I kissed him good-bye and left feeling rather sad.

I went to see Papa on Wednesdays after work as I had promised. As I had to pay for my board and lodging now, I was not able to give him as much money as I had before. From week to week the situation at Papa's home seemed to get worse. I went to see the Corinths to talk things over. "What can I do? It cannot go on like this. Papa just cannot continue to live the way he does."

We decided that I should go back and try to live with Papa again. With his drinking problem, he could no longer work. I was planning to tell him about my decision to go back home the next Wednesday. But Frau Behrend's son invited me to a water ball game that evening. "I'll see Papa tomorrow," I told myself, and I left for the game.

The next morning I went to work as usual. About nine o'clock our faithful servant, Wang, who had stayed with us through all the difficult times, came to the bakery and said to me,"Liu Guniang, come home quickly. Your papa is very ill."

I asked permission to leave the store and hurried home. I found Papa lying on the bed, very pale, unconscious, with foamy saliva rolling from his mouth. I did not know what to do for Papa and decided to call a rickshaw and drive to Tante Corinth's and tell her what had happened. I left Wang to stay with Papa.

Adjacent to Tante Corinth's house was the German-American Hospital. We went over for help. "I'm sorry, but no doctor is available," a nurse told us. "We will send a doctor as soon as one is free."

We quickly returned to Papa. He was still unconscious.

Tante Corinth was unable to revive him. At noon she had to leave to take care of her husband and children. "I will be back soon." she said, and left.

I was alone with Papa. I stayed at his bedside, prayed, and waited for the doctor to come. There was nothing I could do. A little while later, perhaps thirty minutes, Papa opened his eyes. He recognized me, reached for my hand and said in a very low voice, "Mausi, be a good girl; I am leaving you."

"Nein, Papa, don't go! Stay with me, Papa, please stay," I cried. But his hand grew limp, he turned his head, and he died.

Wang came running into the room when he heard my cry. He sat beside me on Papa's bed. I laid my head on his shoulder. He stroked my arm and said, "Bo Yao Ku, Liu Guniang," don't cry."

Wang had been with us a number of years and was our only servant who stayed faithfully with Papa during those last difficult months. He sat with me until Tante Corinth came. While waiting, I noticed that Nelly would not come out from under Papa's bed when I called her, which was strange. I wondered why she would not come, then I remembered someone saying that dogs senses when their masters are dying. She was really Papa's dog. Except for Wang during the day Nelly was the only companion Papa had after I moved out.

After a while I heard Tante Corinth coming. I ran to her, throwing my arms around her neck. I cried, "Tante Corinth, Papa died, what am I going to do?"

She took me in her arms and held me tight and I heard her soothing voice saying, "Erna, we will take care of you. You will be all right." We went to Papa's bed. I cried again when I heard Tante Corinth praying, "The Lord is my Shepherd."

The doctor finally came. He examined Papa and said to me, I am afraid your father committed suicide. He has taken some poison." He bent down and gently stroked my shoulder, saying, "I am sorry, Dear."

"Oh, why has he done this," I wondered. Was it because I had not come to see him the day before? Did he think I had deserted him? And here I had wanted to tell him this very evening that I was coming back. Could I have prevented it had I come yesterday? I felt so guilty and told Tante Corinth about my guilt feelings.

"Ach nein, Erna, don't think like that. He was tired and had no will to live anymore."

"But if I had come yesterday to see him he would have known that I still loved him and wanted to be with him."

She took my hand, "Erna, let us go home now. I'll ask Wang to stay with Papa until Onkel Corinth will come and take care of the necessary things and the funeral. We will have to find a home for Nelly, too."

We went back to Papa's bed for the last time. I stroked his graying hair back from his forehead. He looked so peaceful now. What a sad life he has had, I thought. He has gone through so much. Poor Papa. Now you have no more worries, you are in heaven. "I'll be good, Papa!" I cried aloud.

I petted Nelly, hugged her; she licked my face. "I'll find a good home for you." I shook hands with Wang. "Chija chija nee, thank you, Wang, I will see you soon," I said. I left the house with Tante Corinth.

Papa was buried in the German Cemetery. There was a small gathering at the funeral. A gentleman from the German Consulate came, Herr Kiessling, and a few of Papa's and my friends. "Another 'Old China Hand' died," I heard someone say.

When the ground had settled Tante Corinth and I had a gray tombstone made and put at the head of Papa's grave. I planted both green and flowering plants on his grave.

October the eleventh was Papa's birthday. I bought a bunch of colorful cosmos, a flower I always gave him on his birthday. That October they were in their fullest bloom. I carried the flowers and placed them on his grave that year.

True to her word, Tante Corinth soon found a good home for Nelly. She gave her to one of her friends.

Herr Corinth became my guardian. Papa's business was liquidated, and with the proceeds a percentage of our debts was paid to the creditors. I was not made liable for the debts that were not paid in full. After a few months, Herr Corinth was notified by the German consul that the third, and last, compensation check had arrived. As the liquidation was completed, I was able to keep the money. The money came at the best time. Had it arrived sooner, it would have gone to pay debts.

The money came to about five thousand Chinese silver dollars. Onkel Corinth invested the money in Germany in safe securities. I would not be able to touch the money until my twenty-first birthday. I was only able to use the interest and that only in Germany.

I ordered books and magazines and had some money remitted to my mother on her birthday and at Christmas. When she went on vacation, I sent her a little spending money. My guardian, Herr Corinth, made sure that I would not spend my money foolishly. It made me feel secure that I had some money of my own in the bank to use if I needed it. Feeling secure was a new feeling for me.

Erna at age 16 years in Tientsin,
China. 1925

Erna at age 18 years in Tientsin,
China. 1927.

Karl Heinrich Kluge. 1876-
1928.

CHAPTER SEVEN
On My Own

A new life started for me. It was such a relief not to have that worry about Papa anymore. I had constantly wondered, does he have enough to eat? He had lost weight when I saw him the last time. Was he drinking again? Was the store running low on meat? These had been my worries from day to day.

I was free now. I was free from worries about Papa and free to run my own life. I could buy what I wanted and go to the movies if I felt like it. But, somehow, I had no desire to go and went very seldom. I went a little overboard with buying, though. I loved pretty clothes and began to spend too much. But, I got that out of my system pretty quickly when I found out the money just went so far.

I enjoyed my work, even if I did have to work hard. Herr and Frau Kiessling and Herr Bader and his wife were very kind to me. Their pastry shop had an international clientele and I met many foreign people. They made the finest German, French, Danish, English and Austrian pastries and specialities available for different festivities and occasions. Their goods were not only mailed all over China, but to Africa, Australia, the United States and other countries.

The five languages I spoke were of great benefit to me. German, English, French and Chinese came very easy to me, but I had a little trouble with Russian, especially reading. As all the sales girls were Russian and a big part of our customers were Russian, too, I really needed to improve on it. So, I took a few lessons. Once I learned how to read, I was okay. I knew enough for the pastry business. I could now read the order slips that came to the store.

Herr Kiessling's sister was in charge of the salesgirls, the shop, and all outgoing orders. I worked very closely with her. I was the only German salesgirl and the youngest. After about a year, Fraulein Kiessling married and I was given her position. My confidence rose with my new position. To be entrusted with her job was an honor. And I was allowed to handle the cash register, which meant that they had confidence in me likewise. With my new position, my salary was increased accordingly and I was able to save money every month. My guardian, Herr Corinth, also insisted that I save.

I enjoyed my small attic room in the evenings and on the week-ends. It was peaceful and quiet there and I sat for hours on end reading love stories. Love stories gave me the warmth that I was missing in my life. I embroidered some doilies for the room which brightened up the place. I bought a new mandolin, which I enjoyed playing as I sang. Sundays were usually spent with the Corinths or the Behrends. We often went on picnics, or to holiday activities at the German Club, such as a masquerade ball were I dressed as a Dutch girl.

At times, Tientsin was covered with a cloud of fine sand. When the sandstorms raged in the Gobi Desert it blew all across Manchuria, Peking and down to Tientsin. The sand covered the sky, making the sun barely visible. The sand was so fine it came through every little slit of the doors and windows. The furniture was covered with it. We breathed it, felt it in our nose, our mouth and on our teeth.

I left for work at about seven forty-five every morning. One particular morning there was such a darkness it seemed to me as if it were evening, just after sunset. There was a stillness in the air. It was frightening. I wondered if the world was ending.

I was not the only one that felt as if the world was coming to an end. At Kiessling and Bader's everyone was uneasy and people were saying, "What is going to happen?" This strange stillness lasted for hours. Few people were on the streets. The cars on the streets were covered so heavily with the sand that it was impossible to determine whether they were red or blue.

All of a sudden, a loud thunderbolt rang out, filling the air, and rain and sand poured down from the skies. Everyone ran to the windows to see the mixture of sand and rain pouring down. After about thirty minutes of the strange downpour, the air cleared and the sun shone through. Everyone breathed a sigh of relief. I didn't understand the phenomenon that day, but I was glad the world hadn't ended.

Autumn came and it was the time of year when Herr and Frau Behrend, their two Irish setters, and I took long walks on Sunday afternoons into the nearby villages. Our walks took us into another world. There was even a different scent in the air. I could smell the damp earth, the compost piles near the adobe farm houses, and the smoke coming out of the chimneys. I could even smell the very dirt of the streets. The dirt reeked of animal droppings, sewage, and mud.

On the horizon we could see a few trees and utility poles which lined the highway. All around us were neatly kept rice and vegetable fields. The houses had different shapes, which amazed me. I drew the attention of Frau Behrend to them and said, "Look, Frau Behrend, these houses here have rounded roofs and those over there have regular pointed ones. And look at those fences around the houses, how tightly woven they are!" We went a little closer to look at them.

"These fences will withstand many a sandstorm," she commented.

"I am sure they will," Herr Behrend said.

The children there left their yards and came running toward us. Some had never seen a white person. They ran into the house shouting excitedly, "come quickly! See the "By Guize," (White Devils). Others were afraid of us and hid behind the fence.

I enjoyed our outings. We never went twice to the same village, though, since each was so different from the other.

I was looking forward to my first Christmas party at Kiessling and Bader's. I had heard how nice they were. Both couples and their children lived in apartments adjacent to the bakery. This year the Christmas Eve party was going to be at the Kiessling's. The German employees were invited to the Christmas Eve dinner and the sharing of gifts. We all wore our Sunday best. My dress was made of Kelly green woolen material with a beige lace collar and cuffs. I chose a gold cross necklace which I thought went well with the dress.

The party was lovely and the atmosphere so congenial. We feasted on a Christmas dinner of roasted goose, potato dumplings, red cabbage, apple sauce and, as dessert, English plum pudding. After dinner we were led to the living room where the gifts were displayed—Herr and Frau Kiessling, the Baders and we three German employees—Herr Reichel, Herr Scheel, and I.

Each employee received a "Stollen" (German Christmas cake), a plate with cookies, candies, and marzipan, and an envelope with a month's salary. I thought the gifts were too generous. The two men also received a gift certificate for a suit made by a German tailor. I went over to Frau Kiessling to thank her for the gifts. She said unexpectedly, "Erna, don't you want to try on your new coat that is hanging over there?"

"That fur coat is for me?" I asked.

"Yes it is; go and try it on," she said, giving me a pat on my arm. I tried it on and it fit perfectly. I was so happy. I had never had a fur coat before. Never had I expected such a gift. I had worked for them only for a year. I hugged both ladies with tears in my eyes and thanked them.

After the holidays I went to buy a new hat to go with the coat. I asked Frau Behrend to take a picture of me in the coat and hat. I sent the picture to my mother.

The two young men which were at the Christmas party had earned their masters certification in fine pastry and candy making in Germany. Herr Reichel, the older of the two, came

101

to China with Herr Kiessling when he returned from his repatriation to Germany around 1921. After Herr Reichel's first five years were up, he went to Germany on vacation. The vacation, including the train fare, plus six months leave were paid for by K&B. Herr Kiessling asked him to bring back another pastry chef. He had returned with Wilhelm Scheel who had graduated with him from the same pastry and confectionary finishing school.

When a young man was hired to come to China, he knew it was on a five-year contract. The contract specified that a hired man could not marry within this time. He would receive a two week vacation along with a salary raise each year. At the end of the five years, he would receive a six month paid leave and a round-trip train ticket to Germany. If he decided not to return to the firm, he was given a one-way ticket. Often the young man would go to Germany and come back to China with a wife.

It was important in China to keep up a certain standard of living. To keep up this image, one needed to be able to afford at least a cook, a house boy and an "Amah" if there were children in the family. It was common to have hired help. A European woman just would not stand in the kitchen or clean house, or wash clothes.

If a person had been hired by a bank, an import and export company, or a business firm he would have to commit himself to study the Chinese language, so that he could communicate with the customer in his native language. He was also required to learn some writing which certainly was not easy.

Tientsin had a very large Russian community as well as our German community. They were the so-called White Russians, who deferred from the Communist Reds, the Bolsheviks. The White Russians were predominately Russian Orthodox by faith.

After taking Fraulein Kiessling's place, I had Nina, one of the Russian salesgirls, work closely with me. She was dependable, fast and friendly— all a good salesgirl should be. Her natural wavy hair added softness to her Slavic looks, Dimples appeared when she smiled. A pretty girl! Her parents, with tens of thousands of other White Russians had fled to China from the Bolsheviks in 1917. They were very kind people. I often spent Russian holidays with them.

When I started to work at Kiessling and Bader's, Wilhelm (William) Scheel had already been working there for three years as a "Konditor Meister," or Master Pastry Chef. Wilhelm was short, had steel grey eyes and brown wavy hair — a rather handsome man.

When pastries, tarts, and rolls were brought to the store, they had to be counted and signed for. One day William returned a slip to me with a grin on his face. I was busy at the time and put the slip in the pocket of my white uniform. The purpose of the slip was to confirm that the correct number of cakes or rolls, etc. shown on the slip were received. Later that afternoon I wondered why he had such a grin on his face. But for the time being I put it out of my mind and returned to my job of filling orders of one pound boxes of chocolates. I continued working but the image of his strange grin bothered me. I looked at the clock and realized I was ahead of schedule. I paused and opened the slip and read it. He had put a big question mark after Kluge intending to question my intelligence. (In German the word "kluge" means " clever"). Oh, this made me angry. I did not need anyone to belittle me. When I had a spare minute I went to the bakery, handed him the slip, and said, "You think you are so smart, don't you? Well, this is the last time you put your question mark after my name!" I left him standing there. In the future I signed E.K. This put an end to his little game.

Later William came to me and said, "I'm sorry, I never intended to make you angry." I soon forgot about the incident.

Kiessling and Bader Confectionery and Restaurant, or just K&B, was a very busy place. Except for Chinese New

Year's Day, it was open for business every day of the year from eight o'clock in the morning until midnight, and sometimes later. Christmas Eve they closed at four in the afternoon.

Chinese New Year was a big holiday. This was the day when everyone—male, female, child, young and old—took a bath and wore a new outfit. Only the rich had bathtubs. For a fee people could take baths in bathhouses, which were kept quite clean. Even foreigners went there, if they did not have bathtubs where they stayed.

It was customary for the Chinese people to pay all debts, especially gambling debts, before the end of the year. If these obligations were not met, indebted people often took their own lives. They couldn't stand "losing face."

At this time of the year, all Chinese employees of Kiessling and Bader received their yearly bonuses. On New Year's Day at about ten o'clock in the morning, every employee—from the youngest, who opened the door for the customers or took their packages to their cars- to the Number One baker or cook—came to wish their employer "Kung Chi Fa Tsai," a prosperous New Year. All were invited to the restaurant, and served slightly spiked orange punch and fancy cookies. Before entering the store, they would fire long chains of small fire crackers, hung on trees to chase away the evil spirits. Every year Herr Bader had a treat -the fireworks- for all. He bought the materials and made his own fireworks. Everyone went to the roof garden to see the display. After the fireworks the employees entered the restaurant for a time of singing, joking and showmanship. One would imitate a crowing rooster, another a dog or horse. Another would recite a poem, tell a funny story, or sing a comic song.

After this, the Chinese employees left, each to go to his own home for a big New Year's dinner. The rest of us went on a picnic with several other German families and their children. Usually the picnics were held at the abandoned Mandarin Graves, far out of town. There was always a lot of food and drink. We played games and went on sled rides on the frozen river that was nearby. The sled rides were called "Peitze" rides. The Peitze was a sort of sled or raft. It was made of boards, about three by six feet, fastened to two iron rails, covered with a blanket or piece of fur.

When an empty Peitze came by, William said to me, "Fräulein Kluge, do you want to go for a ride?"

"Oh, yes," I said. I had been secretly hoping that he would ask me. I had become attracted to him. He called out to the man to stop. He took my hand and we ran the short distance to the frozen river and boarded the Peitze. There was no place to hold on in the sled, so we held on to one another. I liked the feel of William's strong arms around my waist. The owner of the Peitze stood behind us. With a sharp-pointed bamboo pole he pushed into the ice, and off we went on the frozen river. The man stayed on one end of the sled and William and I on the other. It was my first Peitze ride and my first time alone and close to William. It was so exciting. I knew he liked me.

After a while I noticed that William was backing off and was cool toward me. I could not understand it.

Then one day at work he said, "Erna, can I see you this evening?"

"Sure. Will seven-thirty be all right?"

"I'll pick you up at the boarding house."

I wondered what it was all about. William had been so serious.

That evening we walked to the Victoria Park in the British concession. After strolling around and admiring the rows of red roses and the beautiful yellow tea roses, we found a bench in a secluded area.

William commented on the beautiful evening and something trivial that had happened at work before he finally came out with it. "I have been wanting to tell you this; it is not easy. A girl in Germany is waiting for me. Her name is also Erna.

She is a very nice girl. When my contract is over next year, I was going back to marry her. I have been trying to put you out of my mind and avoid you, but we see each other daily and you have become more and more dear to me." He took my hand.

I did not say anything, I just put my hand over his, and moved closer to him.

"I'll write her that I am not coming back and for her to release me from my promise."

He put his arm around me and I leaned my head on his shoulder. "Are you sure that this is what you want to do?" I was silently praying that he would say "Yes."

"Yes, but I know it will hurt her. She was my first love and I was her first love, but I have found you, and I want to share my life with you. Will you be my wife, Erna?"

"Yes. I love you Willie." I looked up into his grey eyes and our lips met for the first time.

That night when William walked me home he kissed me again at the front door of the boarding house. I could feel my pulse in my throat.

I lived in tension for several weeks until the letter finally came from William's girlfriend in Germany. William had been anxiously awaiting the letter and tore it open eagerly when it arrived. A slow smile spread across his face. He read the words of his ex-fiancee to me. She wished him happiness with his Erna in China.

William grabbed me into his arms as if he would never let me go.

A grand ball was planned in January at the German Club. William and I decided to go. We were going to have dinner at the Astor House Hotel and then go dancing at the Club. I wore a new evening gown, especially for William. It was made of pale green chiffon with matching lace. There were yards and yards of material in the skirt. I wore matching silk shoes and evening purse. When William saw me he took my hands, held me away, and looked at me.

"You look very pretty in that dress, Erna. What a lovely color for your golden braids and your grey eyes."

He pulled me to his chest and said, "I love you, Dear." This is the first time that he ever said, "I love you."

That evening we found out that we were both very poor dancers. It was the time of foxtrot, tango, blues, and the waltz. William was not too eager to dance, but to please me he tried. After a few tries and after looking at my pretty new shoes, I said, "Willie, I think we should take some dancing lessons, don't you?"

"Erna, I think it is positively silly to hop around the dance floor like this. I guess we should. But, from whom are we going to take lessons?"

"There is a studio not too far from the Club. I will find out more about it," I laughed.

Although we did little dancing that night, we had a lovely time, just being together.

We had to keep our courtship a secret because William was not returning to Germany. He intended to open his own business and wanted to collect the money that was due him from the firm to start his own pastry shop. We wondered if he would get his six months vacation pay. We were afraid that Herr Kiessling and Herr Barder would not be very pleased to hear that he was leaving to open his own business. William intended to go to Mukden, Manchuria, which is far away from Tientsin, so he would not be a competitor to them. Until these matters were settled he thought it best not to announce our engagement.

William's contract with Kiessling and Bader ended in the summer of 1930. They treated him fairly. We could have married and stayed with K&B for a while but William wanted his own business. He was a man with a strong will and did not like to be told what to do. He found a silent partner who was willing to invest in his enterprise. The man was an architect and had a good sense for business.

A modern building was constructed for us in Mukden. William left immediately after his contract expired to supervise construction of the bakery and to manage that which pertained to it. I was busy getting my trousseau together. While William was in Mukden we wrote each other daily. I couldn't wait to write him about everything that I had been thinking and doing every day.

Tante Corinth, her daughter, Elfriede and I took a short trip by boat to Tsingtau to visit some friends who had moved there. The city was a port on the south coast of Shantung Province. After German missionaries were murdered there in 1897 negotiations resulted in a lease of land to the German Government for ninety-nine years to establish a German colony. At the end of World War One the Japanese had captured the city, held it until 1922, then returned it to China. Many Germans were still living there and it retained the look of a German town.

While we were in route, and the two days we stayed in Tsingtau, William, of course, did not receive his daily love letter. When I returned to Tientsin I found several letters from him, the last one very upsetting. He wrote, "I have not received a letter in three days. Have you changed your mind?"

Rather than write a letter I sent a telegram; "Don't you realize that the letter cannot reach you when I am on board the ship, that I was farther away in Tsingtau? Surely I will come, and I do still love you!"

Erna dressed as a Dutch girl at age 19 years in Tientsin, China. 1928.

Chinese Village Dwellings near Tientsin, China. 1928.

Erna wearing Christmas gift from employer
Kiessling and Bader in Tientsin, China. 1928.

William Scheel as a Kiessling and
Bader "Konditor Meister" in
Tientsin, China. 1928.

Erna and a Chinese man on a "Peitze" or
sled on a frozen river in Tientsin, China.
1929.

The German Club in Tientsin,
China. 1929.

The city of Tsingtau, China.
1930.

CHAPTER EIGHT
Married Life

I arrived in Mukden, Manchuria on the first of October 1930, and we were married on the third at the German Consulate. William was twenty-seven years old and I was twenty. I wore a midnight blue velveteen dress for my wedding day. Besides William and me, only the Consul, our partner, and a witness were present. After the wedding ceremony, the Consul invited us to a champagne breakfast consisting of delicious assorted canapes and champagne.

For the evening, our partner, Mr. Pankow, invited us and ten guests to a dinner at his home. For this occasion, my dress was made of pale blue silk and lace. William gave me a corsage of pale pink sweetheart roses. The dinner was exquisite — pheasant as the main course, and an apricot mousse as dessert. It was a most enjoyable dinner.

My new husband and I did not go on a honeymoon. I was not disappointed as I realized that it was important for William to be at the building site. We hoped to open in just three weeks.

Our business was in a very attractive building on the main street of town. Upon entering, the pastry shop was located to the left and the restaurant to the right. Straight ahead, in the back, were the bakery, candy-making rooms, fine pastry room, and kitchen. A staircase between the pastry shop and the restaurant led to the second floor where there was a large hall for private and special parties. Our apartment was also on this level, to the right.

The staircase continued upward to the roof garden which covered the whole length and width of the building. We opened our store in November, just in time to take advantage of the Christmas season. I was really proud of what William had accomplished and proud to be Frau Scheel.

A mature German woman, Frau Ludmilla, and two young Russian girls helped me in the store. The woman was born in Russia. Her husband had been killed during the Revolution and she had fled to Manchuria with her two children and her parents. She was a very pleasant person. I was just twenty and it felt good to have an older person at my side .

Herr Zaudig was in charge of the restaurant. He was an elderly gentleman from Riga, Latvia. He and his wife had moved to St. Petersburg, Russia, where they became victims of the Revolution. He lost his wife and escaped to Mukden. A young Russian was his helper.

William took care of the rest of the business. All of his employees were Chinese. For our apartment we had a Chinese house boy who did the cleaning, washing, and ironing. He was a trustworthy and efficient helper to us.

It was an exciting day for us when we opened the doors of the store to the public. Especially for William—a lifelong dream attained. I celebrated with him. On that first day I took in our first ten dollar bill—a lot of money in those days. I was elated. I ran into the bakery, swinging it high in the air and shouting, "Look, Willie, our first ten dollar bill." I hugged and kissed him in front of the bakers, which embarrassed him immensely.

The bakers laughed and said, "Ding hau, ding hau," very good, very good. William thought I was rather childish, but I could not help myself. I had an exciting day.

Most of our clientele were middle class and wealthy Europeans, Russians and well-to-do Chinese; they all enjoyed the good service and quality foods we provided. Our motto was "Quality not Quantity."

The restaurant was always well attended. A quartet played soft and relaxing music. Some days our guests would enjoy a tea dance at five o'clock. In the evening, dim light enhanced the atmosphere during the dinner hour. People had to make reservations for tables. Again the orchestra played delightful music. After dinner we provided dancing, if the public asked for it. We intended to offer this same atmosphere on the roof garden come summer.

During those winter months, we arranged for several fancy dress balls. They were always well attended, mostly by our Russian clientele. The last ball always took place the night before the Lenten season began. Lent was a very strict fasting period of seven weeks for the White Orthodox Russians, so they really "lived it up" the Tuesday night before Ash Wednesday. The ladies wore beautiful, richly beaded costumes and headdresses, made of pale colored satins. The men wore boots and the typical Russian peasant shirts, worn over the trousers with a belt around the waist.

The culinary specialty for that day was 'blinis'—a yeast pancake served with sour cream, melted butter and black or red caviar. These blinis were baked and served all night long. They drank vodka, wine and beer in great quantities. Everyone danced and sang into the wee morning hours. On those occasions, we had two orchestras playing, one downstairs, and the other in the large room on the second floor.

I stayed up the first part of the night and William the second. William had to be in the bakery early the next morning anyhow.

The winters were very cold, often twenty eight degrees Centigrade below zero. It was in this very cold climate that I had chill-blains on my hands and feet. Wearing fur-lined shoes and woolen gloves which only revealed the tips of my fingers did not help. As soon as the first frost came the redness appeared. The awful itching started whenever my hands and feet got warm and moist. The condition would not leave me until the frost was gone. It started all over winter after winter.

Because of the cold weather, the window pane on our display window was often covered with a centimeter of ice.

We used a small electrical fan to defrost it, especially around Christmas, so that people could see our pretty display.

The ceiling of the window was covered with midnight blue crepe paper. I cut small star-shaped openings and a half moon into the paper. I spent many evenings preparing window displays. In the evenings, a light installed behind the paper would shine through the openings. A glittering snow scene covered the back and floor of the window. Live fir branches, simulating a forest, were fastened to the floor.

The bakers had prepared a large honeycake house. It stood in the background with a witch standing in the doorway and Hansel and Gretel at the side of the house. They were also made of honeycake. In the foreground, little wooden dolls on sleds came down the hillside. Different sized Santas made of chocolate or honeycake, as well as various kinds of animals and fruit made of marzipan and almond paste, were displayed in one corner. Our customers told us, "Your display is so attractive to everyone passing by on the streets."

For our American customers we honored George Washington's Birthday and had small petits fours made into the shape of logs. Larger ones we made with cherries and a hatchet made of red caramel sugar on top.

When Easter rolled around, our window decorations were also attractive. Bunnies, all sizes of chocolate eggs, little nests, and houses made of chocolate—all made in our candy shop— were on display.

We even made elaborate Halloween and Thanksgiving Day displays. And off and on we exhibited fake birthday and many tiered wedding cakes. My husband was an artist in cake decorating and I had the knack for displaying them.

Our apartment was small, but cozy. We had two bedrooms, a living and dining room separated by an arch opening, and a bathroom. We seldom used the kitchen as we had all our meals prepared in the restaurant kitchen. We ate our meals at a table in the corner of the store. Mostly we had the cook prepare simple meals for us since we did not care for the rich restaurant food. Herr Zaudig ate with us. After dinner the cook and I prepared the menu for the next day. I consulted my cookbook often. I felt that I was a poor cook compared to Papa and William.

It was not long before we had a dog and cat frisking about our place. "Flippy," the dog, was a small black and white mixed breed. "Muschi," the cat, was grey and black. The two got along tremendously together. A bakery had to have a cat to keep the mice away. Mice and rats liked to hang around the bakery and they could do a lot of damage. A cat or two took care of the problem.

Our cat usually stayed in the bakery, while the dog had his place in the store behind the counter on a chair. At feeding time the cat always ate first, and the dog watched from about two feet away. When Muschi finished her meal, she walked away with her tail held up high, as if she were saying, "It's all yours now." I had fun watching my new dog and cat.

After being in Mukden for a while we were invited to parties at the German Consulate or at important people's homes. We also attended functions given at the German Club, such as New Year's Day, May Day festivals, and carnivals.

I soon became aware that I needed to learn protocol and etiquette. From a book I ordered from Germany, I learned how to conduct myself in society. Papa had taught me table manners and how to be polite, but that was not enough. In time I learned and became comfortable and at ease in these circles.

I learned to play bridge and played once in a while in the afternoons at the German Club. Sometimes I played tennis in the mornings before the store opened. When William had time, he went to the Club and had a beer or two with some other businessmen. We knew that all work and no play was not good for either of us. We had a growing business, which meant hard work and long hours.

Herr Zaudig was a Christian and as time went by he became a good friend to me. I was able to talk to him when my heart was heavy. William worked very hard with very long hours. Not getting enough sleep made him irritable and short tempered at times.

William rose at five o'clock to go to the bakery. The sales girls came to work at seven-thirty to take out the left-over cakes and pastries and to clean the showcases. We sold our left-over cakes at half-price. I went down at eight o'clock when we opened the store.

The bread bakers had come in at four in the morning. William saw to it that the warm rolls and breads were delivered in time to reach our customers before seven o'clock. Our helpers made bread deliveries in large wicker baskets, which were attached to the backs of the bicycles. We made several deliveries a day, including desserts for luncheons and festive dinners, and cakes for teas and coffee parties.

Our first Christmas, New Year, and Easter holidays were behind us. I was looking forward to warmer weather and was so glad to see the first soft green buds on the bare trees. Spring was here and soon summer would follow. The roof garden had to be ready for the first warm day. Many customers had already been asking, "When are you going to open your roof garden?"

We arranged our tables and chairs early. We placed the furniture around groups of blooming oleander and pomegranate bushes growing in huge wooden containers. The furniture arrangement and bushes would give people a little privacy. The tables were covered with red and white checkered tablecloths and on each one was a vase with fresh flowers. I could visualize our clientele sitting around the tables enjoying our delicious specialities. I could taste the refreshing iced chocolate and iced coffee topped with vanilla ice cream and whipped cream. I could smell the various kinds of fruit and butter cream pastries which we would offer. I knew no Viennese cafe could offer anything more delicious. We would entertain with music there too.

The roof garden opened in May and was a great success.

We did have a few slow days, but when we did, Herr Zaudig took over, so William and I had some time to ourselves. This precious time to ourselves helped our marital relations.

1931 - The Japanese in Manchuria

Little by little, more and more Japanese infiltrated Manchuria. They had invested much effort and money to develop the area of Southern Manchuria. Under them the entire area later became the puppet state of Manchukou—the Land of the Manchus. After the Nationalists came to power in China, their goal was to recover all foreign-held rights in China. This threatened the Japanese interests. On September 18, 1931, the Japanese claimed the Chinese had bombarded the railroad near Mukden. With this "incident" they took all of Manchuria. In the following weeks they occupied several strategic points and erected new buildings around Mukden.

In the North, the Chinese and Soviets were struggling over the Chinese Eastern Railroad, which had been in the hands of the non-Soviets until the Revolution. The non-Soviets had grown up with the railroad and it was their life and livelihood. Neither the Japanese, nor the Russians, were ready for war.

The Japanese also became our customers. I did not speak the language, so I was obliged to take some lessons. I at least had to be able to tell the customers the prices and what the specific ingredients of a cake or pastry were. I needed to know how to say "Thank you," "Please," and "Good-bye," and to bid the time of day. I enjoyed learning another language and it helped me to communicate with these new customers.

The Japanese were good customers and very polite. But the men were frightening to me when they were intoxicated. I tried to avoid them and would hide behind a pillar in the store when I saw them coming into the restaurant, unsteady on their feet.

1932 - Our First Child

In the spring of 1932, I realized that I was pregnant. I was very happy, yet I knew that William did not want a child at this time. I chose a quiet evening to tell him. A thunderstorm had kept our customers away so we had closed early. William and I were sitting in our living room. He was reading a letter from his mother which had arrived that afternoon and I was leafing through a German magazine that had also come in the mail that day. In the background "Eine Kleine Nachtmusik" was playing on our phonograph. We seldom were able to relax like that.

Suddenly I nervously blurted out, "Willie, we are going to have a baby. I am so happy about it, aren't you?"

William put his letter down, looked at me and said, "Erna, you know this is not a good time to have a baby. The business is still new, we are so busy! And the political situation is so uncertain."

I moved closer to him, put my arms around his neck. "It seems no time is the right time. But we will manage. It will be so nice to have a little one in our life."

I felt him soften. He gave me a kiss and asked, "When is it due?"

"Beginning of January, I think. I will see our doctor this week, then we will know more. I am glad that you are not angry. You'll see it will be all right."

"I hope so," he answered and smiled.

The doctor confirmed my condition. The child would be due in the first week of January. A friend of mine, who was expecting around the same time, and I would walk for an hour every time I could leave the store. I was hoping that I would make it through Christmas. I felt good. I even made the window display, crawling in and out of the window, working through all the Christmas rush.

On the evening of December 25—the day before my birthday—I was in our apartment, getting some things ready for an afternoon coffee with friends the following day. At eleven o'clock William came upstairs. He had heard me roaming around. "'Now Frauchen, you know what time it is? You should lie down. It is after eleven."

"All right, Dear. I'll just finish straightening up the candles on the Christmas tree, and then I'll go to bed."

"The last customers have just asked Herr Zaudig for their checks. I'll go down and lock up. I'll be up soon," William said.

"You will find me in bed by then," I answered him.

But William and I were in for a surprise. My labor pains started and my water broke. At one o'clock William ordered a taxi, which took us to the little private hospital. No doctor was there! He was at a Christmas party, in "high spirits," so he had to be called.

The doctor arrived shortly. He had to take something to get himself halfway sober. He approached my bed, still unsteady on his feet. I did not feel good about it at all. I had the feeling that he would fall on me. The inhaling, exhaling, and pushing was an unpleasant experience. I didn't think he knew when I had to do what. With the help of his wife, who was a nurse, I delivered a healthy baby boy. He was born at four o'clock in the morning, December 26, 1932, "at the same time the hot rolls come out of the oven!" his wife said.

Everything seemed just fine—but, it was not.

After a few days, the fever started. I had childbirth fever and hung on between life and death for many days. The doctor had failed to remove all of the placenta.

William came to the hospital to see me daily. I was delirious and often did not realize that he was sitting by my bedside holding my hand. When my mind was clear, I prayed, "Lord, please let me make it through this; make me well again."

I made it. William told me later when I was feeling better, "I would have killed the doctor if you had died." He really was beside himself. I was just very thankful to be better.

I named the baby Konrad Wolfgang. I was not able to nurse him and we had quite a time with him. The powdered milk, "Klim," did not agree with him and our doctor, the same one who had delivered him, was no help at all. He told me to try different quantities. I was not about to experiment with my baby. Instead I changed to an English missionary lady doctor. Under her care our baby gained weight and thrived.

After a few weeks I was back in the store. We found a good live-in Russian woman to take care of the baby. I needed a reliable person, as I was in the store most of the day and often part of the night. She was clean and trustworthy. I knew that I could depend on her.

To our dismay, she moved after about two years. Little Konrad missed her. Fortunately for him, and us, a good, clean and dependable Chinese Amah was recommended to us. Because we had an Amah, and Konrad was exposed to the Chinese language day after day, he began to speak Chinese. He would not speak German to us. We spoke German to him, he answered in Chinese. So, we had a Chinese-speaking German boy.

The year 1933 was a restless one. The combined military and economic position of Japan in Manchuria made it most difficult for foreign businesses to exist and therefore the future for us was uncertain. One foreign business after another closed and moved south. We wondered when we would have to go. Also, the wealthy Chinese companies closed their doors and moved to other cities, mostly south. Consequently, our business suffered and we had to make the same decision as the other business people.

William left for Nanking in 1934 to look for a house suitable for a bakery and living quarters. Our Chinese employees who had come with us to Manchuria either left for Nanking or their home towns, with assurance from us that we would send for them as soon as our business was set up. Herr Zaudig and a few of our Chinese employees helped me pack and to liquidate the business in Mukden. Our partner, of course, was also a great help. I needed his support. I needed all the support I could get. I don't know how I could have managed without all the help I received.

It was a consolation for me that my good friend Herr Zaudig moved with us. When things did not go so well with my husband, I had someone dear that I could confide in. I felt close to Herr Zaudig. He must have been in his late forties. He was tall and slender. His greying hair was parted in the middle and he wore a small mustache. I knew that he was fond of me too, but he never made any advances. He was always a gentleman around me. He was a friend.

1934 - We Start Over In Nanking

So, in 1934 we landed in Nanking and started all over again. The partnership with Mr. Pankow had to be dissolved. Our stay in Manchuria had lasted only four years.

During that time we did not lose contact with Kiessling and Bader in Tientsin. Business interests were awakened and the new store in Nanking opened under the name of Kiessling and Bader. My husband became a partner and the manager of the Nanking store.

I had a good feeling about moving to Nanking. Even though I would have to make new friends I was thankful for Herr Zaudig and the Chinese helpers that moved with us.

Konrad still had his Amah who also came along. I was very thankful for the warmer climate of the area which meant an end to my winter chill-blains.

Nanking was the capital of Kiangsu Province and was located on the south bank of the Yangtze River, about 160 miles west-northwest of Shanghai. The city of Nanking dated back to the Ming Dynasty of 1368. In 1853 it had been attacked by the Tai Ping rebels and many of the national monuments and public buildings were destroyed. In 1899 it opened its doors to foreign trade. Then in 1909 it was connected by railroad with Shanghai and became the well known southern terminus of the Tientsin-Pu-Kou Railway.

The national government moved the capital of China to Nanking in 1928. The city developed rapidly and many large buildings were constructed and broad boulevards were built. It seemed to be the "City of the Future," the center of communication. By then, it had a Christian College for men and one for women, also a Chinese National University.

The house William found was not big, but for the beginning, it was just right. Again, everything was in one building. The store was in the front of the first floor and the bakery and the kitchen in the back. On the second floor was the restaurant and above it, our small apartment. A new, large brick oven was built, work tables put up, a new kitchen for the restaurant installed and showcases ordered for the store. At least we did not have to train new bakers and cooks, as our own soon followed us.

We advertised and our customers advertised for us by word of mouth and our business grew rapidly. The name Kiessling and Bader helped too since it was well known all over China. My husband's quality baking made a name for itself. We had the only foreign bakery in Nanking. We catered to all nationalities; croissants and Bûche de Noël for the French, plum pudding and English fruitcake and scones for the British, paska and Kulich for the Russians, boterietters for the Dutch, stollen and lebkuchen and marzipan and hutzelbrot and all sorts of fancy torten and pastries for the Germans. All foreign embassies ordered cakes from us. Even Chinese Chairman, Chang Kai-shek and his wife were our customers. They often sent their servants to us to pick up orders for them.

Business was very good and we began contemplating enlarging. Unfortunately, we could not expand because we were sandwiched in between other buildings. We started looking for a new location and found a vacant corner lot on the main street—ideally located. An architect began drawing up plans for a new building for us. We were excited and really looking forward to our new venture.

It was 1937 by now. The Japanese were occupying one city after the other and were closing in on Nanking. Negotiations with the architect were postponed.

It was about this time that I received an announcement of Onkel Corinth's death. I did not even know that he had been ill. Poor Tante Corinth—I knew it was hard on her.

1937 - Our Second Child

I was pregnant again. My pregnancy came along normally and I was expecting the baby in July. It was the hottest month in Nanking. Nanking was surrounded by mountains and the heat became trapped in the valley. There was no breeze and I had difficulty sleeping. There were no fans. There was no relief, although we opened all windows. We slept on finely woven bamboo mats because even the sheets were too warm. I said to William, "I do not wish my worst enemy to be pregnant in July in Nanking."

The heat in the city was just too much for me to bear. On cool days I would take a boat ride on Lotus Lake outside the city walls. Konrad and his Amah enjoyed coming along on the ride. In the distance we could see the Purple Mountains.

124

We were surrounded by hundreds of rosy lotus blossoms which lay open on the surface of the lake. The delicate fragrance lingered in the air. The boat ride on the Lotus Lake was always so peaceful and enjoyable to me.

I lived through my pregnancy though, and our little girl was born on July 22, 1937, in the Chinese-American Hospital. My Chinese obstetrician was out of town on some family emergency. His replacement, a tiny female doctor, delivered the baby. I felt a little uneasy when I saw her, recalling my first experience of giving birth. However, she was adept and all went well.

My little girl was the only European baby among forty Chinese babies, and as she had yellow jaundice, she was just as yellow as the others. All the young Chinese mothers wanted to see the little white baby but, to their amazement, she was just as yellow as theirs. I could hear them saying, "Kang-Kang, look she is yellow like our babies, and her hair is black. But look, her eyes are blue." She opened her little eyes and blinked for them.

We named our baby girl Agnes Else Erna. Agnes after my dear Frau Corinth, Else after my mother, and Erna after me. This was the traditional way of naming on my mother's side of the family.

The hospital room was unbearably hot. They placed a big block of ice in a pan by my bed and a fan blew the cool air on me. It was a most effective air conditioner.

1937 - The Rape of Nanking

After the Japanese conquest of Manchuria in 1931-1932, everyone was sure that they would stop at nothing to gain control of all China. Generalissimo Chiang Kai-shek realized his country's weakness. There was no unity in the country. Although he had made great progress in modernizing his Army and industrializing the country, such as building railroads and modern highways, he was unable to hold back Japan.

In the North, the war quickly expanded and in 1937 the Japanese army closed in on Nanking. Rumors were coming from the surrounding towns that the villages were in a horrible state; burning of houses, mutilating and raping women, mutilating children, and looting by the Japanese soldiers.

Thousands fled the city. This was the time of "The Rape of Nanking."

Then the first bombs fell on the outskirts of Nanking. When the alarm sounded, people ran to the nearest bombproof shelter. The safest place in our house was in the bakery behind the large brick oven. Agnes was just a few weeks old. Bye Dah Djea, our Amah, held Konrad, and the rest of the employees huddled around us. I was very frightened, we all were. This went on for weeks. We would return to our shelter behind the brick oven again and again. Our business was at a standstill.

One day the Japanese announced a major air raid on Nanking. All European women and children were evacuated by their respective embassies who chartered boats for this purpose. They were waiting for us at the dock to depart as soon as everyone was on board. With a heavy heart I said goodbye to my William and to Herr Zaudig. Our dear Bye Dah Djea was going to leave Nanking with her son who worked in the bakery. I wondered if we would see her again. This was a trying time.

The boat took us up the Yangtze River. If it had not been for the terrifying situation we were in, it would have been a lovely little cruise. It took two or three days. The Yangtze River is the longest river in China and its principal waterway. It is very wide in some places and passes through beautiful mountains. About midway, we passed a little island called the "Little Orphan Rock." On the very top we could see a pagoda and a cloister. We passed by as the sun was setting. The tip of the mountain and the pagoda stood out against the red, setting sun. The green of the trees seemed brighter in the intense light shining there. I was lonely leaving William, and I stared and stared at the scene, my breath caught in my throat. I prayed, "Lord, give me courage and protect William and Herr Zaudig."

1937 - Escape to Kuling

Arriving in Kiukiang, we got off the boat and here the chair bearers were waiting for us, four men for each chair. Agnes and I were in one of the chairs and Konrad was in another one with a friend of mine. They actually tied us to the bamboo chairs. They carried us across the plains until we arrived at the foot of a mountain. Here more chairs were waiting for us with six mountain bearers for each one. These men were used to the mountains and the narrow paths. They were bony and muscular and they wore coolie hats and straw sandals. Each pair of bearers had a relief coolie walking beside him. Coolies were also hired to carry our luggage.

From that point on, the trip was exciting and sometimes frightening. About a third of the way up the mountain, we stopped at a teahouse where the chair bearers refreshed themselves with a bowl of rice and a cup of hot tea. Then, with a rhythmic stride, they carried us up a flight of steep steps. Up and up the mountain we went. The men did not speak with one another. Sometimes I could hear them humming softly. They were concentrating strictly on the path. One misstep and all of us would have fallen down the ravine.

The path wound around rocky cliffs and beneath us we could hear the rushing mountain streams and waterfalls. The path often twisted so abruptly that sometimes my chair was hanging over a precipice while the front bearers were beyond the bend and the rear bearers were still around the corner behind us. At one point I looked down and became so scared that I quickly closed my eyes, held my breath and then I just fixed my eyes on the sweat stained blue shirt and the queue hanging down the chair bearer's back.

I thought of Konrad and when the path leveled out I carefully turned and saw that my friend was pressing his head to her chest, covering his eyes with one hand because he, too, was afraid. Motioning with her head, she told me Konrad was okay. Agnes was sleeping in my arms. I had heard that there had never been an accident on that specific route, but that was of little consolation to me at that time.

As we approached the summit, the wind was blowing quite strongly, but the chair bearers carried us with an even pace to the top of the mountain. We were now up to a height of 4,000 feet. A beautiful panorama unfolded in front of our eyes; we had arrived in Kuling.

August in Kuling is a pretty time of the year. I saw nice brick houses with well-kept gardens and meadows with sheep, goats and cows grazing lazily. Here and there I noticed some black pigs—white pigs were a rare sight in China. A stream and a small brook rolled down the hills into the valley below.

Kuling was a vacation resort and it looked very much like a small German town in the hilly area. It had many hotels, several stories high, built of red- and sand-colored brick. Each hotel had a few cottages close by. The cottages were ideal for families with children. On rainy days the children could play on the verandas which went around the whole cottage.

It was in Kuling that the families of well-to-do European and wealthy Chinese spent the hot summer months, away from the heat of the city.

Most of us rented a cottage and had our meals in the hotel dining room. The cottages were clean and nicely furnished. The climate was ideal, the days pleasantly warm and the nights cool.

As Konrad was with me all of the time now and had no one to speak Chinese to, he quickly learned to speak German. It was surprising how easily he adjusted. Many of my friends from Nanking were there. It was a relaxing time. We took long walks or sat in the grass talking. The children loved to play in the nearby brooks. Because we did not have to cook or do house cleaning, our minds and thoughts had too much time to worry and wonder about our husbands. We prayed for more mail to come, bringing us messages from home.

I was nursing Agnes, but not successfully. I was told it would help me to have soup with my meals and goat's milk in the mornings. I arranged for a goat keeper to bring milk to my cottage. Every morning at six o'clock he rang a bell, brought his goat and milked it right there. I drank it, but I surely did not like it. The smell and taste was strong and unpleasant. And the goat's milk didn't even help. When Agnes was three months old the milk production stopped and I changed her to the bottle. This relieved me of the goat milk drinking.

After ten weeks it was safe to return to Nanking. The trip down the mountain was again quite exciting. The six chair bearers almost ran down the mountain until we came to the place where we changed to the chairs with four bearers. It had taken about three and a half hours to be carried up and only two hours to go down the mountain. Then on to the steamer and back to Nanking where our husbands awaited us at the pier.

Konrad ran to his father when he spotted him and said in German, "Vati wir sind zurück," ("Daddy we are back"). And he hugged his father. My husband was startled at hearing his son address him in German for a change.

"Well, my boy, you learned to speak German; that makes me glad." And he snatched him up into his arms. William then turned and hugged and kissed me as if he would never let me go. I was glad to find William well and everything the way that I had left it.

It was good to be back home again. I unpacked and put things in order. Business started to pick up again. The fighting and looting went on, however, in the surrounding villages. Hundreds of farmers with their families fled into the city. Torturing, looting, and raping was the talk of the day. Once again we could hear the cannons and Nanking experienced an air raid occasionally. During one of these air raid attacks a shelter was hit by a bomb. It was overcrowded and many, many people were killed and wounded.

We and our household and bakery help still gathered in the bake shop around the oven when the siren sounded. It was the safest and, naturally, the hottest place to stay. One day a bomb hit close to a German hotel not far from us. Many windows were broken there but no one was hurt. Everyone was tense and wondering what to do. Then the answer came sooner than anticipated.

Evacuation to Hankow

One evening about ten o'clock we heard a loud, persistent knock at the front door. "Who could that be?" I asked William. "The business is closed and the streets are deserted."

William just said, "I'll go down and see," and he went to open the door. I followed him to the top of the stairs and listened.

It was a messenger from the German Embassy. He handed William a written paper. It was an order which read: "The Japanese have announced a major air attack on the city of Nanking. All foreign citizens—men, women and children—are urged to leave the city. The German Embassy has chartered a boat to evacuate all German Nationals to Hankow." After the messenger left, William and I just stared dumbly at each other. We sat at the bottom of the staircase. William took me into his arms and said, "Be brave, Erna. Together we will make it!"

The order had also told us that we could only take a few personal belongings and that we had to be at the pier at six o'clock the next morning. Tired as we were, we stayed up all night packing and sorting clothing for warm and cold weather. We did not know when and if we would return. While packing, I said to William, "I hope our store will not be bombarded."

"Erna, we just don't know what is going to happen. We are the only European store in the whole block. How can the Japanese distinguish us from the Chinese stores? How will they know?" he said.

William went through all the business papers and money matters. He made out payroll checks for the employees who were still with us. Herr Zaudig decided to stay behind, handle the other business matters for us and just mainly to protect the store from being looted. Most of our employees had already gone to safer places or to their home towns.

At dawn we hired several rickshaws to take us and our luggage to the pier where the ship, chartered by the German Embassy, was docked. Herr Zaudig accompanied us to the pier. Every embassy in Nanking had chartered a boat for its nationals.

The pier was packed with thousands of Chinese refugees who tried to find some sort of boat in which to escape. We found a place in the German section —among luggage, boxes, cases, furniture, bathtubs, and rugs. I could not believe my eyes when I saw what people were taking along. I said to William, "if they can take so many of their belongings, even bathtubs, let us at least get our portable sewing machine. We have two small children and don't know when we will return and where money will come from, at least I could sew clothes for them."

"That's a good idea, Erna," he said, and turning to Herr Zaudig, he said, "Take good care of them. I'll be back as quick as I can," and he left. There was no sign that we would get on board soon, so William knew he had time to go back and get the sewing machine.

It was almost noon and I had not fed the baby nor changed her. She had begun to cry. People were pushing and crowding into us. Herr Zaudig said, "Don,'t worry, Frau Scheel, I will protect you." He was standing in front of me and the children. With his arms over us he formed an arch by pressing his hands against some boxes and he protected us from being crushed. Agnes was scared and began to cry louder. Konrad clutched my hand and whimpered. I was determined to be brave for their sakes.

When William returned he found a place where we were more secure and where I could feed the children. He had brought some liverwurst sandwiches, pears and plums, and a thermos of sweet tea which we shared with Herr Zaudig. Late that afternoon we were finally allowed to go on board. Saying goodbye to Herr Zaudig was not easy for us. I hugged him and said, "Take care of yourself and be careful. I hope to see you again very soon, good friend." Times were so uncertain I wondered if I really would ever see him again.

None of us knew our final destination. I prayed, "Lord, protect this good Christian man, as you protected him from the Bolsheviks. Please don't forsake him now. And I pray, Lord, that our guardian angel will continue to protect and be with us."

Everyone was pushing and shoving. Hundreds of Chinese refugees in sampans were trying to board the ship. The authorities used long bamboo poles to keep them from climbing up onto the boat. They screamed, "Let us on, let us on!" but the water patrol forced them back. When everybody was on board, the boat whistle sounded and the boat pulled away from the pier. Our four-hundred mile trip to Hankow had begun.

Dozens of small boats filled with refugees continued to follow and attempted to board our ship. Day and night our husbands had to stand guard with bamboo poles. The Chinese were shouting, "Lau yea, Tai Tai, kang kang wadee x'y-tze" ("Master, Missee, see my children!") and begging to let them on board. But it was not possible. Our boat was overcrowded as it was.

Our boat was a passenger ship, which ordinarily took passengers and tourists on excursions. Our cabin was spacious, clean, and comfortably furnished. We had a built-in wash basin and toilet facilities. I felt we were fortunate to have as much luxury as we did.

Again we traveled up the Yangtze River beyond Kiukiang where the river made a sharp turn to the northwest. Arriving in Hankow, our destination, some of us were placed in schools, others in private homes. We were given a small apartment in a school that belonged to a bachelor teacher who kindly made it available for a family. With the apartment came a dog. We were asked to take care of him. The teacher was not able to keep him at his friend's apartment where he now was staying.

I felt strange trying to cook again. Having no servants, naturally, I had some difficulty with cooking, since I had not cooked for years. I could not remember how long it took to cook potatoes. One day I tried my luck with oxtail soup. It was terrible. The meat was tough. We simply could not eat it. Even the dog refused it and crawled under the bed. It would have taken hours to get that tail tender. After a few not-so-good meals, I managed to serve some edible ones. I finally learned to cook a delicious roast with browned potatoes.

Soon Christmas would be upon us and there was no possibility of returning to Nanking. It was difficult to get into the holiday spirit, even though Hankow residents arranged Christmas parties and school children performed their annual Christmas pageant.

We did hear from Herr Zaudig about this time. Hearing from him was a good Christmas present. He was well. Our store had not been bombarded.

We Flee to Hong Kong

Unexpectantly, all foreigners were given notice that the Japanese had announced a major air attack on Hankow. They had been advancing rapidly and the Chinese Army was not able to stop them.

An international refugee train was assembled and huge flags of all the nations of the people leaving were tied to the roofs of the railway cars. They did this so that the Japanese would not bombard the train. We hurried to leave with the train.

The train left on Christmas Eve. We were told to take food along for four days. William bought several large thermos bottles and we filled them with boiled water. By now Agnes was five months old.

That was the saddest Christmas we had ever experienced.

There was no singing of "Stille Nacht," no Christmas tree, no gifts. But nevertheless, many silent prayers went up to God in Heaven.

We were crowded into a small, dingy, cold compartment on the train which smelled musty. I tucked the children in a quilt and woolen blanket. Konrad cuddled his beloved teddy bear in his arms. William and I wore our warm coats and wrapped a blanket around our legs.

I had made hot chocolate and put it into one of the thermos bottles. I reached for it and poured some for us. It was the best hot chocolate we had ever tasted.

Konrad suddenly said, "Mutti, read Little Red Riding Hood to me, please. Please?" He knew I had the story book in my overnight case. He was always so excited when I read in a deep voice; "The wolf said, so I can see you better!" I

134

read by the beam of a flashlight until he fell asleep. Agnes was already sleeping soundly.

William and I were left to pursue our own thoughts; neither of us felt like talking. The night was endless.

During the night those in command had a bad experience which we knew nothing about until the following day. The next morning we were told that the Japanese had destroyed the tracks ahead of us. A reconnaissance troupe was sent to investigate, but thank God, it was a false alarm.

In barely two days we arrived in Hong Kong, our destination. At the railroad station everyone was separated by nationality and taken in by a family from the same country. We were sheltered by a very gracious family. They had three children, ages eight to fourteen.

They had a gorgeous two-story brick house, which was enclosed by a tall stone wall with a massive cast iron gate. I delighted in their well-kept garden. A large terrace led to the entrance of the house. The rooms were spacious with tall ceilings and French windows in every room of the ground floor. The windows led to the garden or the terrace. The polished hardwood floors were covered with thick, lush, flowered Chinese carpets. One room was completely furnished with Chinese furniture. It was teakwood, richly carved and inlaid with mother of pearl and ivory. The other rooms had European furniture.

The eight days we had stayed with our hosts were pleasant and relaxing. During our stay we were treated as special guests. It was a tremendous feeling to be safe after so many months of anxiety and uncertainty. They took us up to Victoria Peak, from where we had a splendid view of the harbor and a section of Hong Kong. And one evening we had dinner on a floating restaurant that took us on a tour around the harbor. Lights twinkling from the tall commercial and bank buildings lit the night sky. In awe, I tried to absorb all the beauty of the night.

Still, we had no word from Herr Zaudig. We were eager to go to Shanghai, where we hoped to find mail from him. News from Nanking was disturbing. Bombing, looting, fires, raping—we did not know what to believe. We heard that the Japanese were ruthless and cruel. William and I decided to leave as soon as we could get passage on a steamer. Finally, with thankful but sad hearts, we said adieu to our hosts and Hong Kong.

On to Shanghai

Now we were on our own and could choose our next destination. We boarded the steamer and were on our way to Shanghai. We passed through the South China Sea, the Strait of Formosa, and entered the East China Sea. About half-way to Shanghai, we made acquaintance with a sea quake. I was very frightened. The boat was tossed about in every direction. Our cabin was at the rear of the ship above the rudder and the propeller. When the propeller was out of the water, it sounded and felt as if the ship would break up into bits and pieces. The noise was deafening. Almost everyone on board was seasick. Our family was well, except Agnes, who was vomiting and crying continuously. There is not much one can do except keep a child with seasickness clean.

In the cabin next to ours was a young mother who also had a small child. I had seen them in the dining room. The continuous cry of the child made me check on them. I knocked, and then I heard a feeble voice saying, "Come in, the door is open." I went in. Oh, what misery I saw. The mother and child were both very seasick. The sour smell of their cabin almost made me ill. But the mother was so grateful that I had come. She said, "I am so very glad you came! No one is answering the bell."

"The steward may be sick also. There are just not many people around. Let me help you and your little one," I said. I cleaned the child first and then helped the mother. She thanked me over and over. I assured her that I would check on them again and see if I could find a steward to help them.

I went to check for her. The dining room was practically empty. Even the cooks—and, yes the stewards—were seasick.

But someone must have been well, because we were served good meals. There were three elderly missionary ladies who enjoyed every meal that was served. And so did we.

Miraculously, the next day the sea was calm again. We had good weather for the rest of the trip.

Arriving in Shanghai, we first stayed in a hotel until we found a room in a boarding house. Shanghai was overflowing with refugees coming from all parts of China. Everyone who was able to spare a room or two rented it.

We listened to the latest news from overseas. We were not sure if letters from home were censored. Therefore, we were eager for news from people coming from Germany. They reported that life there was normal and we trusted that what they told us was the truth.

Weeks passed and still no news from Herr Zaudig. Finally a letter arrived from him. He had addressed it in care of the German Consulate. He wrote that the whole complex of stores in Nanking had gone up in flames. There was nothing that he could have done. He was just able to take his suitcase and run to the nearest bomb shelter. He would come to Shanghai at the first opportunity.

William read the letter to me. At first I was stunned. We were sitting on the bed, he had his arm around me, and he said, "Everything is destroyed. But how good that Herr Zaudig was not hurt."

"Yes, William, I am glad of that too."

Then I visualized our wedding gifts, the fine German china, the silk embroidered pictures, and the collection of first edition books signed by the authors. All gone. I started to cry and scream. "Willie, I can't believe that we have lost everything! All our nice things! All the machines and appliances?

What are we going to do?" In a state of shock I repeated, "What are we going to do? Everything burned and gone! I can't believe it."

William took me into his arms and said, "We'll make it, Dear, we are still young and healthy. I will write to Kiessling and Bader; they will help us."

I could not stop crying. Then I heard Konrad say, "Mutti, Agi is crying, she needs to eat." That helped me stop crying and I went to take care of my little girl.

One day William brought home a box of chocolate candy from the Swiss bakery. He knew how much I loved chocolate candy. I was able to smile and thank him with a hug and a kiss. He took our loss much better than I did.

Erna at the Scheel's "Cafe Royal" in Mukden, China. 1932.

Wedding cake made by William
Scheel in Mukden, China. 1932.

Erna and her tennis coach at the German club in Mukden, China. 1934.

Erna, William, and son Konrad in
Mukden, China. 1934.

Konrad and Chinese "Amah" Bei-da-dje in Mukden,
China. 1934.

Erna in front of the Scheel Kiessling and Bader store in Nanking, China. 1936.

Showcases in the Scheel Kiessling and Bader store in Nanking, China. 1936.

Little Orphan Rock in the Yangtze river. 1937.

The "Escape to Kuling." Erna and the Scheel children were carried up the mountain to refuge during the "Rape of Nanking." 1937.

The village of Kuling, China. 1937.

Erna and Konrad at Kuling, China. 1937.

CHAPTER NINE
We Begin Again In Shanghai

William thought that Shanghai would be a good place to begin again. Shanghai was the largest and most important import and export harbor in China. It was located close to the mouth of the Yangtze Kiang River. Its population in the late 1930's was about five million. There were also about 50,000 to 60,000 foreigners living in the city. It was a busy town. There were several Chinese universities, colleges, institutes for foreign languages, the Shanghai Conservatory of Music and hospitals. The Russian Opera Guild performed often. Famous musicians and singers from all over the world performed and the most recent movies from England, France, Germany and the Unites States were shown there.

William began looking for a suitable business location. His partners from Tientsin assisted us and it took a year to find a suitable building for a business and living quarters. We lived on our savings and money loaned to us by our partners.

Herr Zaudig came to Shanghai and with the help of the German Consulate he was able to find us. With joy we welcomed our friend. The children were especially thrilled to see him. He found a job as a caretaker in a factory. He did not earn much but it was better than nothing. He visited us often. Agnes was the apple of his eye and she returned his love in her childlike manner.

The house we finally found was a small one, but in a good location — opposite the race course on the main thoroughfare of the city on Bubbling Well Road. It was squeezed in between some Chinese shops. Down the street to our right was the China United Hotel, the W.M.C.A. Building and the very modern, seven story Park Hotel. To our left in the next block was the very modern Sun Department Store and a movie theater.

As our house was located on the main street it was a noisy place. Early in the mornings the air was filled with the stench of human waste as the wagons, pulled by coolies, traveled from street to street and house to house to empty and clean the portable toilets which were put out the night before. One could hear the swooshing of bamboo brooms for blocks. A little while later the street cars began to run. The clinging, clanging and squeaking of their wheels, combined with the noise of the venders praising their wares was awful. In the summertime when our windows were open it was especially annoying.

Many people thought we would not be able to compete with the old established Swiss Bakery there. It was well known and well patronized. "Shanghai is a large city with a huge foreign community. There will be enough business for two pastry shops," William said in his logical way.

Being an excellent pastry chef (William's motto remained; "Quality not Quantity") put him ahead again. Of course, the name Kiessling and Bader helped too. The layout of our new place was much the same as in Nanking, only smaller.

So, in 1938 we started from the bottom up again. It did not take long before we had a thriving business. We proved ourselves to the European community. Herr Zaudig was hired to supervise the restaurant as he had done in Mukden and in Nanking.

Family Health Problems

Shura, a young Russian girl took care of the children. Konrad had started school at the Kaiser Wilhelm Schule. One day after school Shura said, "Frau Scheel, Koni is complaining that his hip is hurting and he does not want to walk."

I remarked, "I think he is just lazy" and I brushed it aside. But after a few days Shura said, "Koni continues to complain of his hip."

146

Konrad said, "Mutti, it really hurts. I am not lazy."

"All right, then Koni, we will go and see a doctor." I gave him a big hug and we were on our way. The first doctor said, "Your son has Tuberculosis. It would be best to send him to a sanatorium in Switzerland." I did not trust his diagnosis. I went to a second doctor. The second prognosis did not satisfy nor convince me either. We did not know what to do.

Then someone recommended a Jewish doctor, a bone specialist. He had recently arrived from Germany. I took Konrad to him. He examined my son thoroughly and said to me, "Frau Scheel, your boy has an infection in the lining of his hip joint. This is very painful because the bones rub against each other. I advise that he be fitted for a cast from his chest to the heel of the leg that is hurting him." He then highly recommended Dr. Saürbruch of Berlin, a specialist, very well known all over Germany. I had confidence in this doctor. I took his advise and Konrad was fitted with the cast.

The year was 1939. Hitler had invaded Poland. The "Blitzkrieg" was a very unrestful time for us. It was not easy to make the decision about whether to send Konrad to Germany or to wait until times were more settled. The headlines of newspapers and news on the shortwave radio were most disturbing. Every evening we listened to the latest news from overseas. We were not sure if letters from home were censored. Therefore, we were eager for news from people coming from Germany. They reported that life there was fairly normal and we trusted that what they told us was the truth. Since the Trans-Siberian train was still running on schedule, we decided not to delay this trip for our son. It was too important.

Konrad's adjustment to his cast was not easy. The cast ran from the top of his waist, over both hips, down one leg and beneath his foot. He was a lively boy and getting used to the heavy cast was troublesome.

His sleep was restless, his activities were cut short and merely climbing a flight of steps was quite an ordeal for him. He especially missed playing outdoors with his friends. Konrad fell often and each time he fell the cast broke. The doctors stressed that it was most important that he be taken immediately to the hospital and be fitted with a new cast. It was necessary too that we buy him new pants to accommodate the size of the cast. All of these adjustments were costing us a lot of money. Just starting out in the new business, it was very hard on us. Sending Konrad to Germany would be very expensive too.

While all this was going on with Konrad, I developed varicose veins in my right leg. The condition had been troubling me for a number of years and the pain had grown worse. I went to a well known professor who suggested injecting a sclerosing solution into the vein. I agreed to the injection. He did it then and there in his office. After a few days my leg started swelling. The pain was excruciating and the skin, where he had injected the solution, burst open. I called the office immediately to make an appointment. I was told that the professor was on vacation but that his colleague would see me.

I visited this doctor that same day. He discovered that the professor had missed the vein and that the solution had been injected into the surrounding tissue and had set up an irritating infection. He recommended ultra violet light treatments.

The treatments consisted of cold rays. Therefore, when the technician set the temperature gauge too high I could not feel the tissues in my leg being burned. Afterwards she bandaged my wound and I went home.

After several days the pain became unbearable. I went again to see the professor's colleague. He was speechless when he unwrapped my leg and saw what the technician had done to me. He treated the area with special salve and gave me more to put on the wound at home. The pain persisted in spite of my having my leg elevated. I continued treating my leg with the special salve for several weeks.

In the meantime, we had to make arrangements to send Konrad to Germany. We also had to look for a person to take him. This was a difficult task indeed. It would be a long trip. Konrad had to go to the bathroom several times during the night because his cast pressed on his bladder. It seemed that complication upon complication was piling up on us.

With the help of the German consulate we were able to withdraw funds from the bank in Berlin where the money I had inherited was deposited. We needed this money for Konrad's travel expenses and treatments. In the meantime my leg continued to grow worse. The pain was constant and deep. I felt as though my leg was on fire. Friends advised me to see another doctor. They recommended a renowned Russian female doctor who had studied in Germany. When I explained my condition to her, she told me to come right away. I went immediately. After she examined my leg, she said to me, "I am sorry, Frau Scheel, I cannot treat this. The wound is very deep and the tendons are infected. The professor must take care of this case immediately. Don't put it off or your leg will have to be amputated." She was kind and understanding. "Please see the professor this very day," she urged. I felt desperate and left her office in tears.

When I told William he was very upset. He paced the floor. Then he sat in the chair beside me. "Perhaps it is not so bad. Let us hope the professor can help you." He tried to comfort me and told our servant boy to order a cab. I left at once.

The professor was stunned when he saw my leg and he started treating it at once. He said, "Frau Scheel, you will have to stay in bed with your leg elevated. I will come every day and dress the wound." He prescribed medication for me.

Every time the professor changed the dressing the pain was excruciating. To suppress screaming, I held onto the headboard of my bed. For over a week he came twice a day to change the dressing.

A young German woman heard of our predicament and offered to take Konrad to Germany. She was going to Germany to buy her trousseau, just like Gertraut had so many years ago.

My dear friend Hedi Spengler, who lived at the China United Hotel, just a few houses away, was such a help. She took care of everything Konrad needed. He needed many clothes and other necessities for the long trip.

We had to write to my brother in Berlin and William's mother in Stendal about Konrad. It really was a trying time for me.

The young woman and Konrad would travel by boat to Dairen, then by train through Manchuria to the Russian border where the Trans-Siberian train would take them to Moscow. There they would have to wait two days for the train that would take them to Berlin, where my half brother Walter would be waiting for them.

It was a sad day when my son left for Germany. I was in bed, unable to get up. They left in October 1939. Konrad was barely eight years old. I was upset that I could not even take him to the boat. He did not want to leave and clung to me with his arms around my neck crying, "Mutti, I don't want to leave you! Please let me stay." It was so difficult for me to be strong. I was fighting my tears. I did not want to make it harder on him than it already was.

At last Hedi was able to persuade him by saying, "Koni, you want to get well, don't you? We do have to leave now."

As they left my room, I called out to Konrad, " I'll see you soon; be good to your Omi (Granny)." I don't know how I was able to let my eight-year-old son go to Germany with a stranger. But we wanted him to get well and just could not wait any longer. We had no idea how long I would be laid up.

After Hedi and Konrad left the room, my self-control gave way to hot tears. I just sobbed and let my tears flow. I wished William would come and stay with me for a while. Lying in my bed, I waited for him in vain. I wanted him to come comfort me.

Sometime after lunch, William finally came to my room to talk about an order for a big tea party that had just come in. William had no understanding or feelings for my heartache. He didn't have a kind word for me. I was so hurt, but found peace in prayer.

My brother telegraphed me that Konrad and the young bride-to-be had made it to Berlin all right. My brother and his wife, Trude, had met them at the station.

When they took Konrad to see Dr. Saürbruch in Berlin, he was very pleased with the healing process and said the bone specialist in Shanghai had done the right thing. How happy we were when we received the good news. After several weeks of physical therapy in the hospital, William's mother took Konrad home to Stendal.

While confined to my bed, I was able to help with the business by taking orders from customers over the phone. I also placed orders from the bakery and restaurant to merchants. When I was finally allowed to get up and be in the store, I had to be carried up and down the stairs. While seated with my leg elevated, I could supervise the store and talk to customers and friends. My working made it easier on William. The last few months were very hard on him. He was nervous, irritable, and indifferent to my ailment. His hot temper surfaced often during this period. I longed for a kind word or some sign of affection but William brooded and remained detached. I felt as though he believed I was exaggerating my condition. From the time I had my first injection to the time I was able to walk again took almost six months.

William and I never received a medical bill. And we never asked for one either. After all, my problems were caused by the injection the Professor had given me.

151

Konrad's sickness and my ailment took their toll on both William and me. I could see our marriage steadily falling apart.

1940 - The Vacation in Germany

Both our partners in Tientsin and our friends urged William and me to take a long overdue vacation. In May of 1940 we took a six month long vacation. The Tientsin office sent one of their pastry chefs, Bruno Wolf, to help with the business while we were in Germany. Since William had worked with Herr Wolf in Tientsin he felt confident that with Herr Zaudig's supervision of the restaurant the business would be in good hands.

That trip on the Trans-Siberian railroad was my third one. I had been too young to really remember the first two trips, so I was excited about going.

The political situation did not look good. Germany had just occupied Poland, and Russia did not look with friendliness upon Germany. My friends told me not to let on that I spoke Russian because I could be taken for a spy.

The Trans-Siberian Railroad was the longest in the world. It was 7,500 kilometers (4,500 miles) long and regarded as the most important railroad in Russia. It had only one track and the train left Moscow every fortnight. The train started in Moscow, passed through Swerdlowsks, via Osmsk, Nowosibirsk, Irbutsk, Lake Baikal, Manchuli, crossed through the northern part of Manchuria to Vladivostk, at the shore of the Sea of Japan.

We boarded the train in Manchuli at the Manchurian-Russian border. Our train compartment was very plain as we traveled tourist class. I understood that first class was quite luxurious and even had a samovar (tea maker) in every coach. Tourist class did not.

Our compartment had two upper and two lower berths. Agnes and I had the two lower ones and William had one of the upper ones. There were two small closets, a few drawers and a metal basin with running cold and hot water.

We wondered if someone would occupy the fourth berth. Well, it soon became occupied. A Russian gentleman in his late thirties became our companion.

Foreigners were not allowed to buy anything at the stations where we stopped. We could stretch our legs and walk alongside the train. We fetched boiling water in our thermos bottles to make tea. Our co-traveler always brought something for Agnes and sometimes shared with us whatever he had brought for himself. He was a very nice gentleman. We spoke Russian together and everything went well. During the long hours of traveling, we would stand in the corridor to walk a little and chat with other travelers, mostly Russians.

The compartment next to us was occupied by two Russian officers and their wives. They were so friendly that before I knew it, we were talking away in Russian. I don't believe it ever entered their minds that I might be a spy. We spent some pleasant hours together and everyone spoiled our three-year-old, Agnes.

I enjoyed traveling during the day. The train passed along the southern tip of the Baikal Lake. On our left we saw the majestic Baikal mountains and to our right the lake, still, clear, and green. It is the deepest lake in the world, 1742 meters deep. The lake was a well-visited vacation place. The climate was mild and there were no insects nearby, because the lake's vapor was repellent to them.

In Irkutsk, the cook took fresh black caviar on board. For the next two days it was served as an appetizer in a glass dish on ice with a wedge of lemon on the side. It was the tastiest caviar I had ever eaten. In general, the food was good, appetizing and plentiful. On the other hand, toilet facilities were dirty and smelly, and the floor was wet most of the time.

The trip through Siberia was very monotonous. The ground was covered with snow. In the distance we saw patches of lonely small white-barked birch trees and here and there small houses with grey smoke coming out of the chimneys. Everything seemed grey, desolate, and vast. Rarely did we see people. What a bare and lonely countryside it was.

At first I hoped the train would stop somewhere in the deserted land and I could take a walk in the snow, but after traveling mile after mile I had no desire to do that at all and was glad that the sun went down and darkness covered the country.

After Omsk we approached the Ural Mountains. Swerdlowsk, (until 1924 known as Jekatarienburg) was the capital of the Ural State and lay at the slope of the mountains. From there we passed through Kazan to Moscow. We were glad to stand on solid ground again.

We stayed in a large, old hotel in Moscow. The rooms were spacious and furnished with old-fashioned furniture. There was a nice bathroom adjacent to our room. When Agnes saw the bathtub, she called in delight, "Oh, Mutti, look, we can take a bath! Can I take one now?"

"We will all take a bath as soon as we have our luggage brought to our room," I answered.

We took hot baths and felt very pampered doing so. We had not had a bath for ten days.

We did not see much of Moscow, because I was very tired and did not feel well. We only took walks close to the hotel. After four days, we left by train to Berlin.

My half brother Walter and I had both been small children when I was taken back to China in 1914. Twenty-six years had gone by. I had such heartwarming feelings when he took me into his arms and said, "mein Schwesterlein" (my little sister).

Walter's wife, Trude, had stayed home. When we reached their apartment she greeted us with a "Herzlich Willkommen." What a warm welcome it was. I could smell the coffee she had prepared and the aroma of freshly baked apple cake filled the room. She served sweetened whipped cream with the cake.

We stayed up long into the night. There was so much to tell, so many questions to be answered. I told Walter how much I missed my mother. I could not remember the cuddling arms and love of a mother. I was so eager to meet her. I told Walter about my life with Father and he told me about his life with Mother. He said, "Erna, I believe you were better off with your father. Mother was strict and had a very bad temper." I thought to myself, it could not be worse than when Papa had been drinking. I answered, "Walter, it was awfully tough growing up without a mother and a mother's love. And Papa had a drinking problem."

He answered, "She had a bad temper."

I liked my brother and his wife. Trude was an outgoing and warm person. They had a little five-year-old girl called Sigrid. We stayed with them for a few days and then we were eager to go to Stendal to see our son.

When we arrived at Stendal, a train trip of several hours, I was disappointed to see only William's mother at the station. She was small and looked so frail. Her short cut brown hair did not show any grey at all. I noticed also that William resembled her very much. After exchanging greetings, William and I asked together as if rehearsed, "Where is Koni?"

"He wanted to meet you on our street. He has a surprise for you." And her stern face lit up with a big smile.

As we approached the street where William's mother lived we did have a big surprise! There was Konrad on his bicycle riding toward us, shouting, "Mutti, Vati, you see I am well!" He jumped off his bicycle and ran into my open arms, then he ran to his father, who picked him up. Agnes, who was walking with her grandmother, let go of her hand, ran to Konrad, and then both children hugged each other.

All I could hear was, "Koni!"

"Agi!"

"Koni!"

"Agi!"

Our boy was well. He was healed. We were all together again. Doctor Saürbruch had released him, but he wanted to see him again before we returned to China.

This was my first meeting with Mutter Gottwald, William's mother. I knew her only through her letters. I had imagined her to be a warm, outgoing person. I was surprised when I first saw her. She seldom smiled and she seemed cold and distant. I soon discovered, however, that she was good-hearted, always ready to help. She would share her last piece of bread with you.

Mutter Gottwald was not a happy person. She had lived a hard life. William did not know his father. She had raised him alone—with a stern hand. After William entered his apprenticeship in the bakery, she had married a widower with five children, the youngest a few months old and the oldest a teenager. She never received any love from them. The youngest was the only one who kept in touch with her.

I loved her. She was always sweet to me.

Her house was immaculately clean. She dusted every day, even the pictures on the wall and the clock.

Mutter Gottwald told us that when Konrad first came to stay with her she asked him what he would like for breakfast. He said, "porridge."

"What is porridge?" she asked.

All she found out was that it was a hot cereal. So she began to cook a different hot cereal every morning. None of them was the right one, until that day when she had cooked oatmeal. When Konrad saw the oatmeal, he cried out, "Omi, (Granny), that's it!! That is porridge!!"

Koni said to us, "Omi's canned fruit is so delicious, I ate some every day."

"Yes," Grandmother replied, smiling, "my shelves are almost empty."

"Oh, but it is so good!" Koni went and threw his arms around his granny.

After meeting my husband's relatives and friends, I left him and the children with his mother and went by train to Schwerin to meet my mother. I was just over five years old when we had last seen each other. That had been twenty-six years past. Since the time that my brother sent the post card in 1926, however, mother and I had corresponded and exchanged photographs.

The train trip to Schwerin in Mecklenburg, not far from Hamburg, took several hours. To me it seemed as though the trip would never end. When I finally saw the sign "Schwerin" I gave a deep sigh of relief. As the train came slowly to a halt, I looked out of the window of my compartment and recognized my mother right away. When I stepped onto the platform she recognized me too, and we ran into each other's arms and teardrops of joy filled our eyes. All I could say was, "Oh, Mutti."

And she exclaimed, "Erna, my child, my child."

My chest seemed too small for my pounding heart. At first we could not speak, but then we could not stop. We were both talking at the same time. The letters and pictures we had shared over the years had not begun to reveal our love for each other.

We walked to the apartment where Mother lived with Frau Zahn, the invalid lady that she took care of. My grandmother and an aunt were waiting for us there.

Emotions overcame me when I hugged my grandmother, "Omi" Voss and Tante Klara, her youngest daughter. Oh, how good it was to be with members of my own family, how very good. I never had received so much love, at one time. In China I had no relatives I could lean on, to go to for help or advice. I felt secure, for perhaps the first time in my life.

My grandmother was in her late eighties. She was a little on the heavy side and walked with a cane. Her spectacles were thick; she could only read large and heavy print in the newspaper. Her hair was grey, wavy, and neatly combed away from her face.

157

Tante Klara was a typical spinster. She had never married and had always lived with her mother. Her buck teeth did not improve the looks of her face. Her voice was soft. She had a sweet disposition, I found out later, and I learned to like her.

The little old white-haired lady, Frau Zahn, that Mother took care of joined us. It was so kind of her to let us all meet and dine in her apartment.

Tante Klara had prepared a delicious meal: sauerbraten, red cabbage and potato dumplings, and chocolate pudding topped with vanilla sauce as desert. After dinner, we gathered in the cosy living room for a glass of port wine. That room reminded me of one I had seen in a picture book. The heavy velvet curtains were drawn to the side of the tall windows. I could see the street lights from across the street. The large sofa and the two armchairs were upholstered with a soft maroon plush. In one corner of the room was a carved pedestal on which a huge fern had its place. On the coffee table was an arrangement of fresh flowers. A bookcase filled with books on one wall made me think that some past family member must have loved to read. It was quite late when Tante Klara and Grandmother walked home.

As was the custom in Germany, homemakers went to the baker, the butcher and the grocer every day. Of course, I went with Mother, and we always had a lot to tell each other. One afternoon she related how her husband had died. She told me that one morning she and her husband had an argument at the breakfast table. He was angry and left without giving her a goodbye kiss. After a minute or two he returned and said, "Else, I can't leave being angry with you." He kissed her tenderly and left for the office. At noon he and a colleague went out for lunch. On the way he suddenly collapsed. He had a heart attack and he died before Mother could reach him. Then she said, "Erna, since that day I never leave the house being angry with anyone."

"Oh, Mutti, I will remember that for sure."

I stayed several days. The evening before I left we all had dinner together again. After dinner I helped clear the table and folded the table cloth and handed it to Mother. She took it, looked at it, and in a very angry tone of voice she said to me, "look how you folded this! The creases are not folded right! How does that look?" And she went on and on.

Finally, Grandmother and Tante Klara told her in one voice, "Else, stop already!"

Tears came to my eyes. I was hurt and disappointed. I could not believe that my mother could be so harsh. I then remembered Walter's words, "she has a bad temper." Mother did not apologize.

Not long after that we were reminded that there was a war going on. We experienced three awful night air raids in Schwerin, the city where Mother lived. All cellars were prepared for such events. The tenants kept beds, warm blankets, food and water, and first aid supplies in the cellars, ready for when the air raids came. At the first sounding of the sirens, every tenant of Mother's apartment building went to the cellar.

I always laid Agnes in a bed there. She would go right back to sleep. Konrad stayed awake and sat between Mother and me. He held onto my arm and said, "Mutti, I am afraid!"

"It's all right, Koni, this cellar is built air-raid proof. We are quite safe in here. It is safe." With these words I comforted my little boy. But, I wondered, are we really safe?

We heard the bombs exploding. As one bomb dropped close by, one of the female tennants became hysterical and started screaming. This, naturally, upset everyone and the children started crying. She did not calm down until someone shook her and screamed, "Be quiet! Don't you realize you are upsetting everyone?" When she did not respond, he slapped her face. That stopped her screaming. Then the children settled down. Just this one woman upset our whole group.

There were about forty people in the cellar that night. The next morning we discovered that the bomb had broken windows and destroyed part of the street about one half a block away.

In the evenings we had to cover all windows with black cloth. Not one speck of light was to be seen from the outside. It was the law in Germany during the war. Automobiles and street cars had their lights dimmed. When the air raid sirens sounded all lights went out and traffic came to a standstill. People wore fluorescent buttons on their lapels to avoid bumping into one another. Although restaurants, movies and night clubs were open, no light could be seen from the outside.

It seemed to me that Germany's leader, Adolf Hitler, was doing a good job for the German people. There was no unemployment; there was enough food; there were no beggars. These were the years 1939 and 1940. Poland had already been occupied by Germany. Later Norway and Denmark were also occupied in order to safeguard the supply of iron ore routed from Sweden to Narvik. And also to prevent the dispatch of French and British troops to aid Finland, which was at war with Russia. In April the British troops were driven back to the sea at Dunkirqü where they escaped by boat to England. In May of 1940 the invasion of the Netherlands, Belgium, and France began and the French requested an armistice.

Even with all of these operations going on, life seemed relatively peaceful to William and me. There was seldom an air raid during daylight hours. We could go shopping, sightseeing, and visiting the zoo and museums and movies. Only during the quiet of the night could one hear train after train, hour after hour, passing through the cities. Troops, Panzer tanks, ammunition, and light artillery were being moved to the western front. There was another even more important reason William and I felt peace. We were away from the stress of running a business. We felt fortunate that our vacation was scheduled at this time, for even if the world was at war, this was a time of relative peace in our marriage. I worried that this peace would last only as long as we were away from the business.

In July and August heavy air raid attacks were delivered against British convoys and ports, and in August and September heavy night raids hit the industrial centers of Britain.

The German population was kept well informed of these victories over the radios and in news reels at the movies. Very few air raids hit Germany at this time.

While staying with my mother, we also talked about my marriage. I had written her a little about our marital problems and she had a vague idea that our marriage was not a happy one. On one of our afternoon walks I brought the subject up and said, "You know, I have been contemplating not returning to China."

"Really, Erna?" was Mother's response.

"Yes. William is an honest, sober and hard-working man and a good provider. It could be a good marriage. But that is not enough," I replied. "I can't tolerate his terrible temper and his abusive and insulting language any more. I am losing my self-confidence and my self-worth. Do you know a lawyer I could see, Mutti?"

"We'll see, Erna."

Within a few days Mother did refer me to an attorney. After consulting with him my mind was made up. I would stay in Germany and get a divorce. I had family here and their support. I decided to return to Stendal and tell William about my decision. I told Mother, Grandmother, and Tante Klara that I would return to Schwerin in a few days after settling things with William. I left on the train for Stendal the next day.

When I told William that I had decided not to return to China with him he was very upset and did not want to believe it. We decided to go for a walk and talk things over.

We found a bench on the edge of the forest overlooking a meadow where some cows were grazing. Birds were chirping above us in the trees and a yellow butterfly was sipping nectar, flying from flower to flower. It was so peaceful. William and I always had a difficult time communicating, but this time it was different. Perhaps it was the tranquility of the surroundings which made it easier for us to talk, and talk we did.

When we had finished, William said, "Erna, we have gone through so many hardships and now that things are looking up, you want to leave me. We have our own successful business and our life will be better."

My mind was spinning. I had been so determined to end our relationship when I was still in Schwerin, but now I was not so sure about what to do. It was true that I had enjoyed the days that I spent with my family. But I could not say that I got really close to Mother. It was difficult for me to accept the fact that she had not made more effort to get me back from Father. I was also frightened about the prospect of having to support two children in a country at war. I had no experience other than working in a bakery. I wanted so much to believe William but I needed time to think things over. I was so confused.

"You have promised so often that you would be more tolerant and patient and not fuss with me in front of employees and customers. I just can't take it any longer." I burst out crying. He took me in his arms and said, "It is going to be better. I will try my best to hold my temper." "Willie, you have done it too often. Why do you think it will work this time?" I asked.

"You will see, it will be better!" was all he said. I wanted so much to believe him. I was so afraid of what would happen to me and the children if we stayed in Germany. Although I did not know if I could really trust him, I wanted to so much that I stopped crying and said that I would go back to China and try to make a new start.

We decided to enjoy the rest of our vacation and our time together without business talk. We decided not to tell William's mother about our problems; it would only upset her. "I just hope it will all work out," I thought.

Germany had made a good and lasting impression on me. The streets were kept clean and children and grownups there wore nice clothes. In contrast, I was used to seeing dirty and poorly dressed people and beggars on every street in China. There was no middle class in China, only the rich and the poor. It was so different in Germany; people seemed to have more time for their families and they enjoyed life. Our life in China consisted of work and more work. Very little fun and enjoyment did we ever have. It seemed to me that life in Germany, at least during the daytime, seemed so much more as it should be.

We thoroughly enjoyed the rest of our stay. William was rested and calm and loving to me. More than once I said, "William, why can't we get along like this when we are in the business?" I was happy for a change.

The letters coming from Shanghai were soothing to our nerves. Business was good. Herr Wolf, our pastry chef, had everything under control. William was very glad to hear that.

William and I spent many hours visiting relatives and friends.

I especially enjoyed our visit in Dresden where we stayed with friends we knew from Tientsin. Dresden had so many world famous museums and galleries. The Zwinger, built originally to be a forecourt for a castle, had a valuable collection of pewter and porcelain. Under the reign of August the Great in 1694-1733, it became famous for its Baroque- style arts. The oldest porcelain factory of Europe was in Meissen, a city just a few kilometers from Dresden. Well known Meissen porcelain came from there. Dresden was known as the prettiest of the large cities of Germany.

From Dresden we went to see Herr Bader, who had retired. He owned a beautiful villa in one of the suburbs of Munich. I had not seen him since I left Tientsin in 1930 to get married. I was so delighted to see him.

He had lost his first wife in Tientsin at the birth of their second daughter and had later married again.

Munich, the capital of Bavaria, was another beautiful city. It had numerous famous palaces, magnificent buildings, museums and cathedrals, many from the fifteenth and sixteenth centuries. In 1158, Henry the Lion had pronounced it a city and since 1255 the Regents of Bavaria had made Munich their residency. I was impressed and enriched by the splendor and culture of that period. History and art had always interested me.

After visiting with the Baders, we traveled by train to Lindau, a harbor on the "Bodensee," an inland sea. Lake Bodensee divides Germany and Switzerland. From there we went on an excursion boat to Konstanz. We had lovely weather for our trip.

The children were so excited when we told them we would take a boat trip. "Oh, Mutti, will we be able to sit on deck?" asked Konrad, "And may we go to see the captain on the bridge?"

"May I go with Koni?" Agnes wanted to know.

"Yes, you may go with Koni, but don't let go of his hand," I cautioned her. "If you behave, you may have a dish of ice cream when you return."

"I'll take good care of her, Mutti," said Konrad.

While they were gone, William ordered a glass of wine for us. We sat on deck, enjoying the view of the mountains in the distance. Two accordion players entertained us with delightful music.

In Konstanz we stayed with the Stingels, parents of one of the pastry chefs from Tientsin. Konstanz did not have to be blacked out at night because it was too close to the border of Switzerland. The allies were afraid that they might hit the wrong country if they bombed near there.

Everywhere I went I was captivated by the beauty and cleanliness of the land. From there we took a train to Reutte, a little town in the Tyrolean Alps.

As we descended from the train, I just marveled at the beauty of the country. William, who was born in Germany, had seen many such places. But for me, it was all new. I said, "Willie, isn't it like a picture out of a fairy tale book? Just look at those adorable little houses; every window has a flower box. Overflowing, blooming flowers. Oh, how beautiful! How beautiful!" I turned to the children, "Just look!" I wanted them to take it in too. William was getting a little impatient with me. But I was overwhelmed.

We stayed in a small, but good, hotel. From there we made several excursions by bus and on foot. It was autumn. That was the time of year when the great big purple plums were ripening. Every day that we stayed there we bought a kilo of them. They were so sweet and juicy.

We stayed there eight delightful days, then we returned to Stendal.

Our six months were almost up and we wanted to spend a little more time with Mother. It was not easy to leave my new family from whom I had received so much love and care. I wondered whether I would ever see them again.

I left Mutter Gottwald with a heavy heart. She and my husband had a disagreement and would not make up. It had been only a small matter. But, they would not speak to each other.

It was our last day there. We were leaving the next morning. That evening I asked her, "Mutter Gottwald, come over for a glass of wine. Make up with William." We were staying across the street from her in William's grandparent's house.

"But he should be the one to come and apologize," she said.

"Oh, let it be, already," I pleaded.

It took some persuasion to get her to come over. I had a premonition we would not see her again. I was so glad that she finally did come. William would not have made the first move. He would have left for China without a goodbye. Thankfully, they did make up.

As our train pulled out from the station the next morning, it was so sad to see Mutter Gottwald standing there by herself on the platform, waving her handkerchief. When I could not see her anymore I broke down and cried. She was a good person, but seemed so unhappy. Konrad, too, was most unhappy. He really had become attached to his "Omi."

We stopped in Berlin to say goodbye to my brother and his family. Again, I was sad at leaving Walter, Trude, and little Sigrid.

"Take care, little Schwesterlein," Walter whispered as we hugged goodbye.

We paid a visit to Professor Saürbruch who was very pleased with the healing of Konrad's hip. "Should Koni continue with his medicine and vitamins?" I asked.

He replied, "You can throw them down the toilet! A good diet, that's all he needs."

We said "Auf Wiedersehen!" to Germany and left by train. We had traveled through Russia and Siberia to Germany in May and we returned to China by the same route in November. Both times we saw only snow. In May it had been too early for the trees to sprout and in November winter was already there.

The Growing Business in Shanghai

We were back in Shanghai. Our vacation to Germany seemed to have been only a dream. We returned rested, in good health and spirits, and with a thankful heart.

Business was progressing and William was very pleased, but it made me wonder if our revived marriage could stand the new pressure of our growing business.

166

We now had a bookkeeper who took care of the payroll and general accounting. I made out the invoices, checked sales slips and incoming bills. However, as it was already November and Christmas not far away, I had no time during the day and was obliged to do my paperwork after the store and restaurant were closed.

One particular night, after midnight, I was sitting in the store at a table writing invoices. Behind me was a cabinet on which cake boxes were stacked. The night bakers were in the back, baking bread and rolls as usual. Then, all of a sudden, some boxes fell on my head. I jumped up to check what caused this ... the boxes were only stacked improperly. But I was really frightened.

I went back to my invoices, but my nerves refused to calm down. An hour or so passed when, suddenly, I heard the sound of shattering glass upstairs in the restaurant. I sprang out of my chair and ran to the bakery, my heart pounding. I asked the head baker, "Come with me to check what is going on up there!" He went with me.

Nothing much was going on. Just a mouse or two had been playing among the liquor glasses and had pushed some of them down. "I'll always keep a cat in my bakery," I thought. That was two scares in one night and I was ready to quit. But I needed to finish up with my invoices. So I continued with my work.

Our front door was made of two glass panels that swung open to the inside, and a collapsing, metal lattice security door on the outside. I was tired and was rushing to finish my work when I heard a clang, clang on the metal door and a thump ... something was thrown onto the floor of the shop. My heart stopped. I wanted to scream. I sat still and stared. Finally I gathered up the nerve to go see what the noise was. There lay the morning paper, that the paper boy had just thrown. "Well, enough is enough for one night," I said aloud. I gathered up my papers and went straight to bed.

The experiences of the night were still bothering me the next morning. I shared my frightening night with William and he just laughed. He said, "Erna, you frighten too easy!"

During the holiday seasons there was always a night or two that I did not go to bed at all. At six o'clock in the morning I would take a refreshing shower or bath and go back to work. This gave me temporary energy, but the overwork did catch up with me later in the day. I just had to take a short nap.

It was 1942 and business was growing steadily. Parking was very limited near the bakery. We needed a larger place. There was no way to expand where we were. We found a very nice corner lot away from the center of the city and decided to build. William became very busy consulting with the architect and the builder and spent many hours away from the business. More and more of the responsibilities rested on my shoulders.

At that very busy time, another accident happened. We had running hot water in our apartment, but on busy days, when a lot of hot water was being used in the kitchen and bakery, we did not have any in our bathroom. It had to be heated on the kitchen stove and carried upstairs. It had been one of those extra-busy days. William was sleeping and I finished up a few things in the store. "Please take the bucket of hot water upstairs. Just leave it on the bathroom floor by the side of the tub," I said to the servant boy. After fifteen or twenty minutes I went upstairs, lifted the heavy bucket and started to pour the water into the bathtub when the bucket slipped. The hot water spilled all over my feet. It was very painful. I almost screamed. But I did not want to waken William. I hurriedly mopped up the water with a bath towel. I was afraid the water would seep through the ceiling into the restaurant. I then hobbled down to the bakery and told the Chinese baker what had happened. He applied some oil and cornstarch to my feet. I thought that was the best thing to do.

Luckily, the hot water had not gotten on the still very tender scar on my right leg. That night my feet and legs burned as if they were on fire. I tried to sleep but could not.

The doctor came the next morning. The first thing he looked at was the scar on my leg. Then he looked at my blistered feet. "Frau Scheel, don't you know better than to put oil and cornstarch on a burn!" he exclaimed. "That clogs the pores; air is blocked out and the heat is locked in."

"Oh, I did not know what to do. The baker put it on my feet!" I said.

"Well, you must stay off your feet for several weeks now," he said more kindly. "We'll see how you progress."

I was so disappointed. "Why must this happen at a time when we are preparing for the new business?" I thought.

I did have to stay off my feet. We called for a pastry chef from Tientsin again to help us out. This time a Herr Stingl came. He was the son of the Stingls that we had visited in Germany.

Shura, the Russian girl who had previously taken care of the children, had a new job when we returned from our vacation. So, I was thankful when we found another very responsible young Russian woman who had a good education, spoke perfect English and French, and handled the children very well. She was almost a governess. Agnes was not yet in school; she was with the new girl, Mila, all day. Mila taught her to speak Russian and also to sing a few Russian songs. The children grew very fond of her.

Shanghai was controlled by the Japanese from 1937 to 1945 but we saw very little of them in the city. One morning in 1942 the children came into my bedroom, all excited and shouting, "Mutti, there are Japanese tanks on the race course! May we go over? Come see!"

"Well, we will have to ask Vati first and then wait for Mila." There was no school that day so Mila was coming in a little later.

169

Since everything was quiet at the race course, William and I allowed Konrad and Agnes, with Mila, to go. The Japanese soldiers were very friendly to them and showed them the inside of the tank. One of the soldiers took pictures of them and asked, in English, "Where do you live?"

Konrad answered, "Across the street," and pointed to the bakery. The children were very excited when they returned home and told us all about it.

A week or so later one of the soldiers came to the bakery. He was carrying a few pictures for us. "Thank you so much," I said in surprise, as I looked at the pictures. The soldier turned and left. I thought that was awfully nice of him. I suddenly realized that not all Japanese were so heartless as I had always visualized them to be.

After a short time, the tanks were gone.

Kiessling and Bader - Shanghai

The architect, upon William's request, had drawn the plans and construction began on our new building on Hart Road. The building was located away from the hustle and bustle of the city and close to the German Lutheran Church School, the Information Bureau, and the radio station. Because I was not able to be up yet, the architect brought the plans for our new apartment to my bed and together we worked on the layout of the rooms and the furniture. We selected materials for the curtains and ordered lamps for the various rooms. Every piece was custom made. William and I intended to retire in about fifteen years and we wanted our furnishings to be durable. We were going to move to Germany then and take everything with us.

It was a very exciting time for me. I was looking forward to our nice, spacious new place and all the new furniture. The apartment would also have two balconies, one in the front and one in the back. William said to me, "Erna, all the furnishings are left up to you. Choose what you like—no

170

limit on cost." The architect and interior decorator helped advise me and together we made all the decorating plans.

After several weeks in bed, I was able to go down to the store once again. There was so much to do. William ordered new showcases, trays for cakes and chocolate candy, and utensils. New uniforms for the sales girls had to be made. They were rose colored with the beige initials KB, for Kiessling and Bader. The waiters and servant boys would wear black pants with white jackets; the cooks white uniforms. We had to hire many new people.

Our method of hiring Chinese personnel was quite unique. The head baker hired his helpers based upon the number specified by William. The pastry and candy department personnel and delivery boys were also the head baker's responsibility. The "Number One" waiter hired the waiters and clean-up help. The head cook hired his cooks and helpers. Each department head, more or less, was responsible for his own personnel. It was quite an undertaking. Of course, William still had the last word in hiring. If he was dissatisfied with any one of them, he would talk to the "Number One" person who then took action. If this failed, unsatisfactory employees were promptly released.

William and I hired the European personnel. We started the new business with over one hundred new employees. Since we also kept the small business on Bubbling Well Road, our total employee staff numbered about one hundred and fifty people.

We were glad when, finally, on July 29, 1942, we opened the doors of our new establishment on Hart Road.

It was a beautiful day. Flowers, plants, and telegrams came all day. They were brought and sent in by friends, business associates and suppliers, all wishing us well and wishing us a success for our new undertaking. Customers were complimenting William, "Herr Scheel, what a great place this

171

is. We wish you both much success!" Even one of the owners of the Tientsin business came to our Grand Opening.

I had a dress made especially for the occasion. It was made of navy blue silk. On the left side of the bodice, I had a bouquet of flowers embroidered. They were red poppies, blue bachelor buttons and a sheaf of wheat. The embroidery was exquisitely crafted. I wore a string of pearls which I thought was becoming to the square neckline.

I felt elated that day. I knew we had a very nice place. We were proud—we had made it again. Our bakery, restaurant, and roof garden was a busy place indeed that day.

The new store had very large windows. It had both large and refrigerated showcases. A nice office was next to the store. We would need a full-time bookkeeper now.

On the ground floor was the store, the candy and fancy cake making department, the bread and pastry rooms and the big ovens. The jams and juices were cooked outdoors in a covered place.

On the second floor was the kitchen and the restaurant which could seat one hundred sixty-five people. The seats of the chairs were reversible. A warm orange leather covered one side for use in the winter and the other side was rattan for the summer. The long wall on the street side had a narrow balcony with small tables for two. The wall consisted of glass doors which could be folded back or closed, depending on the weather. In the center of the kitchen was a very large stove, which could be worked at from all sides.

On the third floor were two apartments, one for our pastry chef, Herr Wolf and his wife, Olga. The other one was for us. Our meals were served in our private dining room. Servants brought the food up from the restaurant kitchen.

Above the apartments was the roof garden which extended the length and breadth of the building, very much like the one in Mukden. As in Mukden, we had a four-piece orchestra playing either on the roof garden or in the restaurant.

In the first few months we worked hard and long hours. We had inexperienced help in every department—help that had to be taught and trained. In addition to the work of the business, I also wanted our apartment to be in order. Mila was a big help in keeping the apartment neat. For the cleaning, washing and ironing, I had two Chinese maids.

I was under more and more stress from responsibilities, and I often had severe headaches. Pills did not help. One day we finally called the doctor. "Frau Scheel," he said, "you will have to take it easy. And now and then blow your top! That always helps." He gave me a shot and said, "This will make you sleep for at least twelve hours." The doctor then went outside my room to have a word with William.

I slept.

Herr Zaudig's Concern For The Children

It was shortly after this that Herr Zaudig put a letter into my hand. "Read this, Frau Scheel," he said, kindly. Although the letter was supposed to be from the children it was obviously written by Herr Zaudig. This is the translation:

Sender: Konrad and Agnes
"Dear Parents,

Take a little better care of yourselves. You have to stay healthy, not only that you may once enjoy life, but also for us, your children. Certainly everyone has to work and has his daily cares and problems, but we mean that it need not be carried on in such large scale that you don't have any time left at all for the pleasant diversities and soothing things that life offers.

If Vati does not take time off now and then to play cards with other uncles in the evenings or to go for a walk, it will never, never get better with his nerves, in spite of treatments of all the doctors in Shanghai. And your sick feet, dear Mutti, will only

173

get worse if you will continue and run here and there for days and weeks. Well, your once so famously strong nerves have a lot to be desired now. We have noticed that for a long time already. Life passes us by so fast. You can see this best in us, your children. When I, your Agi think back on my life and state the fact that I have already five years on my back and Koni almost ten. In spite of our youth, we are dead tired at night. We can imagine how you hard-working parents must feel then.

How nice it was in the good old times when Vati had one evening off and Mutti the other. Then, at least, one of you could sleep in. The way business is now you should have at least one day off together. That won't do? Maybe some day we will think of something with our childish heads. "What the common sense of a knowledgeable person does not see, a child will see in its simple mind."

As you, dear Mutti, probably will be called to that awful telephone and Vati is on one of his inspection tours from bakery to roof garden, we don't want to keep you any longer. We beg with all of our hearts, work and care for us but please, please grant yourselves some rest and diversities from time to time. If Uncle Zierle, the doctor, is called from time to time to see us, it is usually just a cold or some quickly healed child's sickness. But if he should be called to one of you, it will surely be a family disaster. That must not happen.

Think of the words: In self control one sees the Master, and apply this to your zealous work and business interests. Because the main reason is, for us, your children, that you may stay healthy and enjoy life with us.

174

You can buy everything; toys, clothes, cakes
en mass,- but not healthy parents-, and to keep that
is your parental duty. "

I laid the letter aside with tears in my eyes. Herr Zaudig
had seen how William and I were doing injustice to our children, to ourselves, and to our marriage. He wanted us to realize these things. He had written the letter in the children's
names, for our benefit. I realized that what he said was true.

I showed the letter to William. He read it and said, "What
business does Herr Zaudig have meddling in our private life?"
He did not appreciate the letter at all and let Herr Zaudig
know his feelings on the matter.

Everyday Life In Shanghai

Life in Shanghai was different in many ways from other
Chinese cities. It had an international population. It was such
a big city. One could only find rich and poor people, and
beggars, but no middle class. It was especially noticeable in
Shanghai. With the exception of a few parks and the foreign
concessions Shanghai was a dismal city. The sidewalks, as
well as the sides of buildings, were spotted with spittle. On
every street were beggars, some without feet, others with legs
amputated at the knees. Some had open sores. Some had a
hand just hanging by the skin, which they would swirl around,
as they called out, "Lao jä-tai tai, Master, Misses!" Before
we opened our bakery in the morning they were already there
sitting and waiting for the day-old bread or cake they knew
we would give them. We had told them they should not come
during business hours. A relative or friend would bring the
crippled ones and leave them at some busy corner or street in
the morning and then pick them up later.

I remember one afternoon when it was raining hard. The
muddy water was just gushing down the street. I was stand-

ing by a window talking to a Chinese customer who was waiting for the rain to stop, when we noticed a beggar on the other side of the street. He had only two stumps for arms and his legs were amputated above the knees. He had a cup hanging on a string around his neck into which people would drop their coppers, but in this downpour, no one stopped to throw him their change. He was hollowing and shouting. He stopped for a while, then he started to roll in the mud. I couldn't stand to watch him. I said to the customer, "Look at that poor fellow. Why does he do that?"

"Don't feel sorry for him, Frau Scheel. His crippled body is his fortune. He may be richer than you or I. His people put him there. They are watching and will gather the money that some throw to him."

"But this is awful and cruel," I said.

The customer did not comment.

I could never understand the minds of the Chinese. I also remembered that there had been, in Tientsin, a beggar whose legs were amputated just below the knees. He always sat at the same place on the main street, his hat lying at his side. He did not beg. He greeted everyone, "Good morning, Master, Missy!" He even called one's name if he knew it. He was always dressed neatly and clean. Everyone was friendly to him. He was the "King" of the "Village Of The Beggars." Outside of the Foreign Concession in the Chinese section of the city was the "Beggar Village." Every beggar brought the money they had collected that day to him and he gave each one their share.

Also common in Chinese cities, and very frequent in Shanghai, was another practice which I considered very inhumane. Almost daily one could find a bundle in the bushes on the roadway medium. It was usually a newborn baby girl, wrapped in newspaper or rags. If it were still alive someone would take it to a Foreign Mission Home where it would be accepted and cared for. These children would later attend the

176

Mission School, learn to cook, sew, knit or be taught another trade. When they were of age, the Mission would find a mate for them. Seldom would one find a boy baby. I asked, "Why do they mostly get rid of the girl babies?" The answer: A girl leaves the house and takes a dowry with her, while a boy brings a girl into the home, whereby the family profits. This happened mostly with the poor.

In the winter many beggars froze to death. Shanghai's climate reminded me of the monsoon characteristic of the China east coast region. There were heavy rainfalls in the spring and summer coupled with frequent cyclonic storms, especially in the spring. Its latitude was almost as far south as that of New Orleans, Louisiana. The summers were hot and humid. The temperature rose into the 90 degree Fahrenheit range and in the winter it would drop to 13 degrees maximum. After a hard freeze at night, many beggars were found frozen to death in a doorway or alley. Wagons, three times the width and height of a coffin, pulled by one man and pushed by another, were drawn through the streets and alleys to pick up the frozen bodies. Each man had a long pole on which a large hook was attached and with these they lifted the corpses and dumped them into the wagon, one on top of the other. Between the years of 1920 and 1940 it was said that 29,000 bodies were picked out of the cities' alleys, or fished from canals, rivers, and sewers each year.

One cold winter afternoon I had to speak to one of our delivery boys who was just leaving. As I turned the corner of our house, I saw two Chinese women leading, almost carrying, an elderly sickly-looking woman. Her face looked awful. I wondered what they were doing with her. I had no time to linger as I had to catch the delivery boy. Her wretched face haunted me all evening. The next morning a pedestrian came into the store and said, "A woman is lying in your alley." The alley separated our house from an apartment building. I went to see what had happened. It was that same poor woman I

177

had seen the evening before. She had frozen to death. I could not comprehend what had happened.

I asked our Number One head waiter, "Why would they leave the woman in the alley to die?"

He said, "When a relative lives with a poor family and is very ill, almost dying, they put that person out to die so they will not have to pay for the burial. Burials are expensive."

"Oh, how inhumane!" I exclaimed.

"But these are poor people," he replied.

We called the city health department and one of those wagons came along and picked her up. That was the first time that I had actually seen such a wagon and the men with the long poles. It was a traumatic experience for me.

We knew never to give the beggars money because they would often buy opium or other narcotics.

A young, educated White Russian fellow was one of our steady day-old-bread customers. He was a drug addict. He did not come every day. I often saw him sitting across the street with his head tucked between his knees. I knew he was under the influence of drugs, probably heroin. He spoke good English. Several times he had asked me for money to buy medicine. He was so thin. He would say, "Frau Scheel, I need to buy medicine—I really do." I gave him a few dollars.

"Mischa, don't spend it on drugs."

"No, no, Frau Scheel." Some time later I would see him sitting across the street with his head between his knees.

The next time he came to the store I said, "Mischa, no more money for you."

"I'm sorry, Frau Scheel."

I still saw him now and then. On one occasion when we were not busy I called him into the store. "I want to talk to you, Mischa. You are an intelligent young man. Do you know what you are doing to yourself?" I had heard that he had relatives in a nearby city. "Write to your relatives and ask them to help you. Your uncle is a doctor, isn't he?"

"Yes, Frau Scheel."

"Well, write to him."

"I'm ashamed if he sees me like this."

"The more he will want to help you, Mischa."

"You are right, Frau Scheel. I will write."

"All right then, and let me know."

A few days later he came to the store and said, "Frau Scheel, my uncle wrote. He will help me if I come. But I will need train fare money. Can you help me out?"

"Mischa, I hope you are telling me the truth."

He lifted his hand, looked toward heaven, and replied, "As the Lord is my witness, I am telling the truth."

I gave him the money and said, "Mischa, I hope to see you well. God bless you."

"Oh, thank you so much, Frau Scheel." He took the money and left. I looked after him and I just hoped that I had done the right thing.

After several months I saw Mischa sitting across the street, his head between his knees ....

The buses in Shanghai were mostly double decker, such as those seen in London. They ran along the main street toward the "Bund," the street along the Yangtze Chiang River, where they would turn. There they would often capsize during a strong storm. The spring typhoons were often very severe.

We had a frightful experience in our new building on such a stormy day. The wind and rain were slashing against our glass doors in the restaurant. Rain was seeping through one of the doors when our waiters noticed the door giving slightly. They called William in.

"Go into the yard for some large boards," William said to some of the men. "And hurry!"

They hurried out. But they could not get around the corner of the house, the storm pushed them back again and again. Then, during a brief lull of the wind, they made it. However, in the meantime, the corner section of the door had blown down and the rain was pouring into the restaurant. With the help of a few strong men, the door was at last put back into place which stopped most of the rain from coming in. What a mess in the restaurant, I thought, as the servants began cleaning up.

As time went by, things got settled and the business ran smoothly once more.

But our marriage suffered again. How different William had been on our vacation. I was thankful that I was busy and did not have much time to think. But more than ever did I seek strength in prayers. When I thought, I just can't stand William's bad temper and fussing any longer, I would kneel down in my bedroom and pray. Prayer to my God gave me the strength I needed to persevere.

I decided to take some time off for myself. I went to parties at the German Consulate on special events. I attended parties and plays at the children's school. On occasions, William and I also had guests. These diversions, along with prayer and my children, helped me to endure life.

My Joy - The Children

In September 1943 Agnes started school. She was so excited. "Now I can go to school just like my big brother," she said. We had a German custom that every child received, on their first day of school, a two-foot long, cone-shaped, brightly-decorated container filled with candies, fruit, and a little toy. It was somewhat like a Christmas stocking filled with treats. When the child came out of school, on that first exciting day, the mother was waiting in the schoolyard with the big cone.

Agnes was so excited when she saw me there with her big cone. I gave it to her and then I had her pose with it while I proudly took pictures of my little schoolgirl.

We had one problem with Agnes, though. She was a slow eater and was late for school almost daily. One day her teacher, Fraulein Pfeilsdorf, came by the store to talk to me about this problem. She said, "Frau Scheel, I cannot allow Agnes to be late daily. Please try to get her there on time."

"I didn't realize," I said. "I will see to it that she is not late again." I was terribly embarrassed.

I straightened this out by asking Mila to come in a little earlier and see to it that Agnes got to school on time. Mila also picked up the children from school and supervised their homework. In the evening we had supper together and then Mila went home. One of the maids bathed the children and saw to it that they brushed their teeth. Then I was called upstairs. Konrad and Agnes shared a large room which was both a bedroom and playroom. A door divided their bedroom from ours. I read them a few stories and afterwards we sang one or two songs together. Of course the children had to tell me what happened that day. This was always a special time for them and for me, too. Before I went back to the store, we prayed together.

We had a fine young minister who taught religion daily. All the children liked him very much and he often had parties for them. Since we lived close to the church now, it was seldom that I did not take the children to church on Sundays.

One evening as I came up to their room, Konrad was sitting on his bed chewing on something. I asked, "Koni, what are you eating?" He would not answer. "You know you are not to eat after you have brushed your teeth. What is it?"

"I am eating an eraser," he replied.

"An eraser! Why?" I demanded to know. He answered, "Pastor told us today, if we lie, it would show in our heart and Lord Jesus would see it. I lied today, and I want to erase my heart before Jesus sees it." I gave my ten-year-old Konrad a hug, as I turned my head away with a smile.

On another evening when I went up to their room, I noticed that Konrad behaved strangely. He was giggling without any apparent reason and would not stay quiet while we prayed. He acted peculiar, but he did not seem to have a temperature. I could not decide what the matter was. I put the children to bed and then went downstairs.

I asked William, "Please go upstairs and see what is wrong with Koni. He is acting so strange. He does not have a fever and he will not tell me anything." I was really worried.

"All right, I'll go see what is the matter with the boy," he said. He went upstairs alone.

He came back down after a while, laughing. I asked, "What was it?"

"Nothing is wrong with him. Your son is drunk!"

"Drunk? What did he drink?"

"Well, Erna, you know how much Koni likes to stay with our German stock-room man." I knew he went in there and tried to help Herr Klee, or just sit by him and talk. "You know our five gallon jugs of rum arrived today," William continued. (We used rum in cakes and candies.) "Herr Klee was syphoning it into quart bottles and Koni asked if he could do it too." William was laughing and having a hard time telling the story. "Herr Klee allowed Koni to help. But, Koni sucked too hard on the syphoning tube and swallowed some of the rum. I see it did not take much of it to make him lose his bearings." I was not so amused as William.

One afternoon Fräulein Pfeilsdorf, who was also Konrad's teacher, came to the store to place an order for a party she was giving. I took her order. We were not busy at the time so I said, "Please come to our apartment for a cup of coffee, Fräulein Pfeilsdorf." She accepted my invitation and we went upstairs.

We sat on the balcony as it was a pleasant afternoon. I found her to be a very nice person. She was slender with blue eyes and greying hair and a kind smile on her face which

182

everyone liked. I knew Konrad and Agnes were fond of her. She was so kind to them, but also strict, a perfect teacher I felt.

Just as she was about to leave, she remembered something Konrad had done in class. We sat back down for another cup of coffee. She said, "Frau Scheel, I meant to tell you this episode, but you were always busy when I came to the store. Today is the perfect time to tell you. We were discussing the onion in class one day and I asked if anyone could tell me something about it. Konrad's hand shot up. "I know a poem about the onion," he said. "Well, good, recite it," I said. He started:

> *"Hab' Sonne im Herzen*
> *und Zwiebel im Bauch*
> *dann kannst Du gut Scherzen*
> *und Luft hast Du auch."*
>
> *o r*
>
> *"Have sun in your heart*
> *and onion in your belly*
> *Then you can joke well*
> *and you'll also have air."*

We both broke out laughing. She said, "Where did he learn that?"

I thought for a moment and then remembered. I said, "When we were on vacation in Germany and visited some friends, one of their sons taught it to him. I am surprised he still remembers it. But I don't think he made the connection with the onion and the air!"

She said, "I could not help but laugh when he recited it."

Most of the children's clothes, and mine also, were made by a Chinese tailor. I had a Russian seamstress, though, who made my better dresses. The Chinese tailor came to the house; I would show him a picture of a dress in a magazine and give him the fabric I had chosen. He would take my measurements and return after a few days for the first fitting. I remember

183

one particular dress he made for me. It was a dress with buttons down the front. I was explaining to him that I did not want the buttons too close together when he said, "I savvy Missy," and pointed with his finger to the places he was going to put the buttons. "Putty button, wait a minute, putty button, wait a minute."

"That's exactly right," I said to him, happily. I knew then he understood where I wanted the buttons placed.

1942 - The American Presence In China

The war continued in the interior of China. Japanese troops concentrated their bombing attacks on Chunking itself. The endurance and the patriotism of the Chinese became stronger as Japan's attacks increased. Generalissimo Chiang Kai-shek hated the Communists. He had two enemies to fight, the Communists and the Japanese. The Chinese Communist Party struggled with and against non-communists for the control of China. In this vast country they annihilated the local anti-Japanese guerrilla units and those who would not cooperate.

In January of 1943 Chiang Kai-shek made it possible for treaties to be signed with England, the United States, Germany and other countries with concessions in China. The treaties would free China forever from any extraterritorial rights those countries might have had. The Chinese National Government had built up its army with American equipment and training. That brought numerous American Army and hospital personnel to Shanghai. Many of these people patronized our pastry shop and restaurant. We furnished bread, rolls, and pastries for the officer's mess; also, we supplied the Army hospital.

We became quite friendly with one American family, Major Anderson and his wife. We exchanged visits at each other's homes. They were awfully nice people. The first time we were invited for dinner, I thought it odd that Mrs. Anderson wore an apron over her nice dress. She was also wearing bedroom slippers instead of dress shoes. She was an attractive lady, tall and slender. She had red curly hair, smiling brown eyes, and an exquisite complexion. Her husband—perhaps six feet two, blond, a little stocky—was a very likable person. They made a handsome pair.

Their little two-year-old son was sitting in the middle of the living room, tearing up magazines and sticking pieces of paper into his mouth. His parents did not seem to mind his chewing paper. He seemed to enjoy the paper as much as if it were chewing, gum. I did not notice whether he swallowed the paper or disposed of it in some other way.

When we sat down to eat, Mrs. Anderson herself served us. I then knew that she did not have a cook. Most people had a cook, so I had taken it for granted they did too. So, I thought, that's why she wears an apron and comfortable footwear. Until then, her American customs had seemed strange to me.

The Long Arm Of Hitler

Adolf Hitler, in the meantime, was deeply involved in the war in Europe. Japan and Italy became his allies.

Many Jews fled Germany and thousands came to Shanghai where many of them opened their own shops and businesses. We started ordering our cake boxes, all of our paper supplies, and eggs from Jewish dealers. They were reasonable and dependable.

The "National Sozialistische Deutsche Arbeiter Partei" was also known as the Nazi Party. The NSDAP, as it was called for short, was quite strong. William was one of the early members of the party. When Hitler first came to power he had shown a number of good characteristics. Numerous people joined the party with honest convictions. However, many joined the NSDAP much later, not out of conviction but because they could benefit by being a party member. For instance, some jobs depended on party membership.

The "Heil Hitler" salute was very common in Shanghai among Germans but, in our store, the customers were greeted with the time of the day. We had an international clientele and William did not think it was appropriate to use any other greeting.

Unexpectedly, the Party came out with a new ruling. The Germans were no longer permitted to buy from or deal with Jewish merchants. William did not see any reason why he should discontinue dealing with those who had served him well. He came to an agreement with them. We would place our orders by telephone, the merchandise would be delivered by Chinese people, and the bills would show a Chinese firm's name. That was the way we continued trading with them. William's practice was never discovered.

Once in a while one of the Jewish people we knew came to see us. The Jewish people were selling their jewelry and other items of value. They needed money to live on. We bought tablecloths, embroidered linens and some jewelry.

One man showed me a delicate diamond ring. Tiny diamonds were set in flowers and leaves. "Oh, look, William. I really want this ring. It's so delicate."

"No," he said, "a baker's wife does not wear diamonds!" So I didn't get the ring. Diamonds, he had said before, would make me appear uppity.

Later, I bought a ring from another Jewish man for myself. It wasn't a diamond, but I liked it. It had three rubies set in a flat vertical golden design.

An Old Friend Needs Help

Herr Zaudig had to quit working. He was getting old and the responsibility of taking care of the small shop on Bubbling Well Road was too much for him. He rented a small room and visited us often. He had to see his little girl, Agnes, and also our dog, Flippy, who was his special friend.

186

When Herr Zaudig was visiting us one day, I noticed he was neglecting himself. His clothes were dirty and he had body odor. I mentioned it by saying to him very gently, "Herr Zaudig, you know you have some spots on your suit. I guess you did not notice them."

"Oh, no, Frau Scheel, I did not see them. I'll take the suit to the dry cleaners. Thank you for telling me," he said apologetically.

For a while he did all right until one cold winter day when he came to visit. He again looked terrible. He was unshaven, and his clothes were all rumpled as if he had been sleeping in them. I saw lice crawling on his coat. To see lice was not so upsetting to me, one could easily get them on the street car, which he had to ride, but I could not put up with that in our home. He just was not taking care of himself at all. I felt sorry for him, but I did not know how to approach him. "I wish William would speak to him," I thought, but, I knew it would be senseless to ask him. So I took heart and said, "Herr Zaudig, you look cold. Would you like to take a nice warm bath? I'll give you underwear and a suit from my husband. They will fit you, I think. Then we will have a nice hot cup of coffee and some sandwiches together."

"That would be nice, Frau Scheel," he said with a pleasant smile. I called the amah and had her prepare a bath for him. His underwear was washed and the suit cleaned for the next time he came. I gave him a warm blanket to take home. After that he always took a bath and changed into clean clothes when he visited.

Herr Zaudig needed someone to look after him. I really liked him. He had always been so kind to me. We had always been close, but now that he was no longer our employee, we had become his family. He was appreciative of what I did for him.

Germany Loses The War -
We Lose Our Business

News from Germany was not good in 1944. In the evenings we tuned in to the German short wave station to listen to the news and Hitler's speeches. Hitler had a powerful, convincing, hypnotic voice. Across the miles his voice kept me fascinated and assured. I got goose pimples just listening to him. He surely had me captivated. So many saw through him, but I was one of those who did not.

The letters we received from home were censored and were not telling us much. But we could read between the lines that things were not so good.

Since 1941 I had been sending parcels to our relatives: coffee, cocoa, tea, spices and chocolates. The parcels could only be sent by boat via the Atlantic Ocean to Lisbon, Portugal.

All through the war the German women in Shanghai had been knitting woolen socks, scarves and sweaters for the soldiers, and sewing baby layettes for folks in Germany.

We tried all kinds of ways to get letters and parcels to them, but in 1943, the sending of letters stopped. We were permitted to send and receive only twenty-five words once a month through the Red Cross.

I was sending dried peas, lard, flour, bacon, soap and sugar to our folks. No chocolate, sweets or coffee could be sent. They needed nourishing food. Clothes were also needed. Ten kilos was the limit we could send. Mutter Gottwald asked us for soap instead of sugar. She had always been so clean. Soap to keep clean was more important to her than sugar for nourishment.

My brother Walter worked behind the front with the telegraph and telephone division of the army. Because Berlin was heavily bombarded, he had taken his family to Silesia where his wife's parents lived. It was safer there. He had two little girls by then.

By 1945 the situation in Germany was bad and the people had lost all trust and confidence in Adolf Hitler. We anxiously waited for news. We wondered if the end was coming soon.

People were acquiring Chinese citizenship so that they could save their properties and businesses. Some were lucky; others were not. Many withdrew their money from the banks and transferred it to banks in other countries. They were the smart ones. Some folks just disappeared into the interior of China to avoid repatriation.

The war finally came to an end in 1945. Germany had lost the war.

Millions of German soldiers and civilians had lost their lives in vain. The devastation of cities, the destruction of museums with their priceless art, churches and cathedrals destroyed, all so uselessly. I thought of the beautiful Munich and Dresden I had visited in 1940, just five years back.

Our dream of living in Germany and enjoying a comfortable retirement there was gone with the war.

All bank accounts were immediately frozen, including ours. The Chinese closed the German radio station and the information bureau. Officials from the NSDAP were interned. Businesses and private properties were confiscated. Many elderly men, who had worked all their lives and had built up good businesses and were ready for retirement, lost everything. Many committed suicide.

We were still doing business. The American hospital and the Army personnel continued to purchase from us. Little by little, though, business slowed down and we had to dismiss a few employees.

The words "repatriation" and "concentration camps" were often heard.

William began contemplating emigration to the United States. He had an uncle, Frank Scheel, who lived in Cleveland, Ohio. William wrote and asked him if he would sponsor us. He agreed to help us.

189

Erna's German "Reise Pass" used during her trip to Germany in 1937.

William Scheel's Foreigner's Resident Certificate which was to be always carried on person to be produced for inspection if required. Shanghi China, 1938.

The German Consulate in Shanghai, China. 1937.

The Scheels and their staff at their first Shanghai, China Kiessling and Bader store on Bubbling Well Road. 1938.

Konrad on his bicycle in Stendal,
Germany after his recovery. 1940.

"Mutter" Gottwald with William,
Konrad, and Agnes in Stendal,
Germany. 1940.

Konrad and Agnes on a Japanese tank in Shanghai, China. 1942.

The Scheel's large Kiessling and Bader Business on Hart Road in Shanghai, China. 1942.

Herr Zaudig and Herr Wolf in Shanghai, China. 1942.

Agnes with her cone when she started school in Shanghai, China. 1943.

Erna and other German women in China sewing for the German troops. 1942.

CHAPTER TEN
China Exodus

We were hoping to leave China for America before re-patriation--which seemed very certain--began. My dream of Germany was gone, so I thought William's idea of emigrating to the United States was the next best thing.

During this trying time I heard that Frau Corinth had died several months back. Friends passing through Shanghai told me. I grieved for my dear Tante Corinth, but I was also very hurt that no one wrote to me about her death. Their daughter had married and was living in Tientsin. She could have written! "This is life," I thought; "everybody lives in their own private world."

Our pastry chef, Herr Wolf, and his wife returned to Tientsin. We did not have enough work for him. We rented their apartment to a German couple whose house had been confiscated.

The children still attended school. The church doors were still open.

Germans were not permitted to transfer money out of the country. But, through a Jewish friend, we were able to secretly send a thousand dollars to Uncle Frank in Cleveland. That was all the cash assets we had because German bank accounts were confiscated by the Chinese government. Uncle Frank invested it wisely for us. William was preparing. We would need all the money we could save for the trip to the States.

One day a list of German names for repatriation appeared in the daily newspaper, names of high officials of the Nazi Party and single men. Herr Zaudig's name was on the list.

They were to be ready to leave by boat for Germany in just two weeks. Each adult was allowed to take three hundred fifty pounds of personal belongings and each child one hundred seventy- five pounds. They were only allowed to take a certain amount of money--very little--and no jewelry. They would be first sent to a transit camp outside of Shanghai for a short time, and then taken on board a ship which had already picked up Germans from other ports.

Herr Zaudig came to tell us good bye. Konrad and Agnes were very upset. "Will we see you, Onkel Zaudig?" Agnes cried.

"I do hope to see you all in Germany," he replied. He hugged them both.

"Take care of your self," I pleaded, "and try to stay in touch. I guess we will be following soon." I hugged my friend good bye. I was so sorry to see him leave. He then went down to the bakery to say good bye to William.

1945 - Our Home And Business Are Confiscated

One afternoon in the fall of 1945, we were visited by three Chinese gentlemen in civilian clothes and two American officers in uniform. One of the Chinese men approached a sales girl and asked to see Mr. and Mrs. Scheel. I heard them ask for us and went to greet them. "Get William," I told the girl, "He's in the restaurant with a customer."

When William came, one of the men said, "Mr. Scheel, we would like to talk to you and Mrs. Scheel privately." I suddenly had a strange feeling deep down in my stomach. "This is it!" I thought. My knees were shaking. I could hardly make it up the steps.

In our apartment, we invited the men to sit down. We offered them something to drink. They declined. After introducing them-selves, the older of the Chinese men took from his brown leather briefcase a sealed envelope and handed it to William. William reached for a letter opener then read the letter. He then handed it to me without a word. The letter contained a short message; "As of this hour your business is confiscated and will be turned over to the American authorities. The building is needed for a mess hall to accommodate military hospital personnel and must be vacated by tomorrow morning."

What I had feared had happened. William's and my eyes met. No one spoke. Several minutes must have passed ... perhaps just seconds. Then I heard William say in an angry voice, "Gentlemen, what your government is asking of us is impossible! Our storerooms, freezers, and refrigerators are stocked with sacks of flour, drums of shortening, cases of butter, and eggs. Our showcases are filled with baked goods. How can we dispose of all this overnight? Where shall I find a place to live for my wife and children in so short a time? I need more time!"

"Gentlemen, what you are requiring from us is unreasonable!" I burst out. I could feel my pulse throbbing in my throat and could hardly control my voice. I fought back tears. I got up and went to the window so they would not see my face.

One of the American officers said, "We need this building for our service men. Yours is the only suitable building in the vicinity."

"Mr. and Mrs. Scheel," one Chinese man said, "we are sorry but these are the orders." We arose and escorted them back through the store and they left.

To our amazement, we saw an American soldier, with a gun over his shoulder, posted at every entrance of the house. Nothing could be taken out or moved. I was shocked. Turning to William I said, "This is the end." He just nodded.

William told our employees what had happened. "We will be back in a little while," he said to them. Then turning to me, he and I went to our apartment.

I said to William, "I knew it all along that this would happen. But not for a moment did I think it would happen in such a cruel way. 'Get out by tomorrow morning!' that's what they said."

We were alone in our apartment. I could not yet comprehend what was happening to us, that we would be losing everything that we had worked so hard for those past fifteen years. We were sitting on our built-in corner sofa. It was upholstered with an off-white material with leaves of muted green colors woven into it. William and I were holding hands. My handkerchief was wet from tears. We did not talk. We knew nothing to say. The situation drew us to one another. All we had was each other to console us. I don't know how long we sat there.

I looked around our elegantly furnished living room and dining room. Heavy gold-colored curtains gathered at the sides with a cord and tassels separated the two rooms. The furniture in the living room was made of mahogany and the dining room furniture of natural oak. Across from where I sat was my favorite chair. It was a graceful, burgundy velvet wingback chair. I got up, went over, and sat down in it. I caressed its soft material.

I recalled the many hours I had set in it in the evenings, knitting a sweater for the children or socks for a German soldier at the front somewhere in Europe. The children had played on the floor as I knitted.

A soft light was shining from a teakwood floor lamp on which a carved dragon wound its body up the post. The dragon's open mouth held a burgundy lantern-shaped silk lamp shade. Several Persian rugs lay on the floor and a few oil paintings and Chinese exquisitely-embroidered silk pictures decorated the walls. My eyes wandered to William.

On a board in the back of the sofa where he was sitting, a few Chinese curios of ivory, jade, and wood were displayed. A crystal vase with pink roses sat on a small round mahogany table.

William's voice brought me back to reality. As if he had read my thoughts he said, "Yes, Mutti, this is the end. What we had feared all along has happened. All of this," he got up and looked around the two rooms, "is gone. And the business too." We had labored hard for everything we had. He got up, came over to my chair, put his arm around my shoulder, and said, "Don't cry any more. We need to go down and tell our people."

"Yes, I know," I whispered. "but this means starting over again. Where will it be this time?"

"I don't know what we will do," he replied in a hopeless tone of voice, "Let's go down now." I had never seen William so crushed.

"Wait a minute; let me just wash my face and put on some powder and I will go with you." Then we went down together to our employees.

They had many questions. We could not answer them all.

William said, "I do want you all to be here in the morning." They had suspected something terrible when they saw the American soldiers at the doors.

All at once a thought came to my mind and I said to William and our people, "I wonder if Major Anderson knows anything about this. I'm sure he would have warned us. I will go to his headquarters and talk to him."

"It will do no good," William said.

"I'll try it anyhow."

"It might help," one of the bakers said hopefully.

I told the cashiers, "Clear the cash registers; there will be no more business today." I told the sales girls, "Start cleaning the showcases."

I went and changed from my white uniform into a dress. Then I left. Going out the door, I heard voices saying behind me, "Good luck Mrs. Scheel, and God bless you."

I turned back to them and said, "Thank you all. I need that."

Major Anderson was in his office and was surprised to see me. He was a nice man. He looked so handsome in his uniform. After we shook hands, he asked, "Well, Mrs. Scheel, what can I do for you?"

"Major Anderson, you are unaware of what has happened, I assume."

"You are taking me by surprise."

I told him what had happened. He was greatly astounded.

"It is not only the business matter," I said, "but where can we find a place to stay? The Germans are already crowded together and other nationalities are not allowed to take in Germans."

He thought a while, then he said, "Mrs. Scheel, go home and stay there. Don't do a thing." He put his arm around my shoulder and said, "Chin up! I'll see you in the store in the morning at eight." I went back to the store with a better feeling.

When I arrived at the business, the tension was awful there. At least I was able to take some calmness into the situation. I had faith in Major Anderson. William sent the employees home and told them to return the next morning, and then he closed the store.

When we went up to our apartment we found Agnes and Konrad upset and frightened. When they had seen the M.P.s standing in front of the doors, they told us they had felt like prisoners in their own home. They were so glad to see us. "Vati, what is happening?" Konrad asked. Mila had been with them during that time, but she did not know what to say to them. She had read and played games with them to divert their thoughts.

William and I sat down with the children and Mila and explained the situation. Konrad said, "I know Major Anderson will help us."

"I believe we shall at least be able to stay in the apartment," I said with confidence.

Mila stayed with us that night. She was going to pack. I said to her, "Mila, just leave everything. It will be all right." William could not understand how I could be so calm. Neither William nor I got much sleep that night. I prayed most of the night.

As I was lying in bed, I thought of the time when the interior decorator and I had selected the furniture, curtains, and lampshades. I thought of the day the furniture had arrived. Curtains were hung, and everything had found its place. Just a little over two years ago. I loved all of our rooms, they were spacious with lots of light. I had been so tired of the small dingy rooms we had previously lived in. I especially liked our bedroom in this apartment. The furniture was made of light birch wood, with beautiful grain. The curtains were made of old-rose colored silk. The matching bedspread was topped with a filet spread.

My thoughts wandered. Questions circled in my mind. I could not tell exactly what my feelings were. Again and again I thought to myself, "Is it true that this is happening? Have we lost everything again?" Sleep would not come. William was tossing and turning in the bed beside me. "Will the night never end?" I wondered. Finally, sleep relieved me of all my thoughts.

Punctually at eight o'clock the next morning Major Anderson and two Chinese officers arrived. William and I met them in the store. Major Anderson introduced us to the two officers. We did not even sit down. Major Anderson said, "Mr. and Mrs. Scheel, you will have three days to sell your products, and it has been decided that you may stay in your apartment--but you will have to share it with a Chinese family with four children." I felt a big sigh of relief escaping my lips. William and I looked at each other. We appreciated Major Anderson's efforts.

One of the officers said, "After these three days an official from the Chinese government will come to take inventory of the business and your apartment."

The meeting did not take more than fifteen minutes. William informed our employees and I ran upstairs to tell the children and Mila that we could stay in the apartment. That meant so much to them and to me. Even if we had to take in a Chinese family of six.

What a turmoil we experienced the next three days. Most of the baked goods and candies were sold at a greatly reduced price. The unbaked goods were baked and brought to the store to be sold. We let our employees take the breads and left-over baked goods.

On the evening of the third day, after we had said goodby to everyone and they had gone home, William and I took a last look at the store and other departments. All the showcases, candy jars, the big glass chocolate candy display case were empty. In the bakery the work benches and tables were scrubbed clean, the big oven was cold. In the kitchen, no fire was in the kitchen stove. Pots, pans, and utilities were clean and put up. No baker, cook, or helper was around. The spacious restaurant, desolate. No waiter, no one at the cash register. "What an awesome feeling," I said. "This does not belong to us anymore." My voice echoed in the vast rooms, rooms that used to be teeming with life.

It was worse than Mukden. It was worse than Nanking. I thought of the year 1919 when I was just ten years old and Papa lost his butchery in Tientsin--in three days. It was worse than Tientsin.

Our Chinese employees took possession of the original bakery on Bubbling Well Road. They just stepped in and took over. We were helpless; we had no rights and had been proved wrong in hoping to keep that store. Another terrible blow--to think that our own people would do that to us. We never once expected that. "What a change of life style from one day to the other!" I thought.

William and our bookkeeper went through the books. Bills had to be paid and outstanding invoices collected. Commodities still had to be disposed of. We were allowed to sell the raw materials.

After school Konrad helped his father. He went on his bike to pay the utility, telephone, and such bills. He also contacted our former dealers, asking them if they were interested in buying back some of the commodities. Most of them did. Konrad did not like to do these errands, but he understood that it was necessary.

The children were sorry when we had to let Mila go, and so was I. She had meant more to me than just an employee. She was a very understanding person. In a way she had replaced "Onkel" Zaudig. I could talk to her. She lived with her mother. They were White Russians and had fled to China. I had often been invited to their house. Her mother was also a kind and a very dear person. Konrad and especially Agnes missed Mila. She would still come often and see us.

I started keeping house. This reminded me of the days in Hankow. I took the cookbook from the bookcase and gave it its place in the kitchen where it belonged. I needed it badly. Quite often I had to go to our German neighbors in the apartment next to ours and ask for advice.

After a few weeks, when most of the business affairs were more or less settled and William did not have much to do, he became very depressed. He began having suicidal thoughts. "I am poorer now than when I started out in 1930, Erna," he said. " I have a wife and two children to support, no income--and the bank account is frozen." William threw up his hands. "What is there to do?" he screamed. "I'll just end my life!" he said.

"Surely we will hear from Uncle Frank soon. He said he would help us get to the United States. We can both work," I pleaded, "Please, don't give up now, William."

William was out of control. I knew he had a revolver and feared what he might do. I tried to find the gun but my search was in vain. To make matters even worse, I was pregnant. I knew I could not tell him in his present state of mind.

I feared he would want me to have an abortion. I believed my pregnancy, nine years after Agnes' birth, must be the Lord's will. I prayed, "Lord, help me to be strong."

Our folks in Germany were in need of food and clothing. As I could not ask William for money, I decided to secretly sell one of my rings. It was one I had bought and not a gift from William. He was a very suspicious man. I often felt he had a sixth sense. One day I found William looking in my purse. "What are you doing? You have no business looking in my purse."

"Where did all this money come from?" he demanded in return.

"I sold a ring, but not one that you gave me! We need money to send parcels to our relatives."

"Why did you go behind my back, Erna? I do not like this!"

"If I had asked you for money, William, I doubt you would have given me any. With this money I can send quite a number of packages."

"We must think of ourselves now."

"We must think of others too, William!" I pleaded.

Some time later William said, "Go ahead and send the packages, Erna."

Shortly after that we received a letter from Uncle Frank. "I have started emigration procedures and am trying to get an affidavit for all of you. Because the children and Erna were born in China, however, they will have to enter on the Chinese quota. It will take some time, but the authorities are working on it. They hope that they may enter on William's German quota."

The children had to discontinue their music lessons. Konrad was taking accordion lessons and Agnes piano. Konrad was fond of his German teacher and liked to play his accordion. But Agnes did not like her strict Russian teacher--she was glad to quit.

There were times when we needed an item that we had left at the store. We would send the children to get it. They were eager to go, they knew some of the soldiers from the time before the takeover. They would stop and talk to them and get a pack of gum or a candy bar, which they enjoyed very much.

One day one of the soldiers heard Konrad playing his accordion.

He said to him, "Koni, come and play for us."

Konrad was glad to do it and went to get his music book. Agnes followed him. He played a few American folk songs; "Home Sweet Home" and "Oh Susanna." Konrad said the soldiers had sung along with joy.

When they returned to the apartment, Konrad continued, "You know, Mutti, some of the men had tears in their eyes. Maybe they have family and children in the States and got homesick, you think?"

"That is quite possible, Koni. The singing brought back memories, I'm sure."

Neither the children nor William nor I had hostile feelings toward the soldiers. They certainly had nothing to do with our situation.

William was even offered a job in the kitchen of the American Military Hospital. He accepted not very willingly, but out of necessity.

Two or three weeks after we lost our business, the Wong family moved in. Mr. Wong worked for the Municipal Government Bureau of Health. They were educated people, friendly, pleasant, and somewhat apologetic. We kept our two bedrooms, kitchen, bathroom, and the little study. The Wongs occupied the living and dining rooms, cooked on hibachis on the roof garden, and used the bathrooms there.

Before the Wong's moved in, we had removed the pictures, rugs, and art objects. We were able to sell the dining room furniture and replaced it with the tables and chairs from the roof garden. We were not able to sell the living room furniture.

After several months, the Wongs asked us to have dinner with them one evening. I was astonished to see what had happened to our beautiful living room furniture. The sofa was dirty with all kinds of spots and stains on it. The family applied a kind of brilliantine to their hair and it was very visible where their heads had touched the back of the sofa. And my favorite wing back chair! Our apartment just had no place for the chair. it made me feel sick when I saw it.

1946 - A New Arrival Provides A Delayed Departure

One evening the children were asleep. William and I were lying in bed reading. I was three months pregnant for our third child. I decided to tell William. I took heart and said, "Willie, I am pregnant."

"What!" he shouted. "Pregnant? It is not from me!"

"Hush," I said. "Don't be so loud; you'll wake the children. You know it is your child!"

He wouldn't hush. "It is impossible. It is not from me!"

"I should know. There is no one else!" I responded.

I got up and went into the kitchen and cried. He came after me and sat on one of the chairs.

"We cannot have another child at this time, it is just not possible. You will have to have an abortion! Go and see our doctor tomorrow!"

I was angry and I was upset but, I did not contradict him. I had my own ideas though. And I was not going to have an abortion!

I went to Doctor Zierle, our family doctor, the next day. I explained my situation.

"Don't worry," the doctor said. "I do not perform abortions." He then examined me. "You are in good health. I will make up a little lie. Go home and tell your husband that there is an infection and an abortion will endanger your life. Tell him to call me."

"Thank you, Doctor Zierle," I said.

"Be in good spirits now. Come and see me in four weeks."

I told William what the doctor had said. "You and the doctor are plotting this!" he shot back, "Make an appointment with the Russian doctor who examined your leg. This time I am going with you!"

When William went to work, I gave Doctor Antonoff a call and explained my predicament to her. She was very nice and said, "Just bring your husband with you. I will take care of him. Don't you worry."

I had an appointment with her the next day. The waiting room was filled with women, William the only man. I could see how uncomfortable he felt. When I was called, he jumped up and wanted to follow me. "Oh, Herr Scheel, just wait here please. I will call you," the doctor said.

She examined me and had the same diagnosis as my family doctor. She laughed and said, "You are in good health. Keep a good attitude and I will take care of Herr Scheel." She called William in and told him the same thing our family doctor had said. There was nothing William could do.

The next six months were not easy for me because William was very irritable and most unpleasant to live with.

Konrad and Agnes were excited and looking forward to having a little brother or sister. When the news spread among the German community that I was pregnant, I was showered with everything I needed for myself and the baby. Times were bad. They knew that after not having a child for nine years, I would be in need of everything. Almost every day a package arrived at our door. Maternity dresses, baby clothes, a bassinet, stroller, play pen, baby bed--even a chest. The only thing I had to buy was diapers. The people were so good. Unpacking and sorting the packages was my happy time. Konrad and Agnes "O-o-oh-ed and A-a-ah-ed" over the little baby clothes.

209

"Oh, look at the little shirts!" Konrad exclaimed.

"Oh, Mutti, I like the cute little white dress!" said Agnes.

William was angry when the things arrived. We unpacked them when he was at work. Then we stored them away where he couldn't see them.

I thanked the Lord for his goodness. It reminded me of the fact that the Lord repays us manyfold when we do good. I thought of the numerous times I had helped drug addicts and given money to missionaries from all nationalities. William had resented my aiding others and told me more than once. "Who will help us when we will be in need?" he had asked. Well, he now saw how we were being helped when we were very much in need.

There was not much to do but wait for our names to come up on the list. A few German ladies with small children would pass the time by coming together several times a month to exchange ideas and news. We talked about the news we received from families who had already returned to Germany. We shared coffee and homemade cakes. Sometimes we left the children with our husbands or older children and played bridge. This was always a nice diversion. We shared news, household hints and recipes. At our last party one of our friends gave us shocking news. "I noticed," she said, "that when my baby cried, the Amah took her in her arms and soon my child was quiet and slept for hours. I watched the Amah closely and discovered that she let my baby suck her fingers. The secret? ... OPIUM hidden under her fingernails!" We were astonished and feared this might have happened to our own children.

I decided to use the waiting to start packing. We could not take many of our valuables. A very nice collection of Chinese bronze incense vessels, a two and-a-half-foot-tall pagoda, and the teakwood floor lamp could not go. They were too heavy and bulky. We had to leave them.

We had not received the affidavit from Uncle Frank so William did not want to leave. He hoped to avoid repatriation and go directly from China to the United States. He got in touch with our Jewish friend who had transferred funds to Uncle Frank. Our friend had a Chinese wife and they agreed to hide us in their house, outside the city limits, at the time of the boat's departure. We hid for several days behind a huge armoire which concealed the door to our room. Agnes was so frightened. She was only nine years old. Fortunately we escaped the authorities.

My pregnancy was going well. Frau Musslick, one of my elderly German friends, offered to stay with the children while I was in the hospital. On the fourth of June my doctor said, "You have three weeks to go, Frau Scheel."

I went home and told Agnes, "I had better get my suitcase packed for the hospital. I want to be ready; you can never tell." And sure enough, next morning at six-thirty, I had to go to the hospital. Our baby was eager to come into the world.

Our little boy was born on June 5, 1946, at ten o'clock in the morning. He weighed three kilo and one hundred forty grams. It was an easy birth for him and for me.

After the delivery I said to Doctor Zierle, "This was so easy, I could have a baby with you every year!" However, my statement did not sound the way I wanted it to sound. The nurse joined in laughter with Doctor Zierle and me. I felt very good.

William's heart warmed up when he saw his little baby boy. The baby definitely had his ears.

Doctor Zierle and Nurse Elisabet were just wonderful. We named our baby Hellmut Wilhelm Franz. Usually Hellmut is spelled with one l and th. Nurse Elisabet was a motherly, warm-hearted person and suggested spelling the name Hellmut which means "bright courage." She said to me, "I wish for him to have the courage you have."

Nurse Elisabet was very kind to me and spoiled me in every way. She did not let me wash myself. She washed my hair and combed it. She brought food to my bed. Well, I loved being spoiled like that. The days under her care were the best I had in a long time.

I had many visitors. The children and William came to see me daily. After three days Konrad asked me, "When are you coming home, Mutti?"

"In a few days. Why?"

"I like your cooking better," he said.

"Frau Musslick is a much better cook than I am," I responded.

He replied, "But you cook with love!" This made me feel good and I thought: my cooking must not be so bad after all.

On my sixth day in the hospital another list of names appeared in the newspaper. Our names were again on the list.

How are we going to work this out, I thought. I had done some packing, but there was so much more to do. And Doctor Zierle would not let me go home.

When it came to packing, William was not much help. Two of my friends and Mila went to the house to pack. The big overseas trunks had to be ready and delivered to the pier in a week, go through customs, and then be stored in the hold of the repatriation ship. Once there, they could not be removed until their final destination. It was such a frustrating and difficult time and I felt so helpless.

Unfortunately for us, the repatriation meant we would be going to Germany first--then the United States.

Doctor Zierle was trying his best to get our names off the list. He said, "It will be totally irresponsible to let you and the baby travel on a troop-transporter at this time." He allowed me to go home on the tenth day. "But stay off your feet as much as possible," he advised.

After I had been home a few days, the front door bell rang one afternoon. William was at home. Konrad went to open the door. Two Chinese and one American gentlemen were standing outside. One of them said, "We are doctors and are here to see Mrs. Scheel and the baby."

"My mother is in bed."

"That is all right. Please lead us to her."

William heard the voices and went to the apartment door. He had heard them say, "We are here to see your wife and the baby."

"Who are you?" asked William.

"We are doctors. We want to see whether they are well enough to travel thirty days on a troop-transporter." I thought, "This is the verdict, to go or not to go!"

"Very well," I heard William reply, as they approached the bedroom.

They introduced themselves. The American doctor shot questions at me. "How are you feeling? When was the baby born? How much did he weigh?" I answered his questions. He then turned to the Chinese doctors and said," This is too soon after the birth and I sincerely recommend that we set the repatriation date for this family back a year. We cannot take the responsibility of letting this mother and the child leave at this time."

My heart jumped with joy! Could it be possible? Silently I said, "Please Lord."

I could not understand what the Chinese doctor answered. Then they all wished me well and left. Doctor Zierle had succeeded!

Konrad and Agnes came dancing and jumping into the room, hugging me close. William had a smile on his face and said, "Well, Erna, we have a year." I said, "Thank you to my Lord!"

What a comforting assurance to know that we could stay another year. William had to rush off and get our trunks from the pier. We were lucky, they were still on the pier--and not on the ship. We were so happy, feeling we could breathe more easy for a year at least.

With every boat that left, the German colony became smaller and smaller. It seemed that mostly families with small children, the sick, and the elderly were all that were left behind. It was during this time that William's aunt wrote to tell us that his mother had died. She had not been ill for very long. I was sorry I would not see her again. She was a good person, had a hard life, and received so little love.

"She is at peace now," I said silently.

Our Lutheran church was still open for worship services for a while. Our own pastor and a missionary pastor took turns preaching until they too had to leave. Then a German missionary from the China Inland Mission held services on Sundays at their Mission Church and Bible classes on Wednesdays. The children and I attended those two services regularly.

The few school teachers that were left taught privately in their homes. The school had been closed.

One afternoon in late summer we had unexpected company. My dear friend Hedi Spengler, who helped us prepare for Konrad's trip to Germany came to visit. She and her three children had come to say goodby. They were to embark on the next boat, which would be leaving Shanghai in a day or two. We had not seen each other since 1939, the year Konrad went to Germany. That was the year, also, that Herr Spengler was transferred to the German Consulate in Peking. They had lived in Peking since then. I was so glad to see her again. I had hoped we would leave on the same boat. She was delighted to see that Konrad was doing so well and of course she was glad to see our little one. We spent a few meaningful hours together and caught up on many happenings. She gave an address in Germany to me where I could contact her when we arrived there. She was another dear friend leaving.

The year went by quickly. All in all we were experiencing a quiet and relaxing time. We had no worries about the store, orders, deliveries, or disagreements with the employees.

William loved our little boy Hellmut. He was a cheerful baby and gave him many happy hours in his time of anxiety.

On sunny days I took Hellmut out in his stroller. He was a healthy child, had blond, curly hair, grey eyes, and a nice tan and rosy cheeks. People stopped us to take a look at him.

Agnes adored her little brother. He was like a live doll for her. She enjoyed playing nurse. Mila had made her a nurse's cap and apron. That is what Agnes said she wanted to be when she grew up, a nurse.

Konrad was interested in electrical things. He built his own crystal radio and repaired irons and clocks. Once he played doctor with one of Agnes' dolls. I was on the roof garden with Hellmut. All of a sudden I heard Agnes crying. She came running up the stairs, "Look, Mutti, what Koni did! He cut up my doll! All the stuffing is coming out of her and he is laughing!" She was terribly unhappy. I knelt down to her and looked at the "operation."

"Agi," I said, "Mutti will fix it again. I will also have a word with Koni. I am sure he will not do it again."

I went down to our apartment to talk to Konrad. He was sitting at the kitchen table reading. I called him into my bedroom.

"Do I have to come now? This book is so interesting."

"Yes! Now, Konrad!"

"What is it?" he asked in an agitated tone.

I was angry. The way he said, "What is it?" irritated me. "Why did you have to cut open Agi's doll? She just got it for her birthday!"

"I was just playing doctor!" he snapped, "She doesn't have to act so silly!"

215

I could never stand backtalk from either of the children. I took my hairbrush from the dresser and struck him across his face, saying, "Don't you talk to me like that!" He grabbed his cheek and ran from the bedroom.

I didn't lose my temper often, but when I did, I really did. It was done. I couldn't take it back. I felt terrible.

That evening when I prayed with the children at bedtime I apologized to Konrad. His red cheek clearly showed the bristle marks of my brush. It grieved me to look at him. "I am sorry too, Mutti and Agi," Konrad said. Then Konrad and Agnes hugged each other. We all made up.

Mrs. Wong was very fond of Hellmut also, and came over often, especially when I was sunning him on the roof garden. Our children also played together. "Wong Tai Tai" (Mrs. Wong) and I got along very well and conversed easily. Like us, they also spoke the Mandarin dialect. They were pleasant and intelligent folks — just not the tidiest, at least not to our liking. We enjoyed Mrs. Wong's cooking. She had invited us over several times for meals.

The Wongs moved out a few months before we had to leave. In less than a year they had totally ruined the furniture. It was hard to believe that people could have lived like that. We closed the doors to the rooms where they had lived and rarely went in there.

I enjoyed going to the market in the mornings on my bicycle. After a while, I got to know the different dealers. I bargained with them about the prices and tried to find the cheapest meat, vegetables, and fruit. I thought I had found the cheapest merchant. One morning I said to the merchant, "Mr. Lee, must we go through this bargaining every time I come? Can't you just give me your best price? That will save you and me time."

"Ding how, ding how Tai Tai." (Good, good Misses). But soon I found out that he did not give me his best price. "This is China," I thought. "Bargaining is in their blood."

Never-the-less, I like the Chinese people, they have a warm place in my heart.

1947 - Our Year Of Grace Is Over

June of 1947 came and Hellmut was a year old. He was starting to walk and talk. In the back of my mind I constantly wondered when the next list of names was going to appear in the newspaper. A year had passed and July came. The list appeared. And on it were our names.

The time had come to say adieu to the country I was born in and in which I had lived for almost thirty-six years. It was time to say goodby to our friends. It was also time to say goodby to our dog, Flippy. That was the most painful thing I had to do, take my Flippy in a rickshaw to the veterinarian to be put to sleep. I cried all the way. No one could ever touch or hold Flippy except the family. He just did not like strangers. So I held him and put my tear-stained face on his head so he could not see the vet as he gave him the shot. I held him a little while until his body was limp and then I went home. It grieved me so.

The children did not know I had taken Flippy to the vet. I did not want them to see me take him away. When I returned they asked, "Where is Flippy? He is not at home!"

I explained what I had done. "You know how Flippy was. He just knew our family. Nobody could touch him. He would never have gotten used to other people."

Konrad became upset and cried, "Oh, no, Mutti!"

"It is for the best Koni. It was really for the best. He had no pain, no pain at all." It was a hard time for all of us.

We had just eight days to pack and get ready. We left our pagoda, the teakwood floor lamp, and the bronze incense vessels with a friend who was going to sell them for us. We did take our Persian rugs, a leopard skin rug, our Rosenthal china, our silver, and some money. We were only allowed to take a very small amount of money out of the country, so I hid ten and twenty dollar bills in my sewing box with spools of thread. I sewed gold coins into my husband's suits. We had learned some of those hiding places from our Jewish friends. That's what they had done when they left Hitler's Germany. We did not have a great deal of valuable jewelry, but what we had was nice and valuable to us.

The day of our departure came. One last look. I went from room to room with William and the children. Konrad saw a book he wanted to take along and Agnes a small card game and a doll. I let them have these things. This was a traumatic experience for them too.

William went to his study that he had liked so much. He had gotten away from the problems there. Here were his book cases, his desk, and the couch on which he had taken his naps. The beautiful leopard skin rug had lain in front of the couch.

Even though my father and I had returned after World War I, I left this time with my husband and children feeling that we would never return. As we went out the front door, locked up behind us, and handed the key to the caretaker, Konrad asked, "Vati, will we come back to our house? Just like Mutti and Opa did?" We hugged him, and William said, "No. But somewhere we shall have a home again, you may be sure of that. Mutti and I will see to it."

The caretaker, a Chinese gentleman, shook our hands and wished us well for the future. We just nodded our heads in thanks.

Our luggage had been picked up first. Then all of us leaving on the boat were meeting at a designated location, where big open trucks were waiting for us. The sidewalks were crowded with angry looking Chinese, shaking their fists at us and shouting, "Bai Guytze, Wang Baa Daan," meaning, "White Devil and Egg Of A Turtle." Those were insulting and upsetting names to us.

"Why this sudden hatred?" I said to William. He just shrugged his shoulders and shook his head. Agnes was holding on tightly to my arm, her face white with worry. Konrad was staying close to his father. I looked at the police cars in front and in back of us. The shrill sound of the sirens filled the air. I felt like a criminal. Hellmut started to cry. In all the noise I heard Agnes saying, "Mutti, why are the sirens going?"

"I don't know. I don't know." I felt helpless. I expected people to begin throwing objects at us at any moment.

The trucks took us down Bubbling Well Road, passing by our small bakery. The sign Kiessling and Bader was still up. "I wonder how long they will have that sign hanging up there? It is not Kiessling and Bader any more," I said to William.

"Who knows?" he said as he looked the other way. It must hurt him so, I thought.

The Voyage To Germany On
The GENERAL BLACK

We were taken to the transit camp where we stayed several days. Germans were taken there from many other cities also. There we waited for the troop transporter, "*GENERAL BLACK*", coming from Japan. Arriving at the camp, I again was surprised to see that the persons connected with the diplomatic corps were allowed to take so many more belongings than we ordinary citizens. "Just as it was in Nanking," I thought, "how unfair."

The *GENERAL BLACK* had arrived the day before we left the camp to board it. Our overseas trunks were already on board, but all of our suitcases were at the pier to be inspected by the custom officials.

We observed that the inspectors were awfully rude. They slashed some pillows and mattresses--probably looking for jewelry and other valuables. Feathers were flying all over the wharf. They found valuables in some of the bedding. I assumed that they had been informed. Our valuables were not found. I had some rings and bracelets hidden in my braided hair.

Our suitcases were placed between the ones belonging to missionaries. I saw the customs officials coming closer. Two more and they would be to us. I was very nervous. One official came to the missionary on our right. He had him open two suitcases; they found nothing.

He came to us. He pointed at two of our suitcases to be opened. On the very top of the first one was a piece of leather for shoe soles. It was wrapped in Chinese newspaper. He unwrapped it and asked angrily, "What is that?"

"A piece of leather," I answered.

"Leather is not allowed!"

"I have three children," I replied. "And I have heard there is no leather in Germany. I do have to have their shoes repaired."

He looked at me as if he were surprised that I told the truth and said, "all right." He searched a little in that suitcase and went on to the other missionary on our left. We did not have to open our other suitcases. I was relieved that our money and jewelry had not been discovered.

Then we went to board the ship. The decks were crowded with people who were looking through the crowd seeking familiar faces. We were looking up to the decks of the ship doing the same. Suddenly I heard someone calling, "Frau Scheel, Frau Scheel! Up here!" My eyes searched up and down the huge ship. Then I saw her. Frau Meyer! Her husband had been our witness when we were married in Mukden. They had lived in Shanghai for a number of years until the German Consulate transferred Herr Meyer to Japan. They did not know we had a little one.

I was carrying Hellmut. She pointed at him and I could read by her lips and by the gesture of her hand that she was saying, "That is yours?" I could only nod my head yes. We were soon lost from each other in the crowd.

My ten-year-old Agnes was holding on to my free hand. I looked down at her frightened little face and remembered the time after World War I when I was ten and was repatriated with my father. It had meant so much to me then that my friend, Maria, was on the same ship. I was glad Agnes had several of her classmates on the same ship with us. I thought, "Is it true that history repeats itself?"

I said to Agnes, "Don't be afraid. It will be all right. You have several of your friends on board. You will have a good time."

"I don't know, Mutti."

"Yes, Agi, you will play games and have fun. It will be better than you think."

"But the boat is so big. Will we ever find one another?"

"Oh, sure!" I said. She seemed to be be satisfied with my answer.

William and Konrad were standing close by talking to some friends. Konrad and his young friend were watching the sailors and deck hands clearing the gangways, getting ready for the Shanghai crowd to come on board.

I turned to William and said, "Carry Hellmut a while. My arm is getting tired. I'll take him again when we go on board and you will have to carry the bags." He aimlessly took Hellmut into his arms.

While we were waiting on the pier to go on board, someone shouted from one of the decks. "Those of you who don't have rubber sandals, better get some!"

One of the men waiting volunteered, "I'll get them!"

Quickly those of us who wanted sandals raised our hands, even though we did not know why we needed them. We were hurriedly counted. Hands for the children's sandals then went up and were counted. Off the man ran to buy sandals at the nearest department store. He returned in time to catch the ship.

When we were all on board, the big horn blew, the gang-way raised, and the ship pushed off from the wharf. People waved goodby to those staying behind. Some people started to sing:

"Muss e denn,
Muss e denn
Zum Staedtele 'naus, Staedtele 'naus,
Und Du mein Schatz,
Bleibst hier."

or

"Must I leave
Must I leave
This town, this town
And you, my dear,
Stay here?"

Somewhere an accordion and a harmonica could be heard in the distance. Oh, how the song gripped my heart. I looked around me. Like mine, many eyes were filled with tears. So many were born and raised in China, like my children and I. It had become our second homeland. I left many people behind who had become dear to me.

What a huge ship the *GENERAL BLACK* was. There were several decks above the main deck. Our sleeping quarters were on the fifth deck below the main one, without any portholes. We numbered between two to three thousand civil prisoners of war. "Civil prisoners of war"-that's what we were called.

Women, girls, and small children were together and the men and boys had separate quarters. Konrad and William were there. Several hundred women and children were put in one huge section. Our beds were simply a piece of canvas stretched between metal frames with ropes, all of which were connected into a single unit. The units of six were stacked four deep to form a group of twenty-four beds. There was not enough head room to sit on the bed. Two feet away, in every direction, was

222

another group of twenty-four beds. This arrangement filled the whole section. Between the three of us, we had several vacant beds to put our luggage on, and a place to sit. Hellmut had the bed next to me and Agnes occupied the one above me. We took ropes from our suitcases and tied them criss-cross-wise to the outside of Hellmut's bed, so he would not fall out.

To take a shower and wash, we had to walk up a flight of steps and then walk about one hundred feet or more to get to the showers. When I saw the showers, I was not surprised that we were advised to buy sandals. The stalls were very dirty. It was quite a distance for me to carry a little one like Hellmut. Some mothers had brought small tubs to bathe their babies in and shared them with others. But that was not convenient, since the water had to be carried to the tub and then disposed of.

There were several laundry rooms. I washed clothes when a tub was available and did not change clothes every day. Often I rinsed them out at night and wore the same thing the next day.

Going to the mess hall was another ordeal. We had to walk up several flights of steps to the deck where the mess hall was located and then stand in line. It was all right when the weather was good, but in rain and stormy weather it was awful. We complained to the captain, then we mothers with small children were allowed to wait inside. The food, served cafeteria style, was terrible. We had red beets almost every day; corned beef, beef stew, and peaches several times a week. The eggs for breakfast were always hard boiled. The best food served for breakfast was cereal and milk. Children under one year old were given a special diet. Because Hellmut was thirteen months old, he had to eat what we adults ate.

Frau Meyer found us the next day. We were so glad to see each other again. When I told her about the inconvenience of bathing Hellmut, she offered us her private bathroom, which

I happily accepted. It was also easier for Agnes and me to wash our long hair there. I surely was thankful for her kind offer. The people with the diplomatic corps, which included the Meyers, were put up in cabins with private bathrooms. They were also served their meals at tables in a private dining room.

After several days, Hellmut broke out in blisters all over his little body. It was the food I was sure. It did not agree with him. I noticed that he was losing weight.

I decided to take him to the pediatrician. "What is it?" he asked in a gruff voice.

"Doctor," I said, "the adult food does not agree with my baby. He is getting these blisters all over his body. Would you let him have baby food please?"

"How old is he?"

"Thirteen months."

"Then he has to eat the adult food."

"But don't you see, Doctor? It does not agree with him."

"No exceptions are made!" was the mean man's reply. He handed me a jar of salve for his blisters. "Next!" he called.

I was so angry when I left. Although we were civilians, we were treated worse than prisoners of war.

Fraternization was not allowed at all. But the sailors were good to the children. They often gave them a Coke, a candy bar, or gum.

There was practically no privacy for washing, bathing, or dressing. It was quite warm where we slept and very warm in the mess hall. We were drenched when we woke from sleeping or when we finished eating. Hellmut was miserable. His whole body was wet with perspiration and the blisters irritated him more and more.

One day the little bit of air conditioning we had in the sleeping quarters broke down. Several days of the unbearable heat--in the Red Sea of all places--was about all we could bear. The mechanics were not able to repair the air conditioner. A few German engineers got together and decided to ask the officer in charge to let them have a look at it. They were given permission. After only a few hours, it was fixed. We were all very happy to cool down a bit--and not a little proud that Germans had proven their ingenuity.

Again I took Hellmut to the pediatrician. "Doctor, please let my child have baby food," I pleaded.

"How old is the child?"

"Thirteen months, but his body is full of blisters!"

"Too old."

"Can't you see? He is so miserable. He is losing weight!"

"I cannot prescribe baby food for him."

I held Hellmut up to him, so that he could see his blistered body in the light. The doctor was an unkind man indeed. I felt he hated Germans. I pleaded with him. "He is really suffering, Doctor. Please let my son have baby food!"

"Here," he said. He handed me a jar of salve for his blisters.

I became very angry. "You are a heartless, unkind man!" I screamed. I turned and left. My eyes were filled with tears.

I took Hellmut back to our beds and laid him down. It was the time he took his nap. I laid down beside him. I was so upset, so angry.

My thoughts went back to Papa when we had to leave after WWI. We had to go because Germany had lost the war. Only the old and sick could stay behind. Now after WWII we went through the same situation. Neither time was one shot fired between the two nations. But we, the Germans, lost the wars, therefore we had to leave the country of our enemy. We had become refugees of China.

The Americans and the Chinese were allies. That was why we were on an American ship. The Chinese had very few, if any, large boats. They paid three hundred fifty dollars for each refugee to the American government to take us to Germany.

When our business had been taken from us, I had asked William then "Why are the Americans doing this to us?"

"The Americans and the Chinese are allies," he had answered simply, "The GENERAL BLACK is an American troop transporter."

"Why was that American doctor so ugly and mean to me?" I asked myself.

After a while laying there next to Hellmut thinking about this I must have dropped off to sleep. The dinner gong rang, waking me.

The voyage would be long and uncomfortable but I tried to make the best of our situation. On nice days we spent most of our time on deck. Hellmut had started walking about the time we left Shanghai, but coming on board the ship, he became unsure of himself because of the motion of the ship and would not walk. I made a wide belt with shoulder straps for him, sort of a harness. And with that contraption he started to walk again.

Before entering the Suez Canal, we stopped at Port Suez for approximately half a day. In a short time the ship was surrounded by merchants in small boats selling leather articles, embroidered table cloths, blouses, and wicker wares, all hand crafted. I bought a hassock made of different kinds of leather, a purse for Agnes, and a wallet for Konrad. I bought a little wooden donkey for Hellmut. His sores were healing finally, and he wanted to play with his new toy. All of the articles had very pretty, colorful, and intricate designs.

The trading was done quite uniquely. We were standing on the lowest deck. The craftsman threw up a basket to which a rope was attached. We fastened the rope to the railing. The basket was let down again, the trader put the articles we pointed out to him into it and we pulled it up. Then the basket was returned with our money for the man.

The Suez Canal was built between 1859 and 1869. It enabled shipping between Europe and the East, thus making

226

the long trip around the dangerous Cape of Good Hope unnecessary. It shortened the voyage immensely. The Isthmus joined the African to the Asian continent.

One warm, still, star-ornamented evening, I was lying on a blanket on deck, watching the stars and searching for the southern cross. Suddenly the color of the sky on the horizon began to change and the slightest sign of the new moon appeared. Throughout all my many hardships and disappointments, I thought, the Lord has blessed my life with so much beauty of His creation. Momentarily the ugliness of the ship and the situation that I was in was forgotten.

At Port Said we entered the Mediterranean Sea. The sea is a body of water situated between Europe in the North, Africa in the south and Asia in the east. The water there was much saltier than in the Atlantic Ocean or the Black Sea. That was due to the extremely fast evaporation of its waters. On the south, we passed these countries: Egypt, Libya, Tunisia, Algeria and Morocco. Between Tangier, Morocco, and Spain, we passed through the Straits of Gibraltar. I remembered when I had sailed through there in 1921 at the age of ten. Twenty-six years back, the Rock of Gibraltar had made such an impression on me. But my father and I were on a much smaller repatriation ship going to Germany then. And I was small.

Leaving the Strait of Gibraltar, we passed through the Gulf of Cadiz. Coming around the Cape of St. Vincent, we made our way into the Atlantic Ocean. In the Bay of Biscay we encountered a rough sea, just as we had twenty-six years ago. Then we came to the English Channel, making an overnight stop at Southampton, England. From there we went to Belgium, Holland, and the North Sea. As we left the places behind us, we docked in Bremerhaven after approximately twenty-seven days on board the troop transporter, *GENERAL BLACK.*

About eight days before we were to arrive at Bremerhaven, our final destination, the civil prisoners of war, men and women, were made to scrub their living quarters before leaving the *GENERAL BLACK*. Every nook, crevice, hole, cranny, lavatory, shower--we had to clean it. No rubber sandals were needed after we were through with the showers! The officers came with flashlights and inspected everyplace. I was sure that they had never seen that ship so clean. When we finished we renamed the ship "*GENERAL WHITE!*"

CHAPTER ELEVEN
Life In Post-War Germany

I just felt so free in August 1947 as I walked down the gangplank and stepped onto German soil. But I did not really know what to expect... Displaced persons were not welcome in a country of ruins with meager food supplies. We had no idea where we would be sent. William's relatives and my mother and aunts were all in the Eastern Zone, occupied by the Russians. My brother and his family were displaced persons from Silesia, occupied by Poland. They were in the British-occupied zone with very limited living space.

We had the choice of staying in north Germany or going south. We chose to go south to Bavaria. We were told that provisions and necessities of life were easier to obtain there.

We were taken from one refugee camp to another. At each we were "deloused." Always the same procedure — opening up the front of our dresses to allow them to spray insecticide powder down the front. Next, they sprayed our hair and down our backs. As we had no lice, I was horribly humiliated.

It was a cold and damp October and the trains were not heated. We were transported from camp to camp and were crowded in with German displaced persons from around the world. People sat on their suitcases in the aisles, leaving no room to get through to the toilets. We had to wait until we came to a train station. People were fussing and swearing, babies cried and children screamed. The air was heavy with body odor and smoke. I was nauseated most of the trip. American soldiers accompanied the trains and we had to ask their permission to go to the toilet. They were frustrated and impatient with us. At times we went into the bushes because the line to the toilet was so long.

At the stations we were given K-rations. They consisted mostly of dehydrated foods. They were not tasty but they stilled the hunger.

Women from the Red Cross were at every station, distributing coffee and hot chocolate. Oh, how we appreciated them. At one of the stations I was able to buy a box of Pablum. I filled one of our thermos bottles with hot water. As I was mixing some in a bowl for Hellmut, the train halted suddenly. It was a mess. Pablum and mush all over Hellmut and me. There was no light on the train and no one had a flashlight. I cleaned as well as I could with a diaper and a small towel. All at once the moon peeped out from behind heavy clouds. "William," I cried, "take Hellmut." Hurriedly, I took advantage of the bit of moonlight and did a pretty good job of wiping up the mess. That was a train ride to remember!

From my window I saw silhouette after silhouette of ruins—a charred chimney here, a church steeple there, bombarded houses there and everywhere more ruins. My heart grew heavy. I prayed for strength and patience. "Lord, keep us well."

The Refugee Camps

The refugee camps were mostly old wooden or brick barracks. Everyone was packed into the walled quarters of bunk beds and straw sacks with no privacy. Our pillows and blankets inside our two duffel bags came in real handy. At least we could sleep warm at night on our straw sacks. The iron stove in the center of the huge room was inadequate for heating such an open area. William and the children searched far and wide for twigs and branches to keep the fire going; so did the people from the other barracks.

At the refugee camps (we stayed at several during the five week period) we got our food on tin plates and drank out of tin cups. Everything tasted of iron. For a long while afterwards, the taste lingered in our mouths.

Our food was not tasty but edible. Cereal, vegetables, potatoes, and very little meat were our daily rations. Konrad and Agnes got milk and Hellmut, still an infant, got extra milk and butter.

At the Augsburg camp we were allowed to go outdoors. We took walks downtown. Everywhere we went we saw burned-out houses, apartment complexes, and skeletal remains of churches. Not much was left of the beautiful country we had visited in 1940.

There was hardly anything to buy. We had not yet been given our merchandise rations cards. This mattered little as the shelves in the stores were practically bare.

Finally we arrived in Bietigheim, the last camp where the men were "de-Nazified." They were housed in separate buildings from their families and had to go through all kinds of interrogations. William said that they were asked when they had joined the Nazi Party, what activity they were involved in, and all sorts of questions related to the Party.

At last, we received all of our luggage, and our folding cots. Those tips of packing our bedding in duffel bags and taking along folding cots were splendid advice. These tips had been included in letters from those who left Shanghai on boats ahead of us. The letters had been shared amongst the women in the afternoons while we were still in Shanghai, and had really helped. Suitcases and trunks were so much heavier than the duffel bags. A limit of three hundred fifty pounds per adult and one hundred seventy five per child was not much to take, so the lightweight duffle bags helped considerably in saving weight. Because we knew we would be staying at our latest camp for a number of weeks, we put up our folding cots and surrounded our cubicle with bed sheets for privacy.

The bathrooms and lavatories were awful. In the bathhouse, a long metal trough-like sink was installed on one side of the wall. It had hot and cold running water, no partitions.

Across from there were showers without curtains. I decided to rise up early in the morning to take a shower--but others had the same idea. No one wanted to take a shower at night because the facilities were not adjacent to the barracks. I decided to buy a basin so that we could wash ourselves in our private cubicle. The toilets were even worse. There were very few separate toilets. Most of the buildings housed four bowls which were separated only by a piece of plywood about four feet high. There were no doors.

The Bietigheim camps were the largest and we had heard the food was better there. We would be given our permanent address there. We wondered where we would be sent.

One afternoon the children and I were sitting on our cots. I had pulled the sheets aside and could see the entrance. Agnes was reading a story to Hellmut. Konrad was busy whittling on a piece of wood. He always found something to do. I was mending. I heard a voice. A very familiar voice. I looked up and there was Herr Zaudig! Konrad and Agnes saw him at the same time. They jumped up and ran toward him shouting, "Onkel Zaudig, Onkel Zaudig!" I ran to him to hug him. Tears came to my eyes as I said, "Oh, Herr Zaudig! How good it is to see you! How have you been? How did you know we were here?"

"I have been following the newspaper announcements. Every time a new batch of German displaced persons from China came through Bietigheim I knew about it. I live here now. I saw that a new group had arrived, so I took my chance and found you. I was searching for you. I went to the camp to ask if you were among the people. But tell me, who is that little boy?"

"Oh, this is my newest one, little Hellmut."

"You surprise me so," he said. He swung Hellmut up into his arms.

He had brought a piece of apple cake for us. He had obtained it with his few food stamps--a sacrifice for him, I knew.

"And how have you been, Herr Zaudig?" I wanted to know. He did not look too well.

"Fine, fine, Frau Scheel," he said. "I receive welfare and I am living in a small room. My landlady is very kind. I eat my meals with her family."

"Oh how nice," I said.

"She takes care of my laundry and cleans my room."

"Well, I am so glad to hear that you are well taken care of." We laughed and chatted happily. We could hardly believe that we had found each other again.

During the weeks that we stayed in Bietigheim he visited us often. One day I took him to the area where William was staying. We always met William at an arranged time at the fence that surrounded the houses. The whole place looked like a prison. I guess that's what it really was--for the men staying there. William was glad to see Herr Zaudig again.

When Herr Zaudig came to see us for the last time he gave us his address so that we could let him know our address when we would finally get one.

Probstried - Rural Life In The Mountains

It was November of 1947 and getting quite cold. We were looking forward to having our own place to stay and to unpacking our suitcases. Living like gypsies for months was not a pleasure. The placement committee had assigned us rooms in Probstried, in the Allgäu, south of Munich.

We were no longer called prisoners of war, but refugees or displaced persons. As such, we were not welcomed by the home folks. It hurt to be unwelcome, but thousands and thousands of houses had been destroyed during the war. People had to double up and take in folks who had lost their homes. The wave of refugees and displaced persons was pouring in from all over the world. Pouring into a country of ruins and rubble. What a change from 1940—when we were on vacation—to 1947.

233

We were the only passengers getting off the train at Diet-mansried, so it was not difficult for our new landlord, his daughter, and the Bürgermeister—the mayor—to find us. After a short "Grüss Gott," (God's Greeting), the usual greeting there, we introduced ourselves to each other.

Herr Lerner and his daughter, Josepha, were plain village people. He wore a faded Tyrolean hat with a gemsbart, which looked like feathers, a jacket and knickerbockers. Josepha looked nice in her colorful hand-knitted cardigan, which she wore with a winter dirndl.

The dialect they spoke there was very difficult to understand. We tried but we could not keep up a conversation.

They helped us carry our luggage to the horse and wagon. We found room to sit on our suitcases, and with a "Hü" and a "Hot" to the horses, we rode to Probstried, our assigned place to stay, a short thirty-minute drive.

We were given two sparsely furnished rooms. After the Lerners had shown us the rooms and the bathroom, Herr Lerner said, "Come down and have supper with us at about six o'clock."

"This will give you some time to unpack for the night," Josepha added. We thanked them for the invitation. We hadn't expected such hospitality.

We sat down on the bed with our coats on. I held Hellmut on my lap. Konrad was sitting on the only chair. The wood burning stove in the room had not yet provided enough warmth. The other room across the hall did not even have a stove. I looked around the room and thought, how long are we going to live in these rooms? Aloud I said, "Did Herr Lerner say how long we are going to stay here?"

"No," William said. "I guess we will find out in the morning. No kitchen facilities. No bathroom of our own. We will need a bigger place. Let's wait until tomorrow."

"There is no bed for Hellmut. May he sleep with me, Mutti?" Agnes asked.

"Yes. We can push the bed against the wall, so he will not fall out. I guess that will be all right." Hellmut slid off my lap and cuddled up to Agnes. He liked to sleep with her.

There was a knock at the door. I wondered, "Who could that be?" Konrad opened the door. An elderly man with a sack in his hand asked, "Are you the Scheel family who has just arrived?"

"Yes," Konrad said. "Come in."

The man introduced himself, "I am Alexander Jurick. My wife and I are refugees from Yugoslavia. We heard you had just arrived and we thought you could use some dry wood." With these words he handed the sack of wood to Konrad. "How the Lord always provides for us and places good people into our paths," I thought.

William and I thanked him and my eyes filled with tears as I hugged the man and said, "Auf Wiedersehen." Later I met his wife and we began seeing each other often. They were Baptists and true God-fearing people.

The next morning we found out that our two rooms were to be only a temporary arrangement. We were going to get an apartment in the schoolhouse. "Oh, what good news!" I said to William. Two rooms were not much space, and we had to share the bathroom and kitchen with the Lerners.

At first the Lerners were a little reserved, but after a day or two they helped us to get settled. It took us a while to get used to their dialect. I often had to ask them to repeat what they were saying. Many of the villagers spoke high German, which was taught in the schools.

But it was good to be settled. It was so good to have our cots, our blankets, and our pillows. This always gave us a place to sit during the day and a place to sleep at night. At night we laid our heads on our own pillows and snuggled up under our blankets. Those few belongings gave us a faint feeling of security and much hope.

Shopping With Ration Cards

Before leaving Bietigheim we had been given our ration cards for groceries, wood, coal, clothing, and fabric. This was all completely new to us. Josepha was a big help to me. She introduced me to the grocer, the butcher, and the baker.

One day Josepha said, "Next week I am going to get my groceries at a store further away. Do you want to go with me? It will take us about an hour and a half to walk, but we do get a better deal on our ration cards."

"Oh yes, I'll go," I answered eagerly. I didn't know what I was getting myself into.

"You will need a good pair of walking or hiking shoes."

"I have those. I bought a pair of comfortable, strong shoes the other day when I was in Kempten."

"Well, that's good."

So, one morning quite early, we equipped ourselves with several strong, large tote bags and went grocery shopping. The going was rough. The road was not paved, and often we had to walk one behind the other on narrow field paths and forest trails. We could not do much talking. Going there was not so bad; our bags were empty, but coming back, I contemplated, would be different. We purchased quite a bit more on our cards than we would have in our village grocery store. I was so pleased and was already preparing meals in my head as I left the grocery. But my bags were so heavy!.... Every fifteen to twenty minutes I had to rest my arms. I was delaying our getting home. Josepha was used to the heavy loads. She had pity on me and said, "We will stop at my cousin's farm, it's on our way. There we can rest a while."

"Oh, that will be great. Not a minute too soon!"

Her relatives were just having lunch and invited us to share the meal with them. They were having "Apfelschmaren", a kind of apple pancake. Small pieces of slightly smothered apples were mixed into the dough. When the pancake was just about done, it was torn into bite-size

236

pieces, fried just a little longer, then sprinkled with a little sugar. It was delicious.

"We'll have to make this dish at home!" I exclaimed.

At that meal I was tested as to how much I really understood of their dialect. They spoke fast. I listened. I laughed when they laughed, but I really did not know why they laughed. It sounded like a foreign language to me. I was glad when we said goodby and were on our way.

Josepha suspected that I had faked my laughing. She said, "Well, Frau Scheel, you did not understand everything, did you?"

I had to admit and said, "You are so right, Josepha: I surely did not." We laughed and we soon arrived at our village. The shopping trip was quite an experience.

The School House Apartment

Soon after that we moved into the schoolhouse. The apartment was on the second floor, above the classrooms. We had two bedrooms, a living room, and a large kitchen. The rooms were big and bright. It was really nice and I was grateful for it. The furniture was modest--a chair came from one farm house, a table from another. But I made the best of it and was happy to have the place.

The first thing Konrad did was to look out the windows. When he came to the living room windows I heard him call, "Mutti, come here! Look at this beautiful view." The window was facing south. In the distance I could see the high mountains of the region. In the foreground I could see the meadows and farmland with a few houses scattered here and there. Long plumes of smoke from the chimneys were rising up in a windless sky.

"Yes, Koni, this is really pretty. Everything is covered with snow now. I think I'm going to like it here, don't you?"

"I think I will" he replied.

Agnes came into the room. "Mutti, may Koni and I go sledding tomorrow? Perhaps Josepha could lend us her sled. We could take Hellmut between us."

"I don't know, Agi, he's just a year and a half."

"Oh, that would be so much fun. Please Mutti!"

"We'll see about that tomorrow. First we will have to get things in order here." I turned back to the suitcases, knowing I should let them go.

Because we had arrived there in November, we had no vegetables, since everyone grew their own. But the farmers did not want money for their produce. They would rather have had coffee or American cigarettes in exchange. Our friends in Shanghai, who were selling the things that we had left with them, sent us CARE packages instead of money. For this we were grateful because included in the packages were coffee and cigarettes. After receiving the packages, I had no problem getting vegetables from the farmers. For one-fourth pound of coffee, I could get all the vegetables I needed for a week.

Protestants In A Catholic Community

Probstried was a village of about a thousand inhabitants, all Catholic. There were sixteen of us refugees, all Lutheran--except the couple from Yugoslavia, who were Baptist. The villagers were not familiar with our religions and looked upon us as if we were heathens. They did not know that we prayed the Lord's prayer.

A pastor from a Lutheran church in Kempten held service in Probstried about once a month. We could not use the Catholic church. The Bürgermeister let us have services in a classroom. We decorated it with flowers and a rug or two. The windows were open during the summer. The villagers could hear us singing our hymns, the hymns they also sang. They could hear us praying the Lord's prayer, the prayer they also prayed. They must have been pleasantly surprised to hear us. We noticed that they became more receptive of us.

238

On alternate Sundays, we had services in a neighboring village, which took us almost an hour to walk to. During the winter months we could not attend church services there because of the deep snow.

Among the sixteen Lutheran folks I made friends with Louise Ebert and Ida Michalowsky. Louise had married a widower. A father of three children. Ida had never married. She said, "Call me Micha, that's what my friends called me back home." And she called me "Scheelchen." My friends had called me that in Shanghai, I remembered. Micha and the Eberts had fled from East Prussia when the Russians were approaching. They met in Probstried and became friends and I was accepted into their circle. Louise's daughter Christa and my Konrad were the same age and took confirmation classes together in Kempten.

Louise was tall, had strawberry blond hair and a reddish complexion. Freckles made her look younger than she was. Although she was hard of hearing, she spoke very softly. I enjoyed listening to her voice.

Micha and I became very close. She enjoyed taking care of Hellmut if I could not take him along on my errands. She was such a dear person. She was in her late sixties, a retired bookkeeper. Her chestnut hair was turning grey. She wore it in a softly fashioned bun and her face was surrounded by little ringlets of hair.

Micha had been assigned a room in the Catholic priest's manse. He and his housekeeper were very kind to her. Once a week I spent an evening with her . She would prepare some hot chocolate or tea and I would bring a few sandwiches or some cookies along. We would spend the evening singing hymns or folk songs. We would also read the Bible to each other.

She told me one evening that her younger sister, who had fled with her, had died six months back. She missed her very much. I knew our friendship made her loss a little easier to bear.

Christmas In Germany

We were ready to celebrate our very first Christmas in Germany. I was nearing my thirty-seventh birthday. The whole family went to Kempten, the closest large city, to buy Christmas gifts for one another. The stores did not have much of a selection and we had to be careful spending our money. I bought Hellmut wooden blocks and a little teddy bear, Agnes a book and a wooden box to keep her embroidery thread and needle in, and Konrad wanted a new pencil box and a book. The children put their money together and bought William an ashtray and me a pair of cast iron candle holders. William and I bought a surprise gift for each other. We needed a few brightly colored glass ornaments, wax candles, and candle holders. We wanted them for the Christmas tree. Surprisingly we found everything that we needed, even in the sparsely stocked stores.

We had lunch at a small restaurant and took the afternoon train to Dietmansried and from there we walked to Probstried. There was no bus or other public transportation. When we arrived home, everyone went to find a hiding place for the treasures until Christmas Eve.

Herr Lerner was kind enough to let us cut a small fir tree from his forest. The decorated tree livened the atmosphere of our apartment and provided us with a holiday spirit.

The Germans celebrated Christmas a little different than most other nationalities. The Christmas tree, a spruce or fir tree, was decorated by the parents on Christmas Eve day. The children were not allowed to see the tree until the evening, when the candles were lit. Even in China, and in other places where Germans lived, they always upheld the tradition.

Since there was no Christmas Eve church service, we had our supper early. After the table was cleared and the dishes washed--I think this was never done any faster than on Christmas Eve--William went to light the candles. Then he called us into the room. Excited, the children and I entered the festive-looking room. A warm glow from the candles greeted us. We held hands and sang a stanza of "Stille Nacht." Then Agnes recited a little poem and Konrad read the Christmas Story from the Bible. "Fröhliche Weihnachten!" our voices rang out to each other. Then we all exchanged gifts. There were also gifts to open which my mother had sent the children. They were so excited!!!

Away To School

After the Christmas vacation, the children started going to school. There was just a village school in Probstried; education was limited. We decided to send our children to school in Kempten. It was not easy on them, especially Agnes, who was not so robust as Konrad. I had to get them up before six o'clock to get to school at eight. It took them a good twenty minutes to walk the field paths to the next small town to catch the train to Kempten, which took another thirty minutes. Then there was a twenty minute walk to the school. It was really hard on them during the winter months when they had to walk through knee-deep snow.

After an all-night snowfall, one morning on the way to school, they lost their way and ended up back in Probstried. Agnes was exhausted. That was the moment we decided to find a place in Kempten for her to stay during the week. She could come home on Fridays after school.

A teacher recommended an elderly lady who took in three or four girls during the week. It worked out well for all of us. The lady was good to the girls and they liked her and her cooking. Agnes preferred the new arrangement.

The following year a bus was put into service which was very much welcomed by all.

One Friday when Agnes was eleven years old, she had a frightening experience coming home on the bus. She told us all about it later. She had noticed, after riding a while, that the bus was not going in the direction that she was used to. She asked the bus driver, who was very friendly, "Where are you going to?" He told her the name of the town he was headed for. She found out he was heading in the opposite direction and it was his last trip for the day. She became frantic. "What am I going to do? I need to go to Probstried!" she lamented.

A lady on the bus overheard the conversation. She and the bus driver knew each other. She approached Agnes, comforted her, and offered to take her to her home to call me. She lived in the same town in which the bus driver was staying overnight. Agnes was very relieved and accepted the lady's suggestion.

In the meantime, I was at home waiting for Agnes. She was to arrive on the last bus. We had no telephone and could only be reached at the post office or through the Principal of the school who had a phone. William and I went to the post office. I called the lady Agnes stayed with in Kempten. She said, "Agnes left at the usual time, Frau Scheel."

"I cannot imagine what has happened," I said. We were getting quite worried. I went home and William stayed at the post office to wait in case Agnes should call in. After an hour or so, the Postmistress received a call for us. William spoke with the lady, Frau Hailer, and also Agnes. He was convinced that she was in good hands. We were so relieved. Agnes took the first bus home the next day. Frau Hailer had been very nice to her and she also invited all of us to visit her the next Sunday.

We met the next Sunday with her. I liked her right away. Agnes spent several weekends with her. When summer vacation came Frau Hailer invited her to stay for a week. I hoped a lasting friendship would develop between her and me.

Konrad had to study very hard in school. He was ambitious and diligent. In Shanghai he had studied French; in Kempten Latin was required. The priest in Probstried tutored him. He was a good teacher and my Konrad quickly caught up with his class. I knew that he would.

Our old portable, hand-cranked, sewing machine from Nanking made the trip with us to Probstried. It had never come in so handy. I was glad I had sent William back to get it in Nanking before we went on board the ship to Hankow. It had traveled with us to Hong Kong, to Shanghai, and all the way to Germany. I really held on to it.

I sewed a lot for Agnes and Hellmut. I saved every piece of clothing and remade it into a shirt, a blouse, or even a dress for Agnes or pants for Hellmut. They appreciated their "new" outfits at that time.

The Candy Business

William met a man at the employment office in Kempten. They were both waiting for their names to be called for their interviews. Neither spoke the local dialect. It was quite natural that they asked each other where they came from and what their trades were. Herr Wancheck was a displaced person from one of the Baltic states and he had been in Kempten for a while. He was an accountant and unmarried. William took an interest in him and invited him to visit us the following Sunday afternoon.

When Herr Wancheck came we had coffee and cake that I had baked with William's help. I was still learning in the culinary department. Herr Wancheck's stature was similar to that of William's, a little taller, blond, blue-eyed, a wide nose, and high cheek bones. His lips were thin and straight. Somehow he did not make an especially good impression on me.

After William and Herr Wancheck met a few times, they agreed to establish a small business. They put their resources together and with the exchange of several cartons of American cigarettes and a few pounds of coffee, they bought what they needed for the candy-making business. It was surprising what people were willing to pay for American cigarettes and coffee on the black market. William rented a small basement room in Kempten and started production there. Their agreement was that William would make the candy-mostly fondants and hard candy--and Herr Wancheck would sell it to grocery stores. It was slow going.

In the spring, after the snow had melted, I began to help out. I visited the grocery stores in the nearby villages. Micha offered to take care of Hellmut for me. Konrad and Agnes were in school and I always came back home before they returned.

I acquired a second-hand bicycle for some coffee and cigarettes. I rode the bicycle all over the area. It was hilly country and I often had to push my bicycle up the hills. This happened several days a week. It was not easy pedaling around from village to village and from store to store.

Some store owners were quite rude. They knew right away that I was not a native when I opened my mouth. Refugees and displaced persons were just not liked. But I tried my best. I knew that every little sale helped.

To avoid commuting to Kempten every day, William rented a small room from a young couple and came home to Probstried on the weekends only.

I still kept in touch with my family. My mother was a housekeeper for a young woman who owned a photography business. The kind lady Mother had kept house for before had died. Mother's younger sister, Klara, the old maid, lived with my grandmother. My brother was back with Telefunken and had moved his family to Dachau in Bavaria, about twenty minutes by train from Munich.

Our Refugee Vegetable Garden

After we lived through the first winter in Germany, we were assigned a section of a meadow for a garden. It was the year 1948. There we cultivated and learned to grow our own vegetables. Each refugee family was given a piece of land according to the size of their family. Ours was about thirty by one hundred twenty feet in size. As soon as the frost was gone, William and Konrad turned the earth. Agnes and I broke up the clumps and prepared the soil for planting. We needed a lot of gardening advice. Other refugees were very helpful. We planted potatoes, tomatoes, green beans, carrots, radishes, beets, and left one row for flowers. I knew the blooming flowers would not only beautify the vegetable garden but provide cut flowers for the apartment. For the tomato plants, we went to the farmers and asked for some horse manure. It was exciting to see the first little leaves shoot up.

Since a bus had been put into service that spring, Agnes was able to commute to school with Konrad. Every day after school she went out to the garden to see how much the plants had grown, if the radishes were ready to pick, and how many there were. She loved to see things grow.

When we had a dry spell, we borrowed a hand wagon to haul water. We placed large buckets of water in the wagon and transported it to the garden. Our first year of gardening was quite successful. We had a plentiful crop — especially the tomatoes.

Wild Berry Picking

Louise visited one day. Over a cup of coffee she asked me, "Erna, have you ever been blueberry picking?"

I was trying to think. I knew I had not picked berries in China. "Oh, yes!" I replied, "I remember when my father and I were in Germany, after World War I, we went blueberry picking with my Aunt Berta. We got up real early and walked two and a half hours to the patch."

"There are blueberries around here," said Louise, and she named a place where they grew abundantly. She also told me about a sunny hillside where raspberries were plentiful. "A good raspberry patch," she emphasized.

I thanked Louise for telling me and decided to make Sunday a family berry-picking day combined with a picnic. And so we did. We got up at six o'clock, had a hardy break-

245

fast of scrambled eggs, buttered crisp rolls topped with honey, coffee for William and milk for the children and me.

The evening before I had made potato salad, bulletten (hamburger), and a thermos filled with fruit juice. That was our picnic lunch. By seven o'clock we were on our way.

William and Konrad carried a knapsack. The hour-long walk through the forest was too much for little Hellmut so William and I took turns carrying him. The blueberry patch was large and the plump berries glistened in the sun. We had the patch all to ourselves. We spread out, but I kept Hellmut close to me at all times. He picked berries too, but put them into his mouth instead of the container. He was blue from his face down to his knees. I observed William as we worked and could see by the relaxed expression on his face that he was enjoying himself. But he said not a word. That was William. Konrad and Agnes stayed close to one another and I could hear them chatting. Each tried to out-do the other. Agnes' fingers were nimble and quick and she filled her container quicker than any of us. We picked until our stomachs cried out for food.

Konrad spread our blanket under a shady tree as it was getting quite warm. We filled our plates and cups and took our seats on the ground. It was so restful and we enjoyed the leisure time. There was a stirring in the brush and William whispered, "Hush, I think I hear an animal." Sure enough, two brown bunnies crossed the field just a short distance away. We were serenaded by birds chirping overhead in our tree and further down we witnessed a pheasant fly across the blueberry patch. I could see Hellmut was getting tired so after we finished eating, I laid him down and he fell quickly into a deep sleep. After tidying up we resumed picking berries.

We picked until all our containers were filled. I felt so in touch with nature, with God, and with my family that day. After roaming the hillside, we started home.

We stopped at a farm house for milk to take home with us.

Once home, we each had a bowl of berries with milk and sugar. After our treat, I cooked the rest into rich blueberry preserves.

One Saturday morning Agnes and I went raspberry picking with a refugee friend. It was such a beautiful morning. Birds were singing, cuckoos calling, and a woodpecker was pecking away at a hollow tree. In a nearby village we heard cows mooing and a dog barking. I had heard that raspberry picking was not too much fun, because the briers were so bad. I had said to Agnes, "Let's put on old clothes and a long-sleeved blouse or shirt, so we will not be scratched too badly."

As we approached the hill, other pickers were there already. But the berries were plentiful, and it did not take too long to fill our containers. At noon we ate our sandwiches and drank our juice from cups. Then we went on our way home.

Again we all enjoyed a bowl of berries for supper. Again I made preserves. I knew that the preserves and syrup I made would be a delight in the winter months to come.

Agnes and I often talked of our two berry-picking experiences in the summer of 1948.

Gathering Firewood

What a different life style we began to lead. We were not poor, but our income was small and I had to budget very wisely. But I enjoyed the new life style. For once I could be a real mother to my children. I had not taken time for my children while being a business woman. At last I had time.

We were allotted a certain amount of firewood and coal for winter heating and cooking purposes. We heated water for bathing in big vessels. We had a large metal tub to bathe in. Once a month I had a big laundry day. On that day I washed towels, sheets, table cloths, and aprons. Our underwear, socks, shirts, dresses, blouses and such I laundered once a week.

For all this, the fuel allotment was not sufficient. All the laundry, bathing, and cleaning required much wood.

In order to supplement our fuel supply we were permitted to gather dead branches and trees in the forest. Agnes, Hellmut, and I went to the nearby forest to gather smaller twigs and pine cones. We had a small rack wagon into which we sat Hellmut when he tired from walking. After about forty minutes, we were in the forest. I gave Hellmut a small sack into which he gathered pine cones. He enjoyed doing that.

Several times on a Saturday when the children had vacation, Konrad and I went to a forest further away where we could find abundant wood. We started out one nice, not too hot Saturday morning. We had borrowed a large rack wagon from one of our refugee neighbors and began our trek early. The path was quite steep but we had no trouble going up the mountain with the empty wagon. Konrad climbed the trees and sawed off the dead limbs and I stacked them into the wagon. He spotted a big fir tree with low green branches. "Mutti look at those branches. Don't you think we could hide one or two between the dry ones?"

"Oh ... Konrad. I don't know."

"I'll cut them into small pieces Mutti."

"All right," I said, "I hope we will not be caught by the forester!" Our green branches of course were much heavier than the dry ones.

After filling the wagon to capacity, we started on our way home. Going downhill, the wagon wanted to roll by itself. We needed all our strength to hold it back. Suddenly, about half-way down the hill, a wheel broke off with a loud crash and rolled away. The wagon tilted, fell on its side, and the rope tore. The wood was strewn all over the place, some of it tumbling downward. We stood there stupefied. I was close to tears.

"Oh, Konrad! Look what happened. We lost so much wood. What are we going to do about the broken axle? How are we going to get the wood home?" And I went on and on.

"Mutti, we will find someone to help us. Why don't you go down to the people who lent us this wagon. They may know someone who can help us out with another wagon. I'll gather the wood in the meantime."

"All right, I'll go down. Just hope that a ranger does not come by , Konrad!"

I was so upset when I rang the door bell. My voice was quivering as I told my friend of our accident. But she was a dear.

"It could have happened to anyone. It was an old wagon," she said, "Don't feel bad about it. Let's go to my neighbor. I know he is home. He has a sturdier wagon than ours. I am sure he will help you."

Her neighbor was more than glad to help us. Together we loaded his wagon with the wood. He showed us an easier path to get down the hill. It took longer, but it was not so steep.

I was exhausted when I got home. I rested while the children unloaded the wood.

Soon our allotted wood would be delivered. It would have to be chopped and so would the branches that we had brought. That was something else I had to learn; how to chop wood! Konrad and William helped when they had time. But I chopped most of it.

Laundry Day

Laundry day was always a very strenuous one for me. I cooked a pot of soup the day before, so I did not have to cook while washing. Also, I soaked the white and the colored clothing separately that night. The next morning at five o'clock I started. First I lit the fire under the metal laundry vessel so I would have hot water for washing. While the water was heating, I prepared breakfast for the children and sent them on their way to school. Later I either sent Hellmut to Micha's for the morning or he would visit one of the farmers. He enjoyed riding into the fields on the manure wagon or on a tractor with the farmer. He stayed in the fields with him until lunchtime.

With Hellmut taken care of, I went to the basement to do my laundry. Washing on a washboard was hard on my back and my hands. By evening I was always sore all over. When the children came home from school, the laundry was on the line flapping in the sun and wind. Agnes liked to help me take the fresh laundry down and fold it. I appreciated her help. The school house had a big attic and when it was raining or cold, I hung the laundry there.

Other New Experiences

Hellmut made friends quickly with the home folks. He quickly picked up their dialect. The villagers really liked that he was one of them. Agnes also started to speak the local dialect with her friends. But at home we insisted that they speak high German, which was taught in the schools.

After a good rain shower, Agnes and I would gather mushrooms in the nearby forest. We learned to distinguish the safe ones from the poisonous. How pretty the little brown heads appeared out of the soft green moss. We enjoyed gathering them and in the evening our family had delicious fried mushrooms for supper. Mushroom picking was another unusual experience for me, after living in big cities almost all of my life.

During apple-picking seasons, the farmers allowed the refugees to pick up the fallen apples. One Sunday evening we went for a walk with the Ebert family and Micha. We took some tote bags along hoping to find some apples. The children were playing ball in a nearby meadow. I was wearing my white sandals, looking ahead for apples, not watching where I was walking. Suddenly, I felt something soft and "squishy" on my right foot. I had stepped into a cow's "visiting card'. "Yuck!" I exclaimed, "what a nasty feeling. My nice sandals a mess!" The children came running. When they saw the mess, they laughed, "ha, ha, ha" and clapped their hands.

"I'll get you for laughing at me!" I cried, and off I ran after them. They helped me find a brook nearby where I could wash my foot and sandal. We soon went back to apple-hunting.

Oftentimes Hellmut went across the street to the farmer to watch him milk his cows. The farmer lifted him up onto a high bundle of hay so that he could watch him as he milked. There he could see the whole stable. When he came home I had to take off his clothes and hang them out in the fresh air. Our whole apartment smelled of cow and stable. But Hellmut liked that.

A Visit From Mother

The following summer my mother came from Schwerin to visit us. I was looking forward to her visit. We would be together for four whole weeks and really get to know one another again. William was still making candy in Kempten and only came home on weekends, therefore, we were not crowded. There was another advantage; he did not like my mother and did not hide his feelings. But the feelings between them were mutual.

Mother and I often got together with Micha and Louise and went on walks through the forest and meadows. We had so much to talk about on our outings.

Rarely did we leave the house without a tote bag. In it we would gather enough twigs and pine cones for starting a fire in the kitchen stove. Hellmut had a little wheelbarrow in which he gathered small twigs. When it was full he came to me and asked, "Is this enough to make coffee, Mutti?" He was eager to help.

"Sure, Hellmut. Every little bit helps." I smiled at his eagerness to help.

A few times Mother and I went to Kempten to window shop. We were pleased to have the bus service. Money was scarce, but a few times we bought something on sale.

I was glad, however, when the four weeks were up. Being together with Mother day-in-day-out for that length of time showed me that it was not easy to live with her. She was very domineering, demanding, and egotistical. I remembered Walter saying to me that he did not think I would have been happier living with them. Well, that was all in the past. I knew that I had made her stay with us as pleasant as I possibly could.

The Little Farmhouse

After living in the schoolhouse for over a year, we had to move. The apartment was needed for a new teacher. We were assigned a small house on the property of a retired farmer. It was quite primitive. To the right of the entry was a small living room. In the corner was a two-by-one-meter high built-in tile Dutch oven. It was greenish-blue in color. It kept the room nice and warm in the winter and gave it a cozy look. We didn't have a sofa. A cot covered with one of the smaller rugs had to be a sofa-substitute. A little table, a few chairs, and our Chinese carved camphor chest made it into a nice room.

Across from that room was the toilet, which reminded me of a primitive outhouse. All it needs is a little heart or a half-moon cut into the door, I thought, the first time I saw it. It had no heat. Well, at least we did not have to go outside to use it.

In the back of the living room was the kitchen with an eating area. Upstairs were three small bedrooms, no heating there either. I used hot bricks to warm the beds in winter. The chimney from the Dutch tile stove did go through one bedroom, which took the chill out of the room. Still, every night the water in the wash basin and pitcher froze over.

252

We took a daily sponge bath, either in the kitchen or living room, depending on which was warmer. Once a week, we took a tub bath. The bathtub was in the laundry room adjacent to the house. It was very unpleasant in the winter going from the hot bath around the side of the house in the cold winter air to the front door. I was surprised that none of us caught cold or contracted pneumonia.

Still, I liked our little house and tiny yard. I looked forward to planting a few flowers come spring. In the winter I often sat by the window and watched the sun set behind the high mountains or between the tall pine and spruce trees. I also enjoyed watching the moon rise. The snow on the trees sparkled like diamonds, twinkling all over. It looked like a fairyland to me.

The farmer and his wife were a very nice couple. They loved our Hellmut. He went over to visit them often and usually got an apple or a cookie. I felt that we were fortunate to have such a pretty little house, and neighbors who were good people.

Sometimes we had electrical storms — magnificent views also ... to me. Lightning flashed on all sides of us and the thunder was intensified by the echo of the mountains. Once we were fortunate in seeing a spectacular "Alp glow." Such a phenomenon was rare. "Alp glow" is sometimes seen at sunrise. But what I witnessed happened just before sunset and lasted only a few minutes. The whole mountain range of the Alps was embraced in a rosy glow. Everyone in the village rushed to their windows or raced outdoors to watch the spectacular marvel.

William and Herr Wanscheck were still in the candy business. It did help support Herr Wanscheck and us. With the CARE packages and the money we were receiving from our friends in Shanghai, we were making it. Our friends were still selling things that we had to leave behind.

I was hoping that we would hear something positive from Uncle Frank very soon. We really were eager to get out of our predicament. We hoped going to the United States would better our situation.

Konrad and Christa, Louise's daughter, were confirmed together at a Lutheran church in Kempten on May 24, 1949. He was sixteen years old. Usually, the youngsters were confirmed at the age of fourteen, but since Konrad came from Shanghai and our pastor had to leave that city, he could not be confirmed sooner.

It was enriching and comforting to see those fifty young girls and boys, all dressed in black--in China they wore white--being blessed and receiving, for the first time, Holy Communion. Konrad had tears in his eyes. "How many of these young people are truly giving their hearts to Christ?" I was wondering.

After the service, Micha, the Eberts, and my family went by bus back to Probstried. There we enjoyed a festive dinner at the village inn. In the afternoon we had coffee, cake, and sweet rolls at Herr and Frau Ebert's house. We finished out the day by taking a short walk in the forest; later we sat chatting softly in a meadow watching the sun set. I felt as blessed as I believed Konrad felt. I felt comforted by my friends and by the experiences of the day.

I kept in touch with Onkel Zaudig. In his last letter he had written that he was not feeling well. Even though it did not sound serious, I worried about him.

About a week or so after the confirmation, a letter I had written to Onkel Zaudig was returned to me with the remark "Deceased." "This cannot be!" I thought.

I wrote several letters to his landlady, but I never received a reply. I was so sorry. I had lost a dear friend. I was very hurt that I was not able to find out what had happened. He had been such a kind man. And he had not had a happy life. I knew I would miss him.

One weekend when William came home I could see that he was not in a good mood. After supper, the children had gone outside and William and I were alone in the kitchen. I said, "Willie, what is wrong?"

He did not answer right away, and I continued washing the dishes, trying to be quiet so as to give him his privacy. Finally he spoke. "I believe Herr Wanscheck is not bringing all the money for the sales he has made."

I knew that William was a suspicious person. "Did you say anything to him about it?" I asked.

"Not yet. I will wait another week."

"Perhaps he made a mistake," I said, as I reached for a towel to dry my hands.

"I'm pretty sure I am right."

"You will have to confront him then, won't you?" I dreaded that for him.

"Yes ... I hate that."

"Maybe he will straighten out when he sees that you know."

"I hope so," he said.

"Let's go out and see what the children are doing. It is a nice evening." I thought that the cool evening air might make us feel better.

We did not talk about it any more that weekend. But when William left for Kempten on Sunday evening, I said, "I hope all goes well with you and Herr Wanscheck. Try not to lose your temper, Willie."

"I'll do my best, Erna."

The next time William came in he told me that his talk with Herr Wanscheck had been fruitful. "I just told him that if he is short of money to tell me and I'll help him out. Still ... I don't trust him anymore."

William decided that it would be best to leave the partnership with Herr Wanscheck and go to Munich and apply for a job at several of the chocolate candy-making factories

255

there. Our money and CARE packages were dwindling down. Almost everything we had left behind had been sold by this time. For some items they just could not find a buyer.

In the spring of 1950 William received an offer from one of the factories where he had applied for work. He could start in two weeks. He immediately dissolved his partnership and went off to Munich to his first job in Germany. After having had his own business for seventeen years, I knew it would not be easy for him to work for someone else. He did not like to be told what to do.

With mixed emotions I watched him leave. Hellmut and I accompanied William to the bus stop. Konrad and Agnes had already told their father goodby and gone to school. William and I said goodby, he hugged Hellmut, then he boarded the bus. As the bus pulled off, my eyes followed it.

I thought of the day on June 20, 1948, when the Deutschmark was devaluated ten to one. Every adult and every child received 40.00 Deutschmark. We had to go to the bank, the post office, or even the school to receive the money. People who had money in the bank had their accounts adjusted to reflect the new value. The measure would certainly stabilize Germany's economy and we thought jobs would perhaps be more easily available. It had been William's and my hope that he would soon find a job. Now it was spring of 1950, almost two years later. "Who would have thought that it would take that long for him to find work?" I mused. I was glad for William and his newfound job, but my heart was heavy for him. I knew how hard it would be for him to work for someone else. I watched the bus until it was out of sight, then turned away with Hellmut to go home.

After William started his new job, he would try to find living quarters for us--another difficulty. We knew that it would not be easy to find a place in Munich, the city that had been so heavily bombarded. It would take months I was sure.

One day Konrad came home from school quite excited. "Mutti, guess whom I met in Kempten?"

"I have no idea; not someone from Shanghai?"

"Yes! Gerhard!"

"Well, what did he have to say? Where does he live? How is his mother?"

Konrad told me that they lived in a small town not far from Kempten. They had left on an earlier ship than we did. His mother had been a teacher in the German school.

Konrad and Gerhard met often after that. They always had a lot to share. Many memories from Shanghai drew them close to one another.

As time went on, we found many of our friends from China. They were scattered all over Germany and all over the world. People working for the government, such as the Consulate, had been placed in good working positions very soon. My friend from Shanghai, Heide Spengler's husband, was sent to Havana, Cuba, to the German Consulate there. Those who were employed by large firms found placements also. But, for individual businessmen, like William, it was not easy to find work, especially in the pastry and candy-making business.

We Move To Munich

After about two months William wrote that he would pick us up the weekend after next. He had found an apartment. We would get furniture through the committee that took care of the needs of displaced families. The furniture would be there by the time we would arrive.

William rented a truck and arrived in Probstried with the driver late Friday afternoon. We were to leave on Sunday morning.

We did not have much time to sit down and talk. But at mealtime he did tell us a little about the job and the people he was working with. "In China I was the boss and gave orders," he said. "Now I am told what to do."

257

"How are the working conditions?" I wanted to know, "Are the co-workers friendly--you being a refugee?"

"Well, so far I have no problems. I hope it will continue. The machines they have are quite modern," he said, with a pleased look on his face.

"I would want you to be happy about your work, Willie," I said, smiling.

We finished supper and I headed toward the bedroom to do some last-minute packing.

We were to depart early the next morning. I was sad knowing I must leave my friends.

Konrad and Agnes had made close friends too. They told me how they hated to leave them. "Mutti, I shall miss Gerhard so much," Konrad said.

"I know, dear," I said. "But you may see him again some-day if the Lord wills."

One Sunday before our departure, Agnes and I had paid a visit to Frau Hailer, the lady Agnes had met on the bus in the cold wintertime. Agnes wanted to see her once again and I wanted to tell her one last time how grateful I was for her helping my daughter. We stayed a short time and Frau Hailer hugged Agnes as she bade us farewell.

On the final morning, I was really sorry to leave Micha and Louise. We had become close and good friends. They came early to see us off. We hugged and said our tearful goodbys and promised to keep in touch. I wondered, "Is this my destiny? Always making good friends, only to part with them ... perhaps forever?"

Our stay in Probstried had lasted for about two years. I had come to like the peaceful and pretty little village in the Allgäu and the people. But we had to leave them.

Having lived in large cities all our lives, we did look forward to Munich. It was the capital city of Bavaria. There would be a lot to see; museums, theaters, movies, and many historical sights. I encouraged the children with these thoughts. We were going back to "civilization."

I was especially glad that my brother, Walter, and his family were living in Dachau, which was just twenty minutes away from Munich by train. I had received a long and detailed letter from him while I was still in Probstried. I had to stop reading it several times, because tears dimmed my eyes. He had written:

Dear little sister,

I wanted to let you know of some of the very difficult times I had to go through before I was able to finally move my family here to Dachau. I didn't have the heart nor the opportunity to write before now. But, thank heaven, we are together and in good health now.

I had taken my family to Schreiberhau in Silesia when Berlin was so heavily bombarded during the war. Trude's parents lived there, you know. In May of 1945 (I was working in Magdeburg at that time) a friend and I acquired two bicycles from a farmer. Our intentions were to take our families West because Silesia was occupied by Poland. We had to endure many hardships, heavy work, and make do on little food.

We rode by night; hid in barns and in the forests during the daytime. We knew if the Russians, who were occupying this part of the country, caught us we would never have been heard from again.

We had some disheartening experiences. At first we were suddenly attacked by some Polish hoodlums, who took away our wristwatches. A few days later, while we were sleeping in the forest, our bicycles were stolen. We had to walk the last two days.

Arriving, finally, in Schreiberhau, I tried everything possible to get my family into the West. Through a Polish businessman, who was friendly toward Germans, I was able to get them out of

259

Silesia. You can imagine how happy I was to have them with me once more. I would have given my life for them. In exchange for the Polish man's efforts I did give him linens, furs, woolens, and silver.

We left for the West on a refugee train. We carried our personal belongings in knapsacks. Trude had even sewn two little knapsacks for our girls, who were then nine and eleven years old, so they too could carry some of their clothing.

From Görlitz we had to travel by cattle train. Our destination was a small town called Schwarme, near Bremen. It took us ten days to get there. Each day the Red Cross provided us with a warm meal at one of the stations. A few times the train stopped long enough for us to wash up or take a shower at a station.

Arriving in Schwarme, we were able to rent one room from a tinker. In that one room we lived, we cooked, and we slept. I earned a little money by helping the tinker in his workshop.

Many days we lived only on mushrooms, which we gathered in the forest. Erna, you can't imagine how hungry our stomachs were. Nevertheless, we were together. And the landlord and his wife were very kind folk.

Anyway, after a few months I was able to contact my firm, Telefunken. They gave me a job at their branch office in Hamburg. But it was impossible to find lodging for my family in that totally destroyed city. So I accepted a position in Munich where my company had an opening. I rented a house in Dachau. I plan to build our own house here soon. It's time my family and I settle down.

That terrible war lasted too long ...."

I read on to the end of Walter's long letter. I wanted to see my brother again.

Our apartment in Munich was in a complex that had been bombarded and rebuilt. There were three rooms, a kitchen, and a bathroom. I was delighted to see a bathtub. Konrad said, "Mutti, now we can take a bath any time! Isn't that great?"

"Yes, I like that," I said, and I tried the faucet. "But, no water yet!" I said.

We found out the water was not connected to the bathtub. The tenant had to pay for his own connection. And these tenants, the Scheel family, did not have the money to do so. That was a big disappointment to all of us. I tried to make light of it. "Too bad," I said, and shrugged my shoulders.

The apartment was furnished, as usual, with odd pieces of furniture. I added two wooden fruit crates which I had obtained from a grocery store. I covered them with a Chinese hand-embroidered tablecloth. The crates added to the appearance of the room and gave us needed storage space. I never thought I'd see the day that I would be pleased with a decorated fruit crate.

The children adapted well to the place. Konrad finished middle school in June of 1950. Walter was able to get a job for him as an apprentice at Telefunken Company. Agnes attended the Volks- Schule.

We did not live far from the Lutheran Church, the Auferstehungs Kirche, the Resurrection Church, where Konrad had been confirmed. The children and I attended church every Sunday. William did not go with us, but he never interfered with our going. I was thankful for that.

Our apartment was located on the Park Strasse, just a few blocks away from "Die Wiesen" ("The Meadow"), where the world-famous traditional "Oktoberfest" was held. It was a folk-fest celebrated every year in the month of September, a unique affair.

Several times I took Konrad, Agnes, and Hellmut to the Fest after school. There were all sorts of amusement games and rides for both children and adults. Agnes and Hellmut raced toward the rides, squealing with delight, Konrad with a fake expression of nonchalance. After the rides and the amusement games, I bought them ice cream cones--a rare treat for them.

The unique city of Munich is not only beautiful but also the home of the Benedictine Monks. The River Isar flows straight through the middle of town. Henry the Lion granted the monks the right to farm their land and later sell their goods at the market.

In 1854 Munich was proclaimed a city. Since 1812 it has been the seat of the Archbishop of Munchen-Freising.

It surely was a contrast from 1940 (our vacation) to 1949 when we moved to the Park Strasse. Many scars were still visible from the bombs dropped earlier but most buildings had been repaired and restored to their original forms — as were the old museums, cathedrals, churches, theaters and monuments.

I especially admired the "Marienplatz" in the middle of the town. The town hall which was bombarded severely was reconstructed. The American military personnel contributed a large sum toward this project. Large islands of colorful flowers were planted on the corners. At noon the Plaza was packed with hundreds of tourists and townsfolk who came to enjoy the music and view the spectacular sculpted figurines that moved mechanically about the tower of the town hall.

One evening during supper we heard the music from the Wies'n. William said unexpectedly, "Erna, let's you and I go to the Wies'n this evening. We'll have a beer in one of the beer tents."

"Oh, Willie, really!" I responded and hurriedly finished with supper. We so seldom went out together that I was flabbergasted that William had suggested that we do that.

"I want to go too," chirped Hellmut, " Please?"

"No. Today Mutti and I will go alone," said William, "We will take you another time."

Willie and I walked to the Wies'n. Each brewery had its own tent filled with rows of tables and wooden benches which would seat hundreds of people. We found two vacant seats in one of the huge beer tents. Everybody introduced themselves to each other. There seemed to be no strangers. The huge beer barrels contained hundreds of liters of beer. Through the open doors drifted the aroma of whole oxen and pigs roasting on spits over open outdoor fires. Plump chickens by the dozens were roasting. I could hardly wait for the costumed waitresses and waiters to serve us the delicious meats. Each brewery had it own particular specialty.

Music filled the air. In the center of the tent musicians, seated on a platform, performed "oom-pah-pah" music as well as folk and beer-drinking songs. I sang along with everyone else. William was so happy that night. His voice soon joined ours.

I watched the people dance, twirling and swirling about the dance floor. I wanted to dance too but I knew William did not like to dance. So, I decided to enjoy watching others dance in their native costumes — women in colorful "Dirndl" dresses and men in their "Lederhosen" (leather pants). I was so glad that William had suggested this outing. As we watched the dancers I thought about how we had been getting along better than we ever had in China.

"Erna, shall we go now?"

The evening was growing late. I noted the spark in William eyes and realized my mind had wandered.

"What were you thinking of, Mutti?" asked William.

"I was just thinking, William, that even though we have very little, we are much happier now than we ever were in China." William smiled and agreed. We walked home hand in hand that night.

It was true that we were happier now. Being together twenty-four hours a day, seven days a week, like we were in Shanghai had not been good for our marriage. Now Willie went to work every morning and I stayed home. I took care of the children and the apartment. I was a "plain old house-wife" for once in my life and I loved it.

Even so, because William's income was so small, I did try to make a little household money by selling encyclope-dias and life insurance. I spent a few hours each day going from house to house, apartment to apartment, knocking on door after door. I did not like this job. I often called on as many as a dozen homes without a single sale. However, I did not give up. I knew how much every sale helped toward gro-ceries and household expenses.

Tante Liete

I hadn't seen Tante Liete, my mother's oldest sister, for ten years. It had always been her wish to come to Munich during the carnival season. Since we were now living in Munich it was a good opportunity for her to visit us at this time. She lived by herself in Hanover which was many miles away.

Tante Liete arrived by train in time for the carnival sea-son. I thought she was the prettiest of the three sisters. She had grayish wavy hair, an oval face and very few wrinkles. Her eyes were hazel in color. Even though they had a twinkle, there was a sadness that showed through. I greeted my aunt, and she looked at me with a twinkle as I kissed her cheek beneath her glasses, sitting on her slender straight nose. I noticed her small golden earrings and how becoming they were to her. My mother would never wear earrings like those, I thought. Silver hair framed her face.

Tante Liete was unmarried. One night as we sat talk-ing Tante Liete began telling me of her past life. "Erna," she said, "I met a man when I was in my forties. A German-American man. A real gentleman. I remember well the night we met. We were at a mutual friend's house. I was attracted to him right away."

"You met in Hanover?" I asked.

"Yes. He lived in the United States but often came to Hanover on business. We fell very much in love. But time passes so quickly it seems. We saw each other for several years."

"Do you think he would ever really have married you, dear Tante?"

"Oh yes, Erna. On his very next trip to Germany, we were planning to be married. How I loved that man. His last trip..."

"What happened?" I asked, knowing that she wanted to continue with her story. I already knew what had happened but I knew she wanted to re-live it again.

"Unfortunately he suffered a heart attack on board the ship. He died. When I received the news I went into shock you know. Yes, I'll never forget that man. Erna, you know how I live, don't you?"

"How, Tante Liete?"

"He left me a pension. A small pension, yes, but enough. He arranged before our marriage date for me to have a small pension from his estate until the day I die." I saw teardrops glisten in her sad hazel eyes.

I rose and put my arms around her. "Yes, Tante Liete," I said, "he surely did love you dearly."

Tante Liete and I got along very well and did many things together; cooking, shopping, and cleaning. As she was a good seamstress, she helped me with altering clothes for Agnes and Hellmut. We even sewed a winter coat for Hellmut. I learned many new sewing skills from her.

One evening Tante Liete said to William, "Let's go out tomorrow night. I'll treat," and she put a fifty mark bill into William's hand. "Let's spend it!"

265

"No! Tante Liete, I cannot accept that," he said, a little embarrassed I thought.

"Now don't be silly William, let's go and have fun. When you come to visit me in Hanover, you can treat. I really want to do this."

"Then it's a deal!" William folded his napkin, then placed the money in his billfold. I was surprised that he accepted her offer.

So the next evening, after the children had their supper, the three of us went to have an evening at the carnival.

The street car took us to downtown Munich. "Well," I said, "Munich certainly is a happy-go-lucky city in carnival season." People were gathering, laughing, walking in all directions.

We looked at the gaily decorated restaurants with the different colored paper streamers, balloons, and flowers. We heard brass music and singing everywhere.

After strolling around the streets for a while, watching the merriment around us, we found a restaurant that was not so crowded. We ordered "Weisswürstle," sauerkraut, and a large pretzel for each of us. And of course--a beer. "Weisswürstle" was white sausage. They were made of veal and were a speciality of Bavaria.

A band was playing and everyone was singing along. People were dancing on a platform. I said, "Willie, let's dance."

"I don't want to, Erna."

Tante Liete said, "Erna, come lets you and I dance." I felt a little odd and hesitated. "Look, there are other women dancing. We are not out of place. Be a sport!" So I gave in and we danced around the floor a few times, laughing like young girls. I knew that no one would ever guess that she was seventy-five years old.

She had a good sense of humor too. William teased her, "Tante Liete, people will think you are looking for a male companion."

266

She just laughed and said, "So what!"

We didn't go home until after midnight.

The three weeks she stayed with us went by too fast. All of us were so fond of her and hated to see her leave. She was my mother's sister, but what different personalities the two women had.

Meager Times And Welfare

The same year that Konrad went to work, Hellmut started kindergarten. Agnes dropped him off on her way to school and picked him up coming home. That gave me more time to do my selling, but I was still not too successful at it. I felt like giving it up. But I stayed with it.

One evening I was in the kitchen peeling potatoes for supper, when William came in and sat down in one of the chairs. He seldom did that. It was Friday evening. "Well, William, how was your day? Another week has passed and you still have a job."

"Yes, but I will lose it in two weeks. I got notice today. Raw materials are hard to get and there is just not enough work."

"Oh! That's awful. What are you going to do? My earnings surely cannot support the family."

"If I cannot find work before then, Erna, then I will have to go on welfare."

"That will surely be hard on him," I thought. I wiped my hands and went over to him. I put my arms around his shoulders and said, "Perhaps something will come up. Don't be discouraged, Willie."

As I was finishing supper I was thinking, here he is almost forty-eight years old, a hard-working, honest man and proud of his profession having to go on welfare.

I felt sorry for him that day when he went to apply for welfare. I said to him, "It is through no fault of yours that we are in this situation. Don't take it so hard."

"That is easy for you to say; you are not going."

"Let's hope it will be for just a short time." I kissed him and said, "Chin up," and gave him a pat on the shoulder.

All welfare recipients were required to do some community work; cleaning streets, parks, or clerical work in the city hall or other offices pertaining to the city. William was assigned an office job. I was glad for him that he did not have to sweep streets.

All the while we were in Germany, William was hoping that we would get to the United States soon, but the immigration laws were so strict. The authorities were still trying to get us there on William's German quota. We needed great patience. Naturally we wanted to enter together. After many trips to the American Consulate we finally received permission to enter under his quota. It had taken years--five long years. Now we needed a visa. It would take months, maybe a year to acquire the visa, we did not know. In the meantime there were five mouths to be fed. I tried desperately to find a better job, so that we could get off of welfare-but to no avail.

Then one day our neighbor came to bring encouraging news. She said, "Frau Scheel, there is a big House and Garden Show opening here soon. They are always looking for extra help."

"Oh! Would you have the name and address of the person I will have to see about the job?"

"Yes, I brought it with me."

"That is great! I'll go first thing in the morning and apply. Thank you, thank you." I gave her a hearty hug.

Thanks to her lead I got a job. The company was selling little machines that peeled and cored apples and peeled potatoes. A neat and practical little household appliance, especially during canning season. And it was canning time. Apples were just getting ripe. My job was to assist the demonstrator. While she demonstrated I observed the public. If I noticed someone interested, I approached that person with an order form. Usually I made a sale. After several days of watching and trying out the machine when there were few customers my boss let me demonstrate it while she went to lunch. Because I was so enthused about what this appliance could do, I demonstrated it well and my sales pitch was convincing. I usually made a few sales while she was out. I made ten marks a day! Working six days a week, I brought home sixty marks, which really helped. I couldn't believe my good fortune.

While I worked, William helped Agnes with cooking. Konrad helped cleaning the house.

I had been working for several weeks when I heard that the House and Garden Show in Fürth, a city near Nürenberg, was looking for a demonstrator. I applied and was hired. I was to be in charge of the booth, receive a salary, and make a good commission on every machine I sold.

The drawback was that I had to leave the family. That would put a lot of responsibility on Agnes' shoulders. She was only thirteen. William said, "Mutti, don't worry; I will take care of the cooking and we will all help with the other chores." Our neighbor also offered to help. William still had to work for his welfare check. Soon I would be making enough that he could get off welfare assistance.

I went to Fürth. Once there, I learned that the company rented a booth. The rest was up to me. I had to rent the tables, exhibit the machines, hang up posters, and demonstrate. Early in the morning I went to the market and ordered apples and potatoes. They had to be delivered before the exhibit opened. I had two helpers assisting me.

I rented a very small room from an elderly couple. Every year, they told me, they rented a room or two during the exhibitions to supplement their meager income. I had breakfast with them, took my lunch to work, and in the evening I ate supper with a few of the demonstrators from other booths. They were all very friendly to me. I made enough money to pay for the small room, my meals, and support the family in Munich.

Some days the public was just not interested in my product. They rushed from one booth to the next without taking time to even listen to my sales speeches. On one such day, it was raining hard, a demonstrator from the noodle making machine booth came by my stand and asked, "How are you doing today?"

"Not much," I said, "they all seem to be running."

She answered, "Yes, as if they have pepper in their pants." She was an old-hand at these shows, and always had something funny to say in her heavy Bavarian dialect.

One day, after a very busy day at the fair, I went home awfully tired. It had been a fruitful day. I had sold many machines. I was looking forward to a good night's sleep. My landlady said as she opened the door for me, "Frau Scheel, the postman brought this express letter for you."

"Oh, I hope it's good news," I said, my heart pounding. I tore the letter open right there. "It is good news," I shouted. "Our visa has arrived! We can enter the United States!"

I grabbed my petite landlady and, to her surprise, swirled her around. All my fatigue left me.

Her husband said, "This needs to be celebrated. I have a bottle of wine in the cellar. I'll go and get it right now," and he hurried away.

We sat in the cosy kitchen until midnight talking. I did not get much sleep that night after all.

We had taken all our physical examinations and inoculations months back. We had just been waiting. The visa would expire in the first week of October 1951, and it was already the end of July. We needed reservations for five on a ship. The agent of the travel bureau told William that he could not find anything for five in the tourist class. He had only one vacancy, so William decided to go ahead and we would follow as soon as we were able to get passage.

A week before William left for the United States he came to Fürth one evening and stayed the following day. I was glad that he was able to come for there were so many things that I had to take care of after he left. He had made a long list for me. We went over it and he explained it all. The most important matter was that we got reservations in time to be in New York about the eighth of October. That's when our visa would expire.

My biggest concern was the children. They would be left on their own for several days, eight perhaps ten, days.

William said, "The family in the apartment below us offered to look after the children and help Agnes with her chores."

"I am relieved to hear this, William. But it is still heavy on my heart."

"Yes, I know and I understand your anxiety," he said.

"Agnes is only thirteen. Are we not expecting too much of her ? I am worried."

"But the children must manage for those few days. Frau Neumann really meant it when she said she would help Agnes. She even said she would have the children over for supper a few times."

"The children will enjoy that. All right, William .... Tell Agnes to just leave the laundry, I'll take care of it when I come."

We talked until late into the night.

As William was leaving the next day, my landlady and her husband wished him well and walked down the steps with us. They parted with a handshake.

William picked up his briefcase, put on his hat and we walked to the station. After we waited about fifteen minutes, I saw the bright lights of the approaching train. Slowly it came to a stop. William looked for a "smoking" coach. We hugged and kissed goodby. "Have a safe voyage to New York, Willie. The best of luck to you. And give Onkel Frank and Tante Ella our love."

"Take care of yourself and don't fret," he said, as he boarded the train. I saw him lowering a window. He had taken off his hat and his brown wavy hair blew in the wind. A sharp whistle pierced the air. The station master called "Einsteigen" and slowly the train pulled out of the station. I waved with my lace handkerchief until I could not see William any more.

Deep in thought, I turned and walked back to my little room.

William was leaving for the States in a week, traveling by train to Le Havre, France, where he would board the ocean liner for New York. What would the future be like for us? I wondered.

William's birthday had been on the eighth of August. On August 10, the evening before he left, he wrote me a long letter:

"... Agnes cooked goulash and baked a spiced cake for me. She wanted to make an especially good cake, used five eggs and a half pound of good butter. She did not want my help; but did accept the few tips I gave her. She paid for the ingredients for the cake out of her allowance.

Konrad and Agnes each gave me five cigarettes and Hellmut surprised me with a bunch of flowers that he had picked. Don't be too concerned, Erna, I know how it is; I am leaving with a heavy heart. I just can't see you working so hard and I worry about you and the children.

The assistant pastor from our church came yesterday and offered to take Hellmut for the time you were in Fürth, but I thought it would be best for him to stay with Agnes. She would not be alone during the day, and Hellmut does want to stay with his sister. Being vacation time, the children would be together.

As soon as I am over there and have a job, I will send some money to you.

I am sorry that Agnes is not feeling well today. It seems as if her spleen is swollen. She says she hurts under her ribs.

272

She promised, though, to go to the doctor (you know, the one who lives in our building) if it does not get better by tomorrow. I didn't want to write this to you, but I think it is best for you to know about her situation .

I wish I did not have to leave at this time, but I cannot put off my departure any longer. Just hope that you will be able to follow soon ..."

He wrote such a dear letter. In writing he could express his feelings, which he could not do in speaking. He very, very seldom said, "I love you, Erna."

I remember asking him once, while lying in his arms, "Willie, do you love me, you so seldom say it?"

"You know I do. I told you when I asked you to marry me. Why do I have to say it?"

"Because I like to hear it," I said sweetly, and I turned over, disappointed.

That letter really touched my heart. I felt like returning to Munich right then and there, especially knowing that Agnes was not well. Oh Lord, I prayed, please make it that all goes well.

The very next day after William left I received a telegram from Konrad which read, " Agnes sick in hospital. Hellmut at Neumanns. Please come!"

Of course I had to go home immediately.

I entrusted the exhibition booth into the hands of my helpers. I was lucky to get a ride with a demonstrator who was on his way to Munich. The few-hour drive seemed ever so long.

Arriving at the hospital, I found Agnes in pretty good spirits. She came running into my arms saying, "Oh, I am so glad you came, Mutti."

"I'm so glad to be here, dear. How are you feeling?"

"I am feeling fine. The pain is gone. Don't worry."

"Agnes, tell me what happened?"

We found chairs along the corridor to sit down and she said, "I had some pain during the night and also the morning Vati was leaving. He told me to stay home, but I insisted on seeing him off. He went to our neighbor and told her about my condition and asked her to take me to the doctor when I returned from the station. He asked me to notify you."

"Were you scared, a little, maybe?"

"Yes, a little, Mutti. Then Vati, Konrad, Hellmut and I left for the train station. While waiting I got severe pain in my stomach. Vati took me to the emergency ambulatory station there. The doctor examined me and said it was my gall bladder."

"Your gall bladder..???"

"Yes, that was causing my pain."

"Oh dear!"

"Poor Vati, he was so worried. His train was arriving any minute, I was sick and you were in Fürth. And Mutti, the people were so very understanding at the emergency room. They assured Vati that they would take me to the hospital where they would take care of me. Konrad said he would take Hellmut to the Neuman's and send you a telegram."

"Oh, this must have been awful for Vati and you." I took Agnes into my arms. "Poor child," I said.

That was the situation when William left. It must have been awful for him; the uncertainty of Agnes' condition, and the wondering who would take care of little Hellmut. I knew that William would not receive any news until his arrival in Cleveland. "What a way to leave," I thought.

After I had spoken to the doctor and had his assurance that Agnes' condition was not serious, I felt so much better.

He said, "Her condition is mostly due to the responsibilities awaiting her at home with her parents not there. It is too much for her tender thirteen years."

"I'm sorry, Doctor. My husband and I cannot help the situation at this time."

"I know, Frau Scheel. We will keep her under observation for eight to ten days. You may rest assured we shall take good care of her."

"Thank you very much, Doctor," I said, and extended my hand to him.

"Agnes, I will be back to you in a week or so."

"Who is going to take care of Hellmut and what is Koni going to do, Mutti?"

I told her, "I have spoken by phone with Walter and Trude. They will take care of them."

Agnes was so glad to be relieved of all responsibilities. It was really too much that we had expected of our little girl. I was sorry that she had to go through such an ordeal.

"But now it is going to work out, Agi. I will dissolve my commitment with the company I am working for and return soon."

Agnes did not mind staying in the hospital. The nurses were friendly to her and there were a few girls her age with whom she could pass time in the same ward.

I went to our apartment in the Park Strasse. I packed a few things for Hellmut, picked him up from the Neuman's, and took him to Trude. Konrad was at work and would come home with Walter. Trude and her two girls were glad to have Hellmut.

"Now we have a little brother!" the girls said happily.

Walter and Konrad came home for supper. Konrad embraced me and said, "I am so glad to see you, Mutti."

"I'm glad to see you, too, Koni."

"How is Agi doing? When is she coming home?"

"Well, Koni, Agi will stay at the hospital," and I told him everything the doctor had said. "I will be back in a little over a week to bring Agi home."

When it was time for me to catch my train to Fürth, I hugged everyone and said to Walter, "You cannot know what it means to me to have a brother so close by. Someone I can come to when in trouble." I had not known this feeling of kinship in China. "I thank you and Trude so much for your willingness to help me."

"I'm glad to have you too, Erna, and to be able to do this for you."

"But I have to go now, otherwise I'll miss my train."

Walter drove me to the station.

Next morning I contacted my boss and told him that I was not able to stay until the closing of the exhibition. He understood. I quickly trained one of my helpers. Before I left, I did ask the manager if I could buy the little machine that I had been working with.

"You may have it," he said, "as a bonus."

"Oh, I appreciate that. I will take it to the United States."

I said goodby to the elderly couple that I stayed with. I had to promise them that I would write and let them know how we made out in the States.

1951 - The Voyage To America

William had arrived in New York on August 20, 1951. He wrote to me that he took the first train leaving for Cleveland. He was glad to find good news from us waiting for him there. Onkel Frank and Tante Ella met him at the station. William had been a teenager when they last saw him.

The travel agency in Munich was trying its best to get the four of us passage on one of the ocean liners. We had to be in New York around the eighth of October, and it was already September. In the meantime, I did all the things William had written on that long list. It was not easy. I did a lot of running around.

Near the middle of September the travel agency notified me they were able to get us passage for four on a Dutch liner, the *S.S. Veendam*. However, only first-class accommodations were available. This would cost an additional two hundred dollars. I telegraphed William about the need for more funds.

We received the funds in just a few days. Onkel Frank helped William financially.

Now we were all going to be there together at last. I was elated, and so were the children. Our long awaited departure was finally in sight. These four years in Germany had not been easy for us. We all had to make adjustments. What would this new country bring us? I wondered. America the great! The land of unlimited opportunities. Where it is easy to make money. One could almost find gold on the streets. So we were told. For years it had been William's dream to go to America. Soon we would be there with him. Soon we would walk the streets of "golden" America.

We made one final trip to visit my brother and his family to say farewell to them. Walter and I both were sad when we parted. We had spent so little time of our lives together and had just gotten to know each other. Trude and I had become very close. I was truly sorry to leave them. "Maybe, if the Lord wills, we will all meet again someday," I said, and the children and I left them.

The last days were hectic but we made it. We left Munich on September 24 by train via Paris to Rotterdam. There we boarded The *S.S. Veendam*. We sailed from Holland on the twenty-eighth of September, 1951.

Our cabin was very spacious, clean, and quite comfortable. After all, we were traveling first class and were treated as first-class passengers. (According to my purse I felt like a third-class passenger.) Our clothes were not of the latest style either. I had to wear my good dresses from Shanghai which I had not worn once during our stay in Germany.

Supper was served at two different times. The first sound of the gong called the families with children. At this time the dress code was not so important. Because we ate at that time, I got by with the clothes I had. All the while, I felt that we were paupers traveling first class.

Konrad and Agnes had a good time on board. There were lots of things for them to do; ping-pong, movies, and all kinds of games. I knew that they were well entertained. The food was excellent. Hellmut, however, was seasick several times.

The closer we came to New York, the worse I felt. I did not even have enough money to leave a tip for the steward. He was such a polite and friendly man. I was so embarrassed. The day before we arrived in New York I asked him, "May I have your address? I want to thank you properly from Cleveland."

I arrived in New York, the United States of America, with five dollars in my purse. We would have to start all over once again. Konrad and Agnes were so excited and eager to see the Statue of Liberty. Konrad pleaded, "Mutti, please wake us before we pass the statue early in the morning so we can dress and be on deck." We turned in early that night so that we would be refreshed come morning.

"Surely we will all get up in time" I said. "Hellmut, you want to come with us?" Of course he wanted to be with us.

I contemplated my past life, my life still to come, and what it might bring. Life has its ups and downs, I knew. Its good and bad times. Its "Ying Yang," the Chinese would say. I knew my life had been so influenced. But, I thought, we were all healthy and would soon be united again with William. I prayed, "Lord, thank you for protecting us so far. Be with us in this new country, continue to protect us and help us to do your will. Praise you, Lord."

Agnes picking blueberries in Algäu, Germany. 1948.

The Scheel Family in Probstried, Germany. 1948.

"Tante Liete" as a young woman in Hannover, Germany. 1916.

Agnes, Hellmut, and Erna on the S.S. Veendam immigrating to the United States. 1951.

CHAPTER TWELVE
The United States - A New Beginning

The next morning we were on deck early to see the Statue of Liberty. All decks were crowded with passengers. "What a majestic lady," I thought, as I gazed at her tall form, the symbol of freedom. As we passed her, I felt chills trickling down my back and tears welling into my eyes. A new country. A new beginning. I wondered, how many refugees and immigrants must have looked up to her, feeling new hope and gratitude in their hearts? Many prayers of thankfulness and gratefulness surely must have been offered.

On October 9, 1951, in New York City, the seal in my entry document was dated.

Entering the harbor I felt disappointment at the pier where the *S.S. Veendam* docked. The water around us was filthy, littered with all kinds of garbage—paper cups, cans, paper, rotten oranges. The pier was dark and dingy and also filthy and littered. I had read that the Americans were so conscious of cleanliness and hygiene. But, my first impression of the United States was disappointment.

William was at the pier to meet us. The children spotted him first and shouted, "Vati, Vati, up here." William looked tired and thin. He saw us and waved his hat. "Now," I thought, "We are all together again!"

"I'm so glad to see all of you!" exclaimed William, "And everyone so well!" He took Agnes into his arms and said, "You look well, Agi, you have a good color. I am so glad."

"I'm feeling fine, Vati."

We had no trouble getting through customs. We were soon on our way.

William hailed a taxi to take us to Konrad Stingl's house. He lived in a suburb of New York. He had been a pastry chef with Kiessling and Bader in Tientsin, and had worked for us

281

in Shanghai when we were in a predicament. Mr. Stingl had come to the States some time before we arrived.

On the way to the Stingls, William said, "Konrad Stingl told me that I could find a job in New York. And I have." "That's wonderful, Willie," I said, and put my hand in his. But, as a new immigrant with no connections, William had to start way at the bottom. He told us that he had to scrub baking sheets, pans, and even floors. It was the most degrading work he had to do since his apprentice days. These, again, were stressful times for him.

Mr. and Mrs. Stingl greeted us warmly. I was happy to be together with friends from China. The pleasant aroma of freshly made coffee filled the house. We soon were gathered around the table, enjoying the coffee and delicious fruit "torte" (tart). We exchanged old memories.

After awhile the Stingl's four daughters came in. I was astounded to hear the parents speaking English with them. I exclaimed in surprise, "Why do you speak English with the children?"

Mr. Stingl replied, "To speak English makes it easier for them to learn the language. They did not want to be different from the other children in school. You are going to find this out for yourselves."

I was very sure this would not happen to *me* and *my* children! I was going to speak *German* with them at home.

Before we were finished with the first pot of coffee Ellinor decided to make another fresh pot. I watched as she poured two or three cups of coffee down the sink drain.

I said to myself, "You don't pour out coffee!" Coffee was so expensive in Germany, I bought only one-quarter of a pound at one time. That much lasted two weeks and longer. Only on Sundays would I make a pot of coffee. Then on Monday I added a little roasted and ground barley and some chicory to the regular coffee grounds left from Sunday. During the week we just drank the barley and chicory concoction we called "Muckefuok." I did not say anything, but thought, "What a waste!"

First the litter and now waste. These were my first impressions of the United States. On the other hand the skyscrapers and the crowded streets amazed me. Oh, and all those eating places! I had the impression Americans didn't cook much at home.

William and Konrad Stingl had a lot to talk about, mostly their bachelor days in Tientsin. They began recalling one particular event that had occurred one New Year's Eve. A few young men and their girlfriends gathered at someone's house. They ate, drank, danced, and played games. Wine was flowing freely. Alex, one of the young men, had too much to drink and fell asleep in an easy chair. Another of the men came up with the bright idea to blacken his face with soot. The party went on while Alex was sleeping. Towards daybreak the party broke up and everyone went home. Alex, with the blackened face, went on his way also. It was getting daylight and he noticed that people were looking at him and smiling. He looked down at his coat, took off his hat, looked at it, couldn't see anything wrong, shrugged his shoulders, and went on home. In order not to awaken his parents, he took off his shoes and went quietly to his room, removed his coat and hat, and flopped himself into his bed.

When Alex did not come down for lunch his mother decided to check on him. She opened the door and,... lo and behold, there was a black man in her son's bed! She screamed and ran down the stairs to tell her husband. Her scream awoke Alex and he went to take his bath. Passing the mirror, he almost fell over—a black man was staring at him. His parents came upstairs and found him laughing at himself.

As Konrad Stingl was telling the true story, we laughed so much that tears sprang into our eyes. I could not remember when I last had laughed so much.

We stayed at the Stingl's overnight and took the train to Cleveland the next morning. In Cleveland we would be staying with the relatives that sponsored our immigration to the United States.

1951 - In Cleveland With Relatives

Onkel Frank, his wife Ella, and four-year-old son Martin, had arrived in New York on the *SIS Bremem* on October 28,1926. He was William's mother's brother and was a painter and paper hanger by profession. Frank and Ella Scheel had become citizens in 1940 and resided in Cleveland, Ohio in 1951 when we arrived.

Onkel Frank and Tante Ella met us at the station. He resembled his sister, only he was broader and taller. Tante Ella was a small lady with snow white hair, blue eyes, and had a very motherly and friendly personality. She was soft spoken and I felt close to her right away.

She greeted us with, "Welcome to Cleveland!" and hugged each one of us. Then we drove to their home in a suburb of Cleveland. We just brought along our overnight suitcase and had deposited the trunks and duffle bags at the station to be picked up later.

Upon arriving at their home, Tante Ella showed us the house. Their living room, dining room, and kitchen were on the ground floor and the bedrooms were on the next level. Hellmut took his great-aunt's hand as if he had known her all his life. I heard him say, "Tante Ella, I like your house." "I'm glad you do, Hellmut," she replied. "And I hope you will be happy here."

Hellmut and Konrad were going to share one bedroom and Agnes and I the other. William would have to return to New York the next day.

I asked Onkel Frank, "Did you recognize William right away?" "Oh, yes," he replied. "He has not changed that much. He still has the steel grey eyes, straight nose and—most of all-the off-standing ears!" I laughed and glanced at William's unique ears. "He has his mother's small stature;" continued Onkel Frank, "I could see a shade of grey in his brown hair."

That night William told me how frustrated he was with the way he was treated at work. It was humiliating to him that the head pastry chef did not trust his ability in baking. He knew perfectly well how to decorate all the French pastries and fancy "torten" and lovely wedding cakes. He was so very mastered in the art. I said to him, "Willie, have patience, your time will come." "I don't know, Erna," he responded. " You have just been here a few months," I insisted. "You will see, there will be an opportunity for you to show your skills."

The next morning William left for New York . We would not see each other again until Christmas. Since it was October the word "Halloween" was mentioned frequently. "What is Halloween?" I wondered. Tante Ella explained it to us, especially what "Trick or treat" meant. She also explained about the "Jack-O-Lantern." "Children wear all kinds of different costumes," she said. My curiosity was not stilled. I looked for an encyclopedia and found more information:

In medieval times "All Hallows" was celebrated on the eve of All Saints Day, on the thirty-first of October. It was connected with the ancient fire festivals and also the returning of the herds from the pastures. Over the years Halloween began to be observed by children going from house to house demanding "Trick or treat." Treats are generally given, tricks rarely played. After reading the encyclopedia my curiosity was satisfied.

On Halloween, Agnes raided Tante Ella's rag bag. Excitedly she pasted bits of different colored material on Hellmut's coat. She taught him to say the important words "trick or treat," and "thank you." Agnes and I set off with our little vagabond Hellmut to go "trick-or-treating." Hellmut was all set with his costume and his first English vocabulary; "Trick or treat? Thank you!" With paper bag in hand, he went with Agnes and me to the houses on our street. Agnes and I stayed behind while he rang the bell and said his little phrase; "Trick or treat?" All went well until we came to a house where the lady asked him, "What is your name and where do you live?" Like a little dummy, Hellmut stood there, looking up at her. I went up to her and explained, "We are the Scheel's relatives, just arrived from Germany and we are staying with them." "Oh, yes," the lady answered. "I have heard that the Scheels were expecting relatives from the old country. I hope you like it here. And do come and see us sometime. Bring Ella along." "Thank you very much," I said sincerely. I was surprised how friendly the people were. "She does not even know me!" I thought, and she invited me to her house. This had not happened to me in the four years we had lived in Germany.

Soon Hellmut wanted to go home and show Tante Ella his treasures. We arrived there and he said, "Look, Tante Ella, what I have! When can I go again?" "Well, dear, next year. This comes only once a year." Hellmut pouted for a minute or two then looked into his bag. He had quite a bit of candy, an apple, and a few shiny pennies. His disappointment was soon forgotten as he surveyed his new treasures.

Before I went looking for a job, Tante Ella and I went shopping. The children and I needed to have our wardrobes brought up-to-date.

On one of the shopping days, we stopped at a department store for lunch. The lunch room was crowded and just as we were about to leave, Tante Ella saw two people get up. We hurriedly occupied the two vacant seats at the counter. I glanced behind the counter and saw only black girls and men handling food and serving the customers. I looked at my aunt and was just about to say, "Is this where we are going to eat?" but I kept quiet. I observed that other people were eating the food these black hands had prepared. Tante Ella noticed my apprehension and asked, "Erna, would you rather eat some-

286

where else?" "Oh, no," I lied, "This is all right." Silently, I asked myself, "Didn't I live all my life among people who were not the color of my skin?" I was ashamed of myself for having felt the way I did. We ordered our lunch and I enjoyed it.

Konrad found a job very soon at a TV repair shop and he went to evening classes. He had to relearn mathematics and algebra in the English language and he needed to improve his English.

Agnes entered Lincoln High School, where all children of immigrants and refugees started schooling. Agnes was lonesome for her Father and for her friends in Germany. She felt very awkward with all the different nationalities in the school to which she went for a whole year. It was necessary for her to go to Lincoln High to improve her English. But this caused her to miss out on a year's schooling.

Hellmut, being five years old, started kindergarten without knowledge of one word of English (except "Trick or treat," and "Thank you!"). But he learned the language fast.

After having all the different errands behind me, I started looking for a job. I found one with the American Greeting Card Company. They hired immigrants from all nations; some could hardly speak a word of English. Most of the time Onkel Frank dropped me off in the mornings on his way to work. In the evenings I took the bus home. The work I did was very easy, but a certain amount of production was expected of each worker per day. We had to prepare boxes of assorted greeting cards for drug stores, supermarkets, dime stores, and card shops. I was able to make my quota and more.

My weekly paycheck was more than enough to pay for our room and board at Onkel Frank's. William sent money to us for clothing and other necessities and I was even able to put some money aside. We had started out in the States with zero savings, but soon William had paid off the two hundred dollars Onkel Frank had lent him toward our passage to the

287

States. William's ambition was to have a business of his own one day. Again he changed jobs often, always looking for something better.

One day the supervisor of my department came to me and said, "Erna, there is a vacancy at an envelope folding machine. It pays five cents more per hour. Would you like to take it?"

Quickly calculating in my mind how much more I would make a week, I accepted the job.

Very soon, however, I regretted it. The paper for the envelopes was pre-cut; the sides had dry glue on them. I had to place the papers very carefully on a platform. There they would glide down, sheet by sheet, to a place where the sides with glue were dampened. They were then folded and dried and the ready envelope came out the other end. Sometimes the glue did not dry properly, the envelope stuck, and the machine became jammed. I would have to call a mechanic to fix it. I was not paid for the time the machine was being repaired, so my paycheck was really not much more than it was before. Also, there was a lot of exasperation connected with this type work. I was always glad when called to do some other work, when they did not need envelopes that day.

We were adjusting to the new life. On a weekend, Onkel Frank drove us to Mansfield where we had some relatives I had never met. And he also showed us the surroundings of Cleveland. But I missed going to church. After a few weeks I asked, "Tante Ella, is there a Lutheran Church that has services in the German language?" She said, "I don't know, but let us look in the newspaper or the telephone book." After looking for a bit, she said, "Look here, there are several." She pointed out one which was not far from their house.

For the next few Sundays Agnes and I tried several different churches, but the services were not the same as we were used to in Munich or even Shanghai. I was disappointed and so was Agnes. I mentioned this to a woman who also worked at the American Greeting Card factory and who lived in our neighborhood. I knew that she was Lutheran. She said, "Erna, why don't you come to church with me on Sunday? Reverend Miller is a very warm and kind man and he speaks German." "I would like to do that," I said. "I'll come and pick you up," she said. "We will be ready."

That Sunday I enjoyed the service very much, even though it was held in English. It was very much the same order of worship as it was in Munich, only in English. We had found our church.

Soon Agnes was confirmed. She had taken her two years of instructions in Germany and since Pastor Miller spoke German he was able to confirm her in her native language. This really pleased her. We were happy and felt welcomed at that church.

During the Advent season, about six or eight of us women were sitting around an oblong table working with embossed cards. The cards had to be torn out of big square paper blocks. This was hard on our hands, and we also had to be careful not to tear the cards. These women, like myself, were immigrants from various countries. Someone asked if we would like to sing some Christmas songs.

"A good idea!" someone else said in her own language.

We sang first "Silent Night," then "O, Tannenbaum," each one in her own language. Behind us the huge printing and embossing machines seemed to be stamping in rhythm to our songs. I couldn't quite describe my inner feelings, but I felt moved. There was warmth and peace. I looked around and saw several women with tear-filled eyes. I thought of Christmas. This would be our first one in a foreign country and not in our own home. I did not want to become sad, and concentrated my thoughts on the cards I had in front of me. We worked together for a few days and every day we sang our songs.

William was able to come for Christmas. He told us, "I don't like my job. But it is better than the last one and it does pay more. The room I am renting is small, very small—cramped, but cheap." "Oh, Willie," I said, "Can't you find a better room?" "No, Erna; this is how I am able to save money every week. Daily I am reading the want ads and the business opportunities sections, hoping to find a better job in another city. I don't like New York." William looked very depressed. Onkel Frank said, "I will also be on the look-out for you, William. Cleveland is a large town and there are quite a number of good bakeries here." I knew William's main desire was to have a business of his own. We were both putting aside every dollar we possibly could. We spent a few quiet days together at Christmas time.

The months went by fast. It was April 1952. I was wondering how long this temporary situation was going to last. We could not stay much longer at Tante Ella's. We had been with them six months already. William was still searching for a better job. He wanted to leave New York. Finally, a ray of sunshine appeared on the horizon. He saw an ad in a New York German newspaper. A cafe in the French Quarter of New Orleans called "The Four Seasons" was looking for a German pastry chef. William answered the ad. The owner flew to New York to interview him. The offer was good and William started his new job two weeks later. We were excited and looking forward to moving to New Orleans.

The children and I stayed with Tante Ella until school was out, but William had rented a room for himself in New Orleans and started looking for a house. This was not easy. As soon as a landlord heard he had a teenage daughter and a six-year old son, he would not rent to him.

Konrad was going to stay in Cleveland. We were looking for a room for him. He had his job and still went to night school to further his education. I was proud of my diligent, hard-working son. Only nineteen, I thought, and so responsible.

Finally good news from William came. There was a family who leased their house during the three months of summer vacation. William wrote that the house was spacious and had a big screened back porch. The back yard would be shady for Hellmut to play in. The house was located in a good neighborhood in Metairie, a suburb of New Orleans. The owners did not mind children. We had a place to live for three months; this would give us time to look for something permanent. I was so happy when I read his letter. William seemed pleased too.

Here I was packing again. I counted the many times that I had moved in my life and came up with the figure forty, and that was not counting the times of traveling by boat and train. *Forty* times!!

Hellmut cried when we said goodby to Tante Ella. He did not want to leave her. She had been like a grandmother to him. And he could not understand why he could not take his sled along. Up until now in his life, there was snow in the winter. "Why is there no snow in New Orleans?" he asked. "It does snow there sometimes, but it is not cold enough and the snow melts away quickly," I had to explain to him. I took him by the hand as he looked longingly at the sled hanging on the garage wall.

I was also very fond of Tante Ella. We got along well, but I was looking forward to having my own household again. Tante Ella and Onkel Frank had both been very kind to us. I was sure it was not easy on them either, to put us up for so long. Eight months was a long time.

The day came for us to leave. We said goodbye and left family members behind. Once again we ventured into unfamiliar territory. We traveled by train to Chicago, changed trains, and continued on to New Orleans. William met us at the station. After so many months we were a family again, except for Konrad, who would not join us until Christmas.

1952 - New Orleans, Louisiana

Our rented house eventually proved comfortable but was in filthy condition when we moved in. Everything we needed was there: pots, pans, dishes, towels, and sheets. All we needed was food. Even though we would be there only three months, we were forced do a lot of cleaning. This required a good supply of "Spic n' Span," and ammonia. As it was vacation time, Agnes was at home and was a big help in getting the house cleaned. The biggest job was the kitchen. The floor was sticky, the windows were filthy, and the stove was covered with layers of stinking grease. Every dish and cooking utensil had to be scrubbed clean before we could use it. It took days to get the house cleaned.

William had quite a distance to travel from Metairie to the Four Seasons in the French Quarter. As neither of us drove, we did not own a car. He took a bus, transferred to a streetcar, and then took another bus. He usually left the house at about four o'clock in the morning.

After seeing a milkman delivering milk to my neighbor, I visited her and inquired about how I could get in touch with him. I introduced myself. I said, "I am Erna Scheel, your new neighbor. We will be living here for the next three months." She said, "I'm glad to meet you. I'm Mrs. Simmons." "I saw the milkman delivering milk to you this morning. I wonder how I could get in touch with him and have him deliver milk to me?" "No problem. I will tell him when he comes in the morning, Mrs. Scheel. He also has eggs, butter, cream, and other dairy products."

She invited me for a cup of coffee and we got to know one another a little better. She was a pleasant lady. She must have been in her early fifties. Her hair was greying. Her bright blue dress made her eyes look as blue as the blue in the cornflower. We chatted easily. She also was helpful to me in many other ways. For instance, she told me where the grocery store was, which bus to take, and in general, how to find my way around.

After that I went over whenever I needed advice. Sometimes we just visited across the fence. She told me that her husband worked at a bank.

When Sunday came around, I was thinking of going to church. I found the address of the Mount Olive Lutheran Church in Metairie in the newspaper. I had called the church office on Friday to inquire how to get to church and which bus to take. The secretary was friendly and helpful. I had no idea how far it was to the church, so we left the house early. Agnes, Hellmut, and I were waiting at the bus stop when a tall, elderly, grey-haired lady joined us. I asked her, "How far is it to the Mount Olive Lutheran Church?" "It is not too far. That is where I am going. I am a member of that church." "Oh, how fortunate!" I exclaimed. "We just moved here from Ohio." I was so happy to have found someone from that church. Her name was Mrs. Mott. When we arrived at the church, she introduced us to her friends and to Pastor Schack. He was a young man and had an outgoing personality. There were many young couples and children in the congregation. We felt accepted right away.

Mrs. Mott visited us the next day and came often ... more often that I would have liked. Her talkative manner got on my nerves.

William was somewhat satisfied with his job, but, of course, he still wanted to have his own business. Our marriage was on the upbeat. I was content. William was off one day a week. We would take the children to the Pontchartrain Beach, to the Audubon or City Park, or sometimes to a movie. I enjoyed being home and spending time with the children. In China I had so little time with them. I did not realize what the children and I had missed.

Daily I was searching in the newspapers in the *Houses for Rent* section. Our three months were almost up. William was searching for business opportunities. Finally we found a modestly furnished and clean house. The owner did not mind children. It was located in the city of New Orleans and was much more convenient for William to get to his place of work. Also, there were schools for the children close by. And ... it was too far for Mrs. Mott to come often.

My thoughts often went back to my dear friends in Germany. Micha and Louise were still writing. Also Mother, who lived in the Eastern zone of Germany, wrote often. She was not well. The lady for whom Mother had kept house for so many years was very good to her. They were like mother and daughter. But now Mother needed care. Because her employer was not well herself, she found a comfortable room for Mother in a home for the elderly. It had a good reputation. Around-the-clock doctors and nurses were on duty. Mother wrote that she enjoyed walking in the beautiful flower garden that surrounded the building. The food was good also. I was thankful that my mother was well taken care of.

During vacation time when the children were around, I did not suffer from homesickness. After they started school and I was alone all day, I often cried. I especially cried when letters came from my friends Micha and Louise, or from my brother, Walter.

One Sunday I went to church and we sang the hymn, "Fairest Lord Jesus," my favorite German hymn. I started to cry and could not stop. Homesickness really overcame me. It took me some time to calm down. I was so embarrassed, but I felt better when the singing was over and I heard the minister say the blessing.

One evening William came home and showed an ad in the newspaper to me. "Look at this, Erna, someone is advertising a bakery for sale. It is in a very good location, not far from here." After I read the ad, I said, "That really sounds like a good offer. Let us go after supper and look into it." I asked Agnes to do the dishes so that William and I could get to the bakery before it closed. We assumed they would close at seven o'clock. It was a short walk to the small shopping center. There was a Winn-Dixie grocery, a Wallgreen drug store, a ladies and gentlemen apparel store, a jewelry store, and a few other businesses. Right in the center was the bakery. It was still open, so we walked in. While I bought a few rolls, William looked the place over.

William asked the salesgirl, "Could I see the owner, please?" "He has gone home for the day." "Would you give me his telephone number?" She hesitated, but then William said, "I saw the ad in the paper and I am interested in buying the bakery." She gave him the number, William thanked her, and we left the store.

On our way home we were both quite excited. "What a clean little place it is and in a wonderful location," I said. "Yes. And Tulane University and Newcomb College are just a few blocks away. Many rich people live in that section of town," William replied. "Willie, did you notice how clean the showcases were and that the refrigerated one seemed in good condition?" I asked. "Yes, I saw that too. I'll call the owner when we get home." Agnes was quite enthused for us when we got home and told her. But , she was already thinking ahead. "Mutti ... then you will be in the store again, all day long and we will hardly see you!" "Oh Agi, you are a big girl now and you will be able to help after school. That will make it a little easier, don't you think so?" "Yes, I guess so," she said hesitantly. "We are thinking too far ahead already," I said. "But, Agi, we should be thankful for the seven years that we have had together." "Yes, Mutti, that is true."

While I had been talking with Agnes, William had spoken to the bakery owner on the phone. They made an appointment for the next evening. We were looking forward to that meeting. William was so eager to have his own business again. But, we wondered if we would be able to get a loan. We were immigrants, and new in the city.

The following evening we went to see Mr. and Mrs. Michaelson, the bakery owners. They were a sympathetic, middle-aged couple. We took to one another right away. Mr. Michaelson said, "We have had the bakery for a couple of years now, but neither my wife nor I are bakers and therefore it is difficult for us to run the bakery. We do not know the trade. That is why we want to sell before we have to close it."

We told them about our situation and our financial condition. They were eager to sell and made us a reasonable offer. William wanted to see the bakeshop. Mr. Michaelson said, "I'll be glad to show it to you," and he drove us over.

Behind the store, which we had seen, was the bakeshop and a three-bedroom house with a small yard. A narrow alley separated the store from the house and bakeshop. "This is just ideal," I thought.

William told Mr. Michaelson, "I am really interested. But I will have to try to get a loan. I will call you in a day or two."

We went home with mixed emotions. All we had in the bank was nine hundred dollars. And the only possession we had, of course, was a twenty-five-dollar, second-hand Singer sewing machine. William suggested to me, "Why don't you go to our neighbor, Mr. Simmons, who works for a bank? Perhaps he can advise us what would be best to do." It was too late to see Mr. Simmons that evening. I decided to go over the next evening when he came home from the bank.

I went to him and told him about our plans. I said, "Mr. Simmons, have you any advice for us? We do have nine hundred dollars in a savings account with the Whitney Bank. But we need to borrow one thousand dollars for a down payment." "Our bank would not give you a loan, I am sure," he said. "But since you have money with the Whitney Bank, I would go and see Mr. Monroe. He may be able to help you. There might just be a possibility of obtaining a loan there." His advice gave me some hope. I went home and told William. He felt good about it too.

I prayed several times during the night. I went to see Mr. Monroe the next day. I prayed in the streetcar on the way to the bank. I asked the Lord to give me the right words to say. I knew my English was not so fluent. I wanted to be convincing, wanted Mr. Monroe to believe my words, make him understand that William was an excellent pastry chef, that I was a good saleswoman. I wanted to let him know we had a prospering business for seventeen years in China. "Lord, just give me the right words," I prayed over and over.

After waiting about fifteen minutes at the bank, Mr. Monroe called me into his office. He was apparently a perfect gentleman. His brown hair was greying at the temples, it was combed back. His keen grey eyes looked straight into mine. But his friendly smile and soft tone of voice gave me courage and composure. After I introduced myself and told him why I had come, the words came easily and I was able to speak with authority. He smiled when I told him the only collateral we had was a Singer sewing machine worth twenty-five dollars. "But," I said, "Mr. Monroe, in the ten months we have been in the United States, we have saved nine hundred dollars which is deposited in your bank. The biggest assurance is that my husband is hard-working, honest, and an excellent pastry chef and baker. And I, Mr. Monroe, am an excellent businesswoman and salesperson myself."

"Is your husband employed now, Mrs. Scheel?" "At present, he is working for the Four Seasons Cafe. All we need, Sir, is one thousand dollars. I plan to work in the business, also."

Leaning back in his comfortable chair, he stroked his hand over his hair and looked at me a few seconds. It appeared to me as if he might be thinking, "Can I trust her?" Then, finally, he said, "I will let you have the money if you will not withdraw the nine hundred dollars in your savings account." I hesitated, then I answered, "We will surely try." "Bring your husband in tomorrow to sign the papers," he replied.

We shook hands and I left as if walking on clouds. In my heart I said, "Lord, thank you, with Your help I made it."

The children were home from school, eagerly awaiting my return. By the expression on my face, they knew that all went well. I called William at work to tell him the good news. All he said was, "Very good." He had a hard time expressing his emotions, but I knew he was delighted. Also, being at work, I knew he really could not say much.

Mr. Michaelson was glad to hear that the loan had been granted and that we would see him the next evening. He was honestly pleased for us and I guess he was glad to have found a buyer.

Again, this was going to be a new start in our life. I was happy and was hoping, too, that all would go well in our marriage now. It would be just William and me, no partnership. He would be working in the bakery and I in the store. It would be so convenient to have our living quarters behind the store. We could not move into the house for six months, though. It was still leased to another family. In the meantime, we rented an apartment on Dublin Street in the Carrollton area, just a few blocks from the store. Agnes finished out the year at her old school at Metairie High. Hellmut could walk to his school at our new location.

Everything at the bakery was in pretty good condition, except the store and bakery needed a coat of new paint and some cleaning. Mr. Michaelson introduced us to the salesmen and the various companies we would be dealing with. He was very helpful. We kept the bakers and sales personnel. William had to give notice to his boss, who was not pleased at all to lose his pastry chef after so short a time.

The New Orleans Bakery - "Quality First"

We named our bakery "Scheel's Quality Pastry Shop" and our motto, printed on our cake boxes was "Quality First." Store hours were long, Monday thru Friday, seven a.m. to eight p.m. Saturday we opened from six a.m. to eight p.m. and Sunday six a.m. to one p.m. and again from four p.m. to seven p.m. Those really were strenuous days.

It was not easy for William, nor for me, to train our personnel. I insisted that the girls treat the customers courteously, no sassiness. And the method of William's baking was different. His helpers had to be re-trained. He prepared most of the European specialties such as tarts, torten, pastries, and cookies, and the decorating of birthday, wedding, and special-occasion cakes. For these items William mostly used pure butter. Our customers really had to get used to these kinds of pastries. They were accustomed to the sugary icing, while ours was soft and smooth. One customer returned a birthday cake, complaining, "You are using oil in your icing." I was not able to convince her that it was butter. "The butter gets soft if not refrigerated," I tried to tell her, but she wanted her money back.

Our prices were higher too. Only our sweet rolls, doughnuts, breads, and ordinary coffee cakes were comparable to the prices of other bakeries. But it did not take long before the customers learned to appreciate our European pastries.

Agnes worked several hours after school and on peak hours on weekends. She also helped with cooking and household chores. She reminded me of myself when I was young, helping Father in the butchery.

Word spread fast that there was a good German bakery on Carrollton Avenue. Our clientele were mostly the "well-to-do." There was also a significant German population in New Orleans. Tulane University and Newcomb College were just a few blocks away. Many wealthy people lived in that area.

I believed because of our quality merchandise, our ambition and hard work, we made it again. But I also knew that this quick success was possible only in the Untied States. The country of unlimited opportunities.

The Christmas Rush

It was October of 1952, just one year after we had arrived in the United States. It was time to prepare for Christmas. Since this was our first Christmas in the States, we asked our customers to place their orders early so that we would have an idea how much to prepare.

We were so busy that I had to hire a maid for the house. Taking care of the store was a full-time job for me. Saturdays and Sundays were our best days. On Sunday, often over one hundred customers came in between the hours of six a.m. and one p.m. They had to take numbers so that every customer was served in turn.

Since Sundays were so hectic, I was not able to go to church every week. The children regularly attended the eight a.m. service. When I did go, I attended that service also. That allowed me to be back for the eleven o'clock rush.

William worked long hours. Sometimes, if the night baker did not show up, William was in the bakery at four a.m. to bake bread, rolls, sweet rolls and doughnuts. These items had to be in the store by seven a.m. when we opened. He worked very hard physically, especially because the bakers were not familiar with the German Christmas specialities. We had many recipes and each one was different. William had little sleep which made him nervous, irritable, and, consequently, our marriage suffered.

My days were long too. The last two weeks before Christmas I seldom went to bed before one or two a.m. There was just not enough time during the day to fill the orders. Gingerbread Hansel and Gretel houses had to be wrapped in cellophane. Also, chocolate Santas and marzipan figures needed wrapping. This took a lot of time.

The salesgirls took turns in staying late. Agnes also helped an hour or two after supper. The streetcars or busses ran less frequently at night, therefore we sent the salesgirls home by cab and also had them take a cab coming to work. This gave them a little extra time to rest.

Our girls were good workers. They showed interest and were polite to our customers. I was quite strict about this.

Being under a lot of pressure, I too became quite short-tempered. I could not tolerate William's fussing and angry words in front of our customers and the employees. He upset me so that tears came often. I endured the pressure and thought it would get better after the holidays when business slowed down. I prayed for strength to overcome this trial, just as I had received the necessary strength so many times in the past. "Surely, after all we have been through I can patiently endure this," I thought. "And I'm sure things will be better after the Christmas rush."

Our German Christmas Traditions Continue

During the Christmas season, I did my own shopping and cooking during the hours between one and three p.m. That was the quiet time at the store. To the family's and my dismay, we were going to use electric lights on our Christmas tree for the second time. Our German tradition was to light our tree with candles, but we could not find the necessary candle holders.

William and I had agreed to close at four p.m. on Christmas Eve, but there were late-comers, as always. Finally, after all orders had been picked up, we turned off the lights, closed the shop, and went home. It was nearly five o'clock. William finished up his chores at the bake shop and soon followed.

While dinner was cooking, Agnes and I dressed and set the table. Hellmut was ready for Santa and was waiting in his room reading comics. As William was getting ready for dinner, I stood in the kitchen putting on the last touches to our table. In the center of a white table cloth, I had placed a small doily from China which had a little pagoda embroidered in each corner. I placed matching napkins at the side of every plate. Some green fir twigs and two red candles made the table look festive. Melmac plates, stainless steel cutlery, and plain white glasses completed the table setting. No fine china, crystal or silver, but that did not matter. We were together and healthy. That was what was important to me.

My thoughts wandered back to our last Christmas dinner in China with our employees. Herr Wolf, our pastry chef, his wife, Olga, the salesgirls and the other European employees were with us in our restaurant dining room. About twenty-five people in all. The tables had been decked with linen, silver, crystal and bone china. Everybody was tired and glad that the rush was over and looking forward to a day of rest. After dinner each employee received a "stollen" (German Christmas cake) and their bonus. We ended the party by singing Christmas carols. When everybody had gone, we went upstairs to our apartment to celebrate our own Christmas Eve as usual.

Agnes' calling, "Mutti, Vati is almost ready!" brought me back to the present time. After our dinner the children and I took a cab to the airport to pick up Konrad, who flew in from Cleveland to spend Christmas with us. Unfortunately, the plane was delayed for three hours and I was worried that we would not be able to attend the eleven o'clock candlelight service.

But he arrived, finally. I was glad to see him. He looked well. He wore a grey suit and carried a brown lightweight suitcase and a cardboard box. "My son has matured," I thought, with a catch in my throat.

We did have time to go home. William had rested while we were at the airport. He was happy to see Konrad and was in a good mood for a change. After visiting for a while, William lit the electric bulbs on our tree. It was just not the same to us as with real candles, but we celebrated anyway. Konrad read the Christmas story. Then we sang one stanza of "Stille Nacht" and opened our gifts. We did not have much time to linger, because we wanted to go to church. The children and I left for church, but William stayed home.

I had not told Konrad that Agnes was to sing a solo, "Oh Holy Night." When he heard her voice, he whispered, "Is that Agi singing?"

I smiled and nodded. She had such a sweet and clear voice. I wished that William could have heard her. I knew that he would have enjoyed it.

William was fast asleep when we returned home. I let him sleep. He must have just been exhausted. The four of us sat around the coffee table, nibbled stollen and Christmas cookies. There was a lot to talk about too. I wanted to know more about Konrad's life. His letters had been short and they did not tell me much. I wanted to know how the elderly Jewish couple, from whom he was renting a room, was treating him. He said, "I really like the old couple. Mrs. Rosen keeps my room clean and often asks me to come and have supper with them. Mr. Rosen wants me to tell him about China and how it was in Germany after the war." "How long have they been in the States?" I wanted to know. "They were both born here, but their folks came from one of the Baltic countries."

All at once Hellmut blurted out, "Koni, what is in that box you brought?" "Well, I was going to show it to you in the morning." "Oh, no! Show us now!!" Hellmut pleaded. Agnes was pleading too, "What is it, Koni?"

"Okay, bring it here. Be careful." Konrad unpacked it slowly. A TV set. "It is one I repaired at the TV shop where I work. The boss let me have it for a good price." Our first television! Konrad turned it on and we watched awhile. After the excitement we decided to go to bed. It had gotten quite late.

Since Konrad had been born on my birthday, the twenty-sixth of December, it was my forty-third and his twentieth birthday. William made an especially pretty mocha butter cream cake for us. We all spent a happy day together. In fact, it was a peaceful day. Business was slow and the girls did not need me in the store.

Konrad had to return to Cleveland and left on New Year's Day.

"Success" - With A Price

Without any difficulties, we opened an account with Sears Roebuck in April 1953. I bought all new furniture, except for Hellmut's room. I found some nice pieces at a second-hand store for him. Our new home behind the bakery had six rooms and a utility room. It had a small, fenced-in back yard. We moved into the house in May 1953, our fourth move in just ten months.

Shortly after we occupied the house, Hellmut brought home a puppy. A cute little mixed breed, with brown eyes, light brown short fur and a wagging tail (complete with fleas!). Of course, we kept him. We named him "Flocky." We bought a dog house for him and he stayed in the yard most of the time. I was happy to have a pet again, and the children were also. And, oh yes, we had inherited a cat with the bakery. The two made friends very soon. Like in Mukden, the cat always ate first while the dog watched, then he ate his share. One day I was in the kitchen when I noticed the cat lying under the table gnawing on a bone, and Flocky lying close by, watching. When the cat was through, it flipped the bone to Flocky with its paw and mewed. I laughed as I thought, "He must have said in cat talk; 'Have it; I'm through'."

That same year Agnes attended Fortier High School. She was sorry to leave her friends at Metairie High, but she soon found a friend at Fortier. Her name was Joyce Savoy. They met each day at a nearby stop of the St. Charles Street car. After several blocks they got off and walked the rest of the way to school.

I enrolled Hellmut in the St. John's Lutheran School. Whenever possible, I went to the Parent Teacher Conferences and other activities that he was involved in. Joining the Cub Scouts and going to summer camp helped him to adjust and to learn English faster.

Every first Sunday of the month I attended afternoon German services at a Lutheran church. The pastor from the German Seaman's home in New Orleans officiated at these services and also served communion. Germans of different faiths came, also several Germans of Jewish faith attended. After church, coffee and cakes prepared by several ladies were served. A different group served each month. These gatherings, usually attended by sixty to eighty people, meant a great deal to us Germans. Sometimes a child of German decent was baptized or a couple was married. During the Advent season, the tables were always decorated with an Advent wreath, candles, and pine or fir twigs. We sang German Christmas songs. It was always a special treat when a German film was shown.

Through these meetings, and the business, I met a few German ladies. Before long we had a circle of four or five ladies. We met once a month. This was our German circle "Kränzchen." My turn had come to have the ladies over for coffee and cake. I didn't drink strong coffee, but most of them did, so I made it stronger than usual, but still not strong enough for one lady. After everybody had sipped some, I asked, "Is the coffee alright?" All but Hilde Seifert said, "Yes." "Hilde, you did not say anything," I said. "Well, Erna, I was taught not to lie," she answered. We all laughed. We remembered that incident every time someone served weak coffee.

The first year came to an end and we had paid off our loan in full. What a good feeling it was to know that we had made it once again. Little by little our business grew and we needed to purchase a larger rotating oven and a walk-in freezer. I asked Mr. Monroe for a new loan of $2,500. He granted it without hesitation.

It took me two years to persuade William to close shop at one o'clock p.m. on Sundays and not reopen at four o'clock as we had been doing. This would give us time to do things with Agnes and Hellmut. William finally agreed. The customers understood our reasons and adjusted to the new time.

Agnes, Hellmut, and I were looking forward to our free afternoons. Not William. He did not take time out. Oh, no. After we had our Sunday dinner, which I usually precooked, he carried the record player into the bakery. He worked alone and played his beloved Richard Wagner records, full volume. He appreciated good music, he had been exposed to it during his apprenticeship years in Leipzig and Dresden. He had heard world famous musicians and went to many concerts. At that time, through a friend, he had been able to get tickets at a reduced price and he went as often as his time had permitted.

While listening to his records, he made his fancy cakes. After working and enjoying his music for several hours, he went to bed. About eight p.m. he got up, ate a light snack with a glass of beer, and then watched TV a little while. That was his Sunday. Very seldom did he spend family time with us.

Our marriage suffered. We did not get along and we quarreled a lot. I was so upset and disappointed.

Business was doing very well and I thought things would straighten out. A new supermarket offered us a section of their store where we could sell our goods and encouraged us to move to larger premises, but we declined. I, especially, was against it. We were working long hours; to take on more would be wrong.

William had difficulty finding good bakers. They were not used to his way of baking and would not stay long. He was also so hard to please. Mr. Kleindienst, a German baker, came to work for us. He was young, willing, and eager to learn new ways. That young man really did his best to please William. I was so happy when he accepted the job and I hoped

William would get some relief and have time for his family. But it did not last long. Just a year or so. No one could take William's constant shouting and fussing, not even Mr. Kleindienst.

Neither William nor I were pleased when Agnes wanted to date. She was only sixteen and we thought too young to go out with boys. Most of her girl friends started dating when they were fourteen and even younger. She shed many tears. We finally gave in. She went out with other boys and girls and usually came home after a show.

We reluctantly allowed her to join a high school sorority, from which she resigned after a few months. She did not like the drinking and smoking that went on. We were relieved when she gave it up. William and I and the children had to learn the ways of this new country.

Hellmut was getting along well in school. He learned to speak English quite well. One day we were on the streetcar. He asked me, "Do not speak German with me in public. I want to be like the other kids." This really annoyed me and I thought of the time we were in New York with the Stingels. I had said this would not happen to me. I would speak German with my children! When I went home I placed signs in different parts of the house; "Sprich Deutsch" ("Speak German"). But I found it difficult to discipline myself and caught myself sliding more and more into English with Hellmut, but not with Agnes and William. All of us spoke German at home when we were together.

Fortier High was offering sewing classes during the summer months. Agnes came to me one day, just before school was letting out for the summer vacation, and asked, "Mutti, may I take sewing courses this summer? I would like to learn how to sew." "Of course, Agi, that is great. I think every girl should know how to sew. Sure, go ahead and sign up for the course."

She made several blouses and skirts for herself. She also made a bedspread for her room to match the curtains. She had a very pretty room and kept it neat.

Sometimes Agnes had a girlfriend or two spend the night. She also stayed at their homes occasionally. Again, this was new to us; allowing our child to sleep at other people's houses. She had adjusted well and liked New Orleans. Her friend, Joyce Savoy, came over often.

Agnes' boyfriend, Edward Kivett, who went to Tulane University, visited frequently on weekends. We called him "Ed." William and I liked the young man. He often watched William at his cake decorating, or he would just talk with him in the bakery.

Ed lived in Sun, Louisiana, across Lake Pontchartrain where his parents owned a big sand and gravel business, saw mill, and a brick factory. Agnes spent a day there now and then. Ed had two brothers and one sister. He was the oldest child.

Konrad wrote regularly. He was still living with the elderly couple, working during the day and attending night classes. He was industrious and eager to get ahead. In his letters he mentioned a girl he was dating. Her name was Mary. She was of Russian heritage. He seemed to see her often. A little later he gave her an engagement ring and asked for permission to marry her. We thought he was too young. He was only twenty, but in a few weeks he would be of age and could marry without our consent. To avoid bad feelings, we gave our permission.

We did not fly to Cleveland to attend the wedding. Our business was too new to be left with the help we had. And having just taken out the new loan of $2,500 we could not afford such extra expenses. Even though we tried to make these reasons clear to Konrad, he was upset and it became a sore spot in out relationship.

We soon realized how good it was that we had not assumed the additional expense. Unexpectedly, I had to have a hysterectomy and we did not have any medical insurance. My surgery would be a big expenditure. I knew that it would take us months to pay the doctor and hospital bills.

The accountant who came for a few hours every week to keep our books, finally persuaded William to take out health insurance for us. He also suggested that I should receive a small salary for my work in the business. I would be glad to have some money of my own. I began depositing my money in a savings account. My secret wish was to save for a trip to Germany.

After the operation, I was not able to go back to work for six weeks. This upset William tremendously. He seemed to think I stayed away that long purposely. One day while I was still recuperating, he came to the house and started an argument. He provoked me so as he held my arms and shook me. He had never touched me in anger before.

"Let go of me, you are hurting me!" I screamed. But, even though I was still weak, I freed myself and hit him on his chest with both my fists. Then I grew scared and ran toward the front door. William went for his revolver. I just wanted to get away from him. I heard Agnes shout, "Vati, don't! Leave Mutti alone!!!" I knew that she was afraid that he would hurt one of us. She went to call the police.

I did not leave the house after all. The whole scene was very embarrassing and troublesome to me. Not wanting any publicity, I met the police with calmness and said to the officer, "My daughter has acted impulsively in calling the police. There is no need for you to intervene." I watched as the police left reluctantly. William was nowhere around. Agnes and I hugged each other and cried. I went into my bedroom and kneeled down to pray. "What is happening to our marriage?" I asked myself. "William is getting worse. He is abusing me and I ... I hit him with my fists. William and I have

both come to a bad point. Lord, please help us and guide us."
Our episode was very upsetting to Agnes. She was afraid that
her father might injure one of us whenever his next outburst
of temper came.

Konrad and Mary drove down from Cleveland. Because
of our problems, they moved to New Orleans. It was so good
to have them near. I found out that Agnes had secretly written
to Konrad about William's and my fight. Mary greeted us
with a friendly smile and a warm embrace for each one.

I said, "Mary, welcome into our family." "I am happy to
meet all of you," she answered, her brown eyes sparkling.

I asked them to have the evening meal with us. William
was also pleased to see Konrad and his daughter-in-law. Mary
was sitting across from me in the living room. I realized that
she definitely had Slavic features. Brown wavy hair surrounded her face. She wore dark-rimmed spectacles, which,
I thought, gave her a stern look. We spent a pleasant evening
together.

Konrad and Mary chose an apartment which they liked.
They both soon found work. Konrad continued to further his
education. I was happy they had come to New Orleans. We
frequently spent time together.

In 1953, our dog, Flocky, and I made the front page of
the local newspaper:

HEADLINE
A SLENDER THIEF BURGLARIZED FOUR BUSINESSES

*A skinny persistent burglar invaded four stores
in the 600 and 700 block of Carrollton Avenue. He
squeezed through a small restroom window and
other tiny openings, but only got away with $65.
He was prevented from getting more by a stubborn
and alert watchdog and a light-sleeping floral shop
owner.*

The heroic dog was Hellmut's Flocky. A reporter insisted on taking a picture of Flocky and me as I was rewarding him with a "Quality" pastry. Hellmut was very proud of his dog.

That summer Konrad convinced William and me to take a badly needed vacation. We closed the store for ten days and spent some time in Biloxi, Mississippi. By closing the store, everybody could have a vacation. We rested a lot and enjoyed swimming and walking on the beach. We had a really peaceful and harmonious time. Away from the business we got along well. I returned to New Orleans full of good cheer. However, I had built up my hopes too soon. Our relationship deteriorated again. What a disappointment. "Will this never end?" I asked myself.

On top of our problems, grey clouds were appearing in Konrad's and Mary's marriage. Their problems were upsetting to me and did not help my relationship with Mary, which had been good up to then. I did not know how to handle all the stress. Of course, Konrad stayed away more often, which hurt me. Mary stopped coming to visit altogether. Their problems, together with ours, was almost too much for me to take.

I was very downhearted and discouraged because it was so difficult to live with William. Never a kind word, only cursing, fussing, shouting. I could not do anything to please him. He constantly belittled me and said more than once, "You just try and work for someone else; you would not earn the salt on your bread!" It was impossible to sit down with William and talk things over calmly. After a few minutes he would curse, rush out of the house, slamming the door behind him, and disappear into the bakery.

The children also suffered. It was not fair to them for William and me to live this way. After another troublesome day with William, I decided to leave for a few days. I spoke to Agnes about it. I said, "Agi, I have to get away for a few days. I need some time to be by myself and to think things over. Do you think you can manage?" "I'm sure Rose (our maid) can do the cooking and cleaning," Agnes said. "And I will take care of Hellmut. He listens well to me. But what shall I tell Vati when he asks?" "Simply tell him that Mutti will be back in a few days. I am sorry I have to do this secretly, but you know Vati would not let me go, and I just need some time to think." "I understand, Mutti."

I planned to stay at a nearby motel. I hoped that some quiet time would be good for my nerves and give me some time to think. After a few days away I came to no solution. I did not know what to do so I went back home.

On my return, William asked me, "Why did you leave? Where have you been!" I told him, "I needed some quiet time. I cannot stand the way our marriage is going." "So you just run off and leave me alone with the children and the business?" "It gave you an idea how it would be if I left you for good, didn't it, William?"

For a little while he calmed down, then it started all over again.

William and I had been married almost twenty-five years. I tried to understand him and get used to his rough ways, but, instead, I had become more sensitive. I was losing my self-confidence. I felt very insecure.

I had such need to share my problems with someone. Since I had no one, I decided to take my anguish to the Lord. I began keeping a diary. Often I ended with a prayer, asking the Lord for strength, help, and guidance in every situation. I started my writings on October 13, 1955. I was reading a book; *How To Stop Worrying and Start Living.* I honestly wanted to try to understand William. I often asked myself, "Why is he so degrading and why does he humiliate me so? I wish William would realize his treatment of me."

One day I wrote this prayer:

"Wie schwer ist oft das Herze mir,
In meiner Not komm' ich zu Dir, Herr,

312

Mein Gott erhöre mein Gebet
Und weise mir den rechten Weg.
Herr, meinen Glauben stärke mir,
Lass niemals mich zweifeln an Dir.
Behüt' und leite alle Lieben mein
Gläubig, Deine Kinder zu sein."

"My heart is often heavy,
In my grief I turn to you, Lord.
My God, hear my prayer,
And lead me the right way.
Lord, strengthen my faith.
Don't let me ever doubt you.
Protect and guide all my loved ones
To become your faithful children."

It did help to write events down as they occurred. Somehow, my writings enabled me to unburden my heart. I often thought about the different circumstances in our marriage. I knew that in our marriage it had been the little things that caused provocation. I could not think of anything better in life than a happy marriage. This I wanted, even then, for us after twenty-five years.

We had our twenty-fifth wedding anniversary on the third of October, 1955. William had not been feeling well. It had been a busy day and he had been extremely nervous. Agnes wanted it to be a special day. She wanted to see her parents happy. She arranged all the gifts tastefully on the coffee table. She gave us a Sunbeam percolator and a toaster. The employees gave us flowers and my German friends sent a white chrysanthemum plant. Anna Dvinarenko, our former cashier from Shanghai, who now lived in San Francisco, surprised us with a lovely stainless steel platter.

I had purchased a silver money clip for William which I had engraved. On a pretty Hallmark card, I wrote a poem for him:

313

*"Fünfundzwanzig Jahre sind vergangen seit
dem ereignisreichen Tag,
Als mit beschwingten Herzen wir uns Treue
schwuren bis in's Grab.
Wehmütig denk ich an die schwere Zeit ,
doch gab's auch Stunden der Heiterkeit.
Drei gesunde Kinder hat uns der Herr
geschenkt, die gemeinsam wir zum Guten gelenkt.
Viel hat uns das Leben umhergetrieben doch
haben wir uns nichtlassen unterkriegen."
USA ist gewiss unser letzter "stop" dies
beweist "Scheel's Quality Pastry Shop." Mit
Gesundheit, Glück and Gottes Segen, wollen wir
glückich noch die "50" erleben."*

*"Twenty-five years have passed since that event-
ful day when with a happy heart we promised
each other faithfulness to the grave.
With sadness I think of the difficult times but
there also were hours of happiness.
The Lord has given us three healthy children.
Together we led them on the right path. Life has
thrown us about a lot but we never went under.
U.S.A. is surely our last stop,
Scheel's Quality Pastry Shop is here to stay. With
health, luck, and the Lord's blessing the "50th"
year we shall meet with joy."*

In the afternoon William sent Agnes to buy a card for
me. And on the back of a piece of scrap paper he wrote; "
Good for a ring at Anthony's Jewelry Store not over $500." I
was so hurt and angry. I would rather have had a kiss. He
knew that I would never spend that much. I tore up the slip of
scrap paper. William made no comment about my gift or the
poem.

Konrad came over in the evening, but, no word from Mary. She had not visited for some time.

That night I prayed, like all the other nights, that the Lord would give me patience and strength. I really wanted our marriage to work and I wanted to show more love for William. But it was so hard to love someone who was always angry. "Oh, Lord, just help us both."

My daily writings helped me and I did find strength in prayer.

But I needed to speak to someone and hear an answer. I could not go on like that. I decided to call Pastor Schack from Mount Olive Lutheran Church. I made an appointment with him for the following day. I told William that I needed help. Of course, he was not pleased.

I spoke with the pastor for an hour. After seeing him a few times, I felt better. I was hoping that William would go also. Pastor Schack suggested that William join us in the counseling sessions and I wanted him to also. But he would not go.

The days came and went. The children's lives continued on.

Agnes graduated from high school and enrolled in nurses training at Mather's School of Nursing at Baptist Hospital. She came home only on her days off.

Konrad entered Tulane University and worked part time.

He wanted to be an electrical engineer. On his and Mary's second anniversary I bought several gifts and a meaningful card. I sent the gifts over with Hellmut.

Konrad came over the following Sunday. He seldom visited those days. We had coffee and cake and just spent a few hours together. I gave him a stamp album that I had started several years back. Since Konrad was born I had become interested in stamps and was collecting them with the thought they would be his one day. Our time of sharing brought us closer.

I saw Pastor Schack for a whole year. I also sought help and advice several times at a Family Service. They, like Pastor Schack, suggested that William should come. He went only once.

I could not battle my continual strife alone. I had begun taking tranquilizers and sleeping pills. I began to plan to go to Germany for six weeks. Such plans only made matters worse, however, so I gave up the thought.

The weeks came and went. I had come to a point where I did not know what to do any more. My emotions were so torn—always having a smiling face for the customers and tears at home. After school, Hellmut would stop by the store. One look at my eyes would tell him whether or not there had been trouble for his Mutti that day. My eyes could deceive others, but not the children. My life had become unbearable.

Finally, I made my decision. I would rent a small apartment for Hellmut and me, go to work in the mornings, and leave after supper. Twenty-four hours together was not good for William and me. Perhaps a separation would help. I wanted to try it for a few months.

When I told William what I had decided to do, his answer was, "No, I would rather have a divorce." "If that is what you want, that's what we will do," I replied. "I will train someone for the store." The training, I knew, would take a few weeks.

I went to see a lawyer to find out about the legal matters. I also found an apartment. It was being renovated and would be ready by the time I left.

1957 - The Separation and Divorce

But the end came sooner than I had expected. It was on a Saturday morning, May 14th, 1957. Konrad and Agnes both happened to be in the house. I had come over from the store to get a clean apron. After a few minutes William entered from the bakery. We got into a heated argument. The four of us were in the kitchen. William's remarks became so foul that I could not bear for the children to listen to him. "I'm leaving now — right now!" I screamed. William left the room. I went immediately to the phone and called my lawyer. "What must I do?" I asked, "I'm leaving William but I don't want to lose my children." I was always afraid something might happen to me as it had to my mother. "Don't worry, Mrs. Scheel," he answered, "You won't lose your children. You can leave now if you wish, but be here early Monday morning. There are things we need to discuss."

While I talked with my lawyer, William left through the back door. That was the last I saw of him for some while. I hurried to the bakery to tell the salesgirls that I was leaving. I met Ed on the way. When I returned Ed and Agnes helped me pack. Konrad did not want to take sides and left. We loaded Ed's car with a few things I had packed and went to the home of my friend, Hilde Seifert.

I took several items of crystal, my sterling silver dresser set, which William had given me, and my finer pieces of jewelry which I had brought from China. Some were gifts from William and others I had worked hard to obtain. I had brought these cherished items half way around the world and I would not give them up easily. I left behind everything else that I had helped to build up in twenty-six years of marriage.

Hilde's son, Volker, was in Washington at the time so Hellmut and I were able to stay in his room several days until my apartment was ready. We moved the following week. On the occasions when I returned to the house to pick up my personal belongings, William did not show himself. I never knew if he was in or out of the house. During the divorce proceedings, when William and I spoke on the telephone, he was always angry, especially if I asked for a piece of furniture or certain utensils which I needed for my partially furnished apartment.

It took me years to get over the hurt and agony of a divorce. For a year I was unable to sleep at night. I lost my appetite and found myself avoiding people. Although there were grocery stores nearby, I took the streetcar to the other side of town to do my shopping. I didn't want to meet my friends. When I met one of our customers they would inquire why I wasn't at the store. When I told them I was getting a divorce, they always looked shocked. They never suspected my marriage was so terribly troubled. Some of them confided that the business was becoming "run down." The showcases were not well stocked and the variety of baked goods was considerably less. The girls were unfriendly and few customers were seen coming and going. I suspected that business must be very poor when William was unable to continue his alimony payments.

I found work in a local bakery but as my experience was limited to sales, I was unable to direct the bakers and left there.

Konrad was hurt and upset by our separation and tried to persuade me to return to William. But I knew in my heart that I could no longer withstand his hot temper and obscene language. I recalled the time that William smashed a dining room chair because I had under-charged a customer twenty cents. I knew that after twenty-six years of marriage I had not adjusted to his fits of anger and probably never would. William and I crossed paths on several occasions but he always ignored me.

Soon afterwards I noticed an add in the newspaper. A fashionable department store, "Kreeger's," was looking for a sales person in their millinery department. I wore my best navy blue tailored suit, white silk scarf, navy shoes and white gloves. My interview lasted quite a while. I suspect the manager, Mr. Rosen, wished to talk with me to be certain my accent would not hinder my sales. Finally he smiled and said, "You are a lucky young woman. You came to my millinery

318

department applying for a job and did not wear a hat. But I am going to hire you anyway." I thanked him and reported for work the following day. I was told that all sales ladies were required to wear a hat to and from work.

One evening after I had returned from work, eaten dinner and washed the dishes I grabbed up the mop and began mopping the floor. I passed a mirror and caught sight of myself. There I stood in my apron, with mop in hand, wearing my fancy pillbox hat. I just stood their and laughed aloud.

I met a number of nice people while working at the shop and the manager and his wife were very good to me. When Kreeger's opened a second store in the Lake Side Shopping Center in a suburb of New Orleans I was put in charge of the millinery department. I did well and received a nice raise. I not only enjoyed what I was doing, but my work gave me a feeling of self-worth. I proved to myself, and to William, that I was able to "Earn the salt on my bread!!!" After my move to a larger but unfurnished duplex I was able to get Hellmut's bedroom furniture. Mr. Monroe from the Whitney Bank loaned me the money for living room and dining room furniture and a washing machine. He trusted me, and in time, I paid back every penny of the loan.

Hellmut and I looked forward to the weekends when Agnes was home. Ed usually drove in from across Lake Ponchartrain and we had good times together playing games and going on picnics. It wasn't long until the business closed down and William moved out of town. Our divorce became final July 8, 1959.

My job at the new store did have drawbacks. I had to take a streetcar, a bus, and another bus to and from work. This took almost an hour and a half each way. On Thursdays I worked until 9 p.m. I was often afraid while waiting for my bus at the corner where strange characters lingered in the dark.

A friend asked if I would be interested in working for a business machines company as an Accounts Payable/Payroll

319

Clerk with weekends off and no late hours. I explained that my only experience with bookkeeping was in our bakery but she insisted that I talk with the office manager, Mr. Gaudin. She said that they were desperate for a mature and reliable person. William's constant belittling had caused me to lose confidence in myself. Still, I knew I was mature and I was reliable and so I agreed. Mr. Gaudin hired me and Mr. Rosen was most understanding when I explained why I was leaving the millinery department. I gave him two weeks notice.

My new job was not easy. I cried often. Mr. Gaudin called me into his office one day. I thought to myself, "This is it!" But to my surprise, he asked me "Are you not happy here, Erna?" "That's not it," I answered, "I am so slow and I make mistakes." "Erna," he said, smiling, "You are doing just fine." "Mr. Gaudin, I will try it three more months. If I don't do better, I will give you notice." He patted me on the shoulder and said, "OK, Erna."

I did master the Accounts Payable and Payroll. After six months I received a raise and continued working there for several years.

On April 4, 1958 Ed and Agnes were married. Ed's mother, Evelyn, wanted a large wedding and offered to help with the expenses. Their family was long established in New Orleans and they had many friends whom they wished to invite. However, Ed and Agnes, as well as myself, preferred an informal wedding. They were married in the Gloria Dei Lutheran church nearby. William proudly escorted Agnes to the alter and presented her to Ed. I wrote a poem for the newlyweds following the wedding and gave it to them when they returned from their honeymoon in the Smokey Mountains.

My landlady offered her living and dining rooms for the reception. William made a three-tiered wedding cake iced with white chocolate and beautifully decorated. About seventy people attended the wedding reception. William and I exchanged only a few words throughout the day.

Ed and Agnes moved to Abita Springs, Louisiana, north of Lake Pontchartrain. Ed's father had died and Ed entered the family business even though he had not graduated from the University. Agnes worked at the state mental hospital in Mandeville, Louisiana as a nurse in the children's ward. In 1961 Ed returned to college at Louisiana State University in Baton Rouge. Agnes worked at Our Lady of the Lake Hospital as a registered nurse. We visited each other occasionally. In 1965 Ed graduated from LSU with a degree in Industrial Engineering and took a job with Union Carbide Corporation, and he and Agnes moved to Brownsville, Texas.

1964 - A Brief Vacation In Germany

In October of 1964 I made my first trip back to Germany since coming to the United States in 1951. My "Tante" Liete had asked me numerous times in her letters to visit her as she was getting up in years. I saved for months to finance my trip. It was cold and raining when I arrived in Frankfort that October morning. Still, it was a warm feeling to step foot on German soil once again.

Tante Liete met me at the airport in Hanover. She lived in one room on the fifth floor of an apartment building. She had asked that I bring some American cigarettes so I bought her a whole carton. Later when I unpacked my suitcase I handed her one pack, another pack, and another pack.... She said, "Erna, how many cigarettes did you bring?" "I bought you a carton" I answered. "A whole carton?" "Yes." "Erna," she said, laughing aloud, "I only smoke one cigarette on Sunday afternoon after having a cup of coffee and a piece of cake!" We hugged each other and laughed. I suspect she shared the bulk of her cigarettes with the postman, the newspaper lady, and her neighbors.

While in Germany I visited Herr Bader who had retired to Bavaria, also Hedi Spengler and a few other friends who had been repatriated. How nice to see old friends from China.

1964 To 1968 - The Healing Years

For the next four years I socialized very little with the exception of church, sunday school and a weekly get-together with the German ladies in our homes. Hellmut and his dog "Blackie," whom he acquired from my neighbor's litter, were my closest companions.

With the passing years, I was able to put the unpleasant times of my married life behind me and I felt no animosity toward William. I still felt sorry for him after our losses in Mukden, Nanking, Shanghai and even Germany. What a prosperous little bakery we had in New Orleans. Within two years we had paid off a $1,000 loan and a $2,500 loan and all other debts were paid when I left William. What a hard-working and honest man he was. It had been because of his temper and uncontrollable fits of anger that I was unable to continue living with him. Our wish had been to retire to Germany and live in peace. Every time I passed that building on Carrollton Avenue my heart ached.

One evening while coming from work I stopped to buy groceries. I had just received my two-week paycheck that day. As I neared my home with my groceries in my arms and my pocketbook hanging over my shoulder, I noticed that the lid on my garbage can was laying on the ground. When I bent down to replace the lid on the can, someone came from behind. He was a young black man of medium height. Suddenly he grabbed for my pocketbook, spinning me around sideways. As my shoulder struck the sidewalk, my groceries spilled out upon the ground. Fortunately my head fell upon the grass. I started screaming, but by the time I got to my feet he had disappeared around the corner with my purse. My neighbors called the police and came outdoors to help me. I suspected the young man had watched me cash my check in the grocery store and had followed me home. I never recovered my purse. Several days later William called. He said Hellmut had told him about my robbery and asked, "Erna, why did you not call me?" I could tell by the tone of William's voice that he was sincerely concerned.

During this period I became acquainted with a very nice man. He had traveled widely, visited Europe and was most interesting to talk to. We had dinner out several times and attended several plays. However, I soon discovered that he had a weakness for alcohol, so I ended the relationship. Sometime later friends of mine introduced me to a friend of theirs who was widowed. He was a quiet friendly person but he did not like outdoor activities which I enjoyed. We attended the Shakespearian play, "Hamlet" and had dinner in the French Quarter several times. Still, I felt that he would have preferred to stay at home. I sensed our relationship would never flourish as I was too fond of outdoor activities.

Later, when Hellmut went away to school in Austin, Texas I spent many an evening alone thinking about William, and the years we had spent together. I fought loneliness by going for long walks with Blackie. Keeping busy also helped ward off sad thoughts of the past. I listened to the opera or classical music on my radio which I moved from room to room or sometimes placed on a rock in the yard while I worked in my garden. Still, there were unguarded moments when the memory of certain events stormed my mind. Once I came upon a recipe for poppy seed cake in a book that I was reading and I suddenly recalled the Japanese advance on Manchuria and the loss of our bakery in Mukden. Our store had been full of William's handy work — shiny showcases of freshly baked bread, fancy chocolates, ornate birthday cakes, and the lingering aroma of sweetness haunted me. I would recall the happy faces of customers who so enjoyed our pastries. "Besonders gut" they would remark, meaning, "Especially good!"

One evening while I was preparing for bed, I heard a loud knocking at my neighbor's door. My neighbor was not at home and the knocking persisted. The continuous noise reminded me so much of that terrible night in Nanking when a messenger from the German Embassy pounded on our door. I recalled how William had raced downstairs and I followed him. The messenger had handed William a letter.

"What is it, William? What is it?" I remembered calling out. William's face was so vivid in my mind. I pictured him clearly as he read the message — "Be on the pier by 6:00 a.m. tomorrow morning. Bring only personal belongings. The Japanese have announced a major attack on the city and all foreigners must depart immediately." I recalled that night so vividly — how William and I had stood speechless looking at each other. We joined thousands of others of all nationalities the following morning and boarded the boat. I recalled our storefront window with the large gold letters that read, "KIESSLING & BADER." I could picture in my mind the shattered glass and the charred showcases. Herr Zaudig had later informed us that the floor of our apartment had collapsed and our collection of rare books, art and china had crashed to the ground and were totally destroyed. I thought of William and started to weep. In order to drive those distressing images from my mind, I grabbed Blackie's leash and the two of us went for a walk around the block.

1968 - Brownsville Texas

In 1968 I moved to Brownsville, Texas. After living for six months with Agnes and Ed I took a job with an Electrical Supply Company. I found a very comfortable two-bedroom house with a front and back yard. Since the house needed painting and some repair, the landlord agreed to reduce my rent payment if I would make the repairs and do the painting myself. Just after we had painted the rooms and made all the necessary repairs to the house, my landlord informed me that he had a buyer for the house. What a bitter surprise. Once again I was looking for a place to live. After several months I rented a cozy garage apartment within walking distance of

Agnes' house. My apartment stood in an orchard and my landlady, Mrs. Cromac, brought me a basket of fresh fruit every week — oranges, grapefruit, bananas and lemons. Agnes' children, Heidi and Edward visited me often. We enjoyed picnic lunches and dinners in the orchard. Sometimes they stayed overnight with me. I enjoyed walking and gathering shells on the beach with my family.

While I was living in Brownsville, William visited Agnes for a week or ten days. Heidi wanted me to come over and see her grandfather. I was not sure I could face him. "Give me a little time, Heidi," I said to her after she repeatedly tried to take me to her house.

One evening after I came home from work, I took courage and went over. Agnes, her family, and William were in the garden. William was petting the dog and had his back turned toward me. Ed saw me coming and came and took me by the hand. He knew I needed support. William turned and looked up at me. I went to him and extended my hand and said, "I came to say hello to an old friend from China." We shook hands. The ice was broken. After that we talked, mostly about our current lives. That was the last time that I saw William. I was grateful that we had parted in peace.

Several years later, Ed, Agnes, and their son, Edward visited William. He had remarried and was living in New York City at the time. They had two children, Billy and Carmella. They found William in poor health and he and his wife, Gail, were living in very unhealthy conditions. During their visit, William accepted Jesus as Lord. About one year later the Lord took him home. Agnes continued for some years to stay in touch with William's wife and her daughter Carmella.

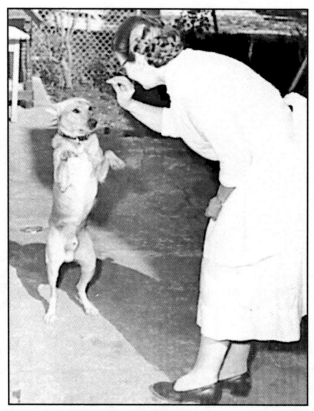

Erna rewarding "Flocky" for scaring away a burglar in
New Orleans, Louisiana. 1953.

William and Erna Scheel in Mukden, China two years after their marriage. 1932.

CHAPTER THIRTEEN
The Joyful Years

During the next fourteen years I lived with Agnes and her family and settled into the friendly little town of St. Albans which is less than ten miles from West Virginia's capitol, which is Charleston. Union Carbide had promoted and transferred Ed to West Virginia in 1973. I helped Agnes with household chores, gardening, and shopping which I enjoyed. I had a cozy room with a private bath and in time made many new friends.

In 1984 I visited my nieces, Margit and Sigrit in Germany. This was the year when the three-hundred and fifty year anniversary of the famous Oberammergau Passion play (1634-1984) was being held. This play is performed every ten years. In the year 1633 when Oberammergau was in the grip of the black plague, the inhabitants took an oath that they would stage a performance of the bitter suffering of Jesus Christ every ten years. For the first time, in 1634, the inhabitants of Oberammergau fulfilled their oath, thus the village in the Ammer-valley celebrated in 1984 the three-hundred and fifty year anniversary of its "Passion Play," and I was there.

When I arrived the little town was packed with thousands of people coming from all over the world to see this famous play. I had reserved a room with a family there a year in advance. The play started around 10:00 a.m. We had a lunch break at noon and were given time to tour the village. There was a specialty store which displayed beautiful hand-carved figures of Jesus, Mary, and the disciples ranging from three inches in height to six feet. I purchased a wooden angel, which was featured playing the violin, for my daughter Agnes. The play resumed at 2:00 p.m. and ended at 5:00 p.m. As I left the theater I could not shake from my mind the image of Christ hanging on the cross. It was so real and the man playing the part of Jesus gave such a heart-wrenching performance. I rushed to my room, picked up my suitcase, and hurried toward the bus stop. In one hand I carried my suitcase and in the other hand my open umbrella. The rain continued and I skipped about dodging puddles in the street. Suddenly a car stopped beside me. A young man rolled down his window and asked, "Can I give you a ride?" I answered that I was on my way to catch a bus to Munich. He opened the door and replied, "I'm going that way. Could I give you a lift?"

At that moment, Agnes' words, "Don't take rides from strangers!" popped into my mind. But as I looked into the stranger's kind eyes and observed the neatness of his clothes I felt he was trustworthy and accepted his offer. The streets were flooded with thousands of people going in all directions and the intersections were jammed with traffic. The young man asked me where I was from and volunteered that he was studying to be a dentist. As we paused at a red light, I turned and looked directly at him. To my astonishment, the man seated beside me had played the part of Jesus in the Passion Play. Spontaneously I grasped his shoulder and cried, "Oh, you are Jesus!" He smiled and said, "Yes!" It suddenly occurred to me that I had seen him on television in St. Albans on an advertisement of the up-coming Passion Play at Oberammergau. We made it just in time for me to catch my bus. We shook hands and wished each other "Auf Wiedersehen!" As I rode along on the bus, recounting my encounter with this young man I regarded our meeting as an absolute blessing from God. After I later related this experience to a journalist, my story appeared in the local newspaper in Charleston.

In October of 1985 my good friend, Betty Girdler, who now lived in California, wrote and asked if I would like to accompany her on a three week group trip to China. I did not have to think twice about making the trip. Betty and I had been best friends when she lived in St. Albans. We got along wonderfully, had many of the same interests, and attended the same church. It had been a few years since we had seen each other. Betty met my plane in Los Angeles and for the next twenty-four hours we talked about old times and prepared for the long journey that lay ahead of us.

The most common way to enter the People's Republic of China was via Hong Kong. It was the British Crown Colony and it was a tax free port. Hong Kong was the bargain hunters paradise. I cannot describe my feelings when our plane touched down there. Thirty-eight years had passed since I was last there on the troop transporter, General Black, as a poor refugee. This was my fourth trip to Hong Kong, but how different it was to be there of my own free will. And yet, my heart became heavy as I remembered the visits of the past and I wanted to cry. The bus was waiting to take us to the New World Hotel where we joined the rest of our group, consisting of thirteen women and one man, along with our group leader, Mrs. Cheng. Following two days of sight-seeing and some shopping we went by train to Gungzhou where we saw the Sun Yat Sen Memorial Hall that was built in 1931 and seats 5,000 people. Sun Yat Sen was the founder of the Chinese Republic.

The next day we flew to Beijing, the capitol of China which means "Northern City." We visited the Summer Palace which was so named because this is where the Imperial family spent their summers.

Next we visited the Forbidden City or the "Imperial Palace" so called because no commoner or foreigner could enter without special permission. This palace is China's most imposing architectural masterpiece. It is comparable to the pyramids and the great wall. The entire complex includes six main palaces and many small palaces and houses. They contain 9,000 rooms.

We visited Tian'anmen Square (Gate of Heavenly Peace.) This is the largest public square in the world.

Although Beijing was only a three hour train trip from Tientsin, I had never been there during my stay in China. I would have loved visiting my birth city, Tientsin, but to do so, I would have to sacrifice my walk on the Great Wall which I had never seen.

After visiting the famous Ming Tombs we traveled to Xi'an, once the largest city in the world and the capitol of eleven dynasties. Only in recent years has it become famous to the outside world. In 1974 the Terra Cotta Warriors were discovered by a peasant digging a well. More than 8,000 life-size figures were eventually unearthed. These were crafted in the third century B.C., and seeing them was a breathtaking experience.

While touring Nanking we passed the hospital where Agnes was born. It was completely modernized. I recalled the small Chinese lady doctor who delivered my little Agnes. I also remembered Agnes having jaundice and brown hair at birth. She looked like a little Chinese baby. Amongst the forty Chinese newborns in the nursery she was the only European infant. The Chinese mothers were disappointed to see a foreign baby looking so much like their own. Of course when Agnes opened her blue eyes her difference was obvious.

Our next stop was Shanghai where I had my most heart warming experience. I located our small shop opposite the Race Course (now called Folks Park.) Mrs. Cheng went with me as my Chinese was not all that good anymore. Our old bakery shop had been enlarged and did not look the way we had left it. A short friendly man approached us and recognized me. When he welcomed us in Chinese my eyes filled with tears. His name was Liang and he was just fifteen years old when we left in 1947. His brother, Wang, was our No. 1 cake baker. Wang had retired a year earlier and Liang planned to retire the next year. He asked about Konrad and Agnes. He did not know about Hellmut. He also asked about William. "Is he still filled with hot air?" (meaning "hot tempered").

Liang served us ice cream and I bought some coffee cake for our group for breakfast. I was glad Mrs. Cheng came with me. Even as I write these lines tears fill my eyes. China was my home for so many years. We had hard times there but also many good years. I left the bakery that day with mixed feelings. It was in Shanghai that we started again for the third time and had our greatest success in business. Also, Hellmut was born there. Shanghai represented the "yin yang" of our lives.

After Shanghai we returned to Hong Kong and boarded the plane for the United States. I stayed with Betty for a week. During this time we had our film developed. There were many occasions where I had taken pictures and she didn't and vice versa. As we later viewed our photographs and slides it was as if we were reliving the whole journey over again. This was a most memorable trip. After I returned home I organized two slide presentations — first, a smaller one, lasting approximately twenty minutes, which I presented several times to school children, and a larger one which I presented to various church and civic groups. My presentations were well received by both audiences. I would later read excerpts of my budding autobiography to many of these same groups. Always I received great encouragement.

A year or two before going on my trip to Germany I had started to write about my life. This is how it came about. Agnes, Hellmut, Ed and I were sitting together looking at my old photo album from China dating back to 1904. As we looked at the pictures I related the different happenings. I had heard a lot from my father. They were spellbound. Agnes suddenly said, "Mutti, why have you never written all these things down. It is not only interesting to us, your children, but also your grandchildren. Our family needs to know this."

"You're right!" Hellmut and Ed agreed.

So this is how I started. I tried to write as often as I could. One afternoon as I was writing my dear friend, Sannah

Jensen came to visit. We had a cup of coffee and some coffee cake I had baked that morning.

"What are your writing, Erna?" she asked.

I handed her a few pages. "Erna," she said, "you should write a book. This is most interesting."

"I don't think my writing is good enough, Sannah," I replied, "but I'll try."

A few weeks later I met Joan McAteer at a Monday night prayer and praise service. Somehow we got to talking about writing and I shared how I was attempting to write the story of my life. She said, "Erna, this is exciting." She explained that she belonged to the St. Albans Writer's Group which met the second and fourth Monday at the library. She urged me to come with her and bring what I had written. Well, that's how it all started.

My golden years are filled with many interests. In 1987 I moved to an apartment building for the elderly in St. Albans. I had a nice one bedroom apartment facing south on the eleventh floor. I made many friends and became involved in church, bible study, ladies circle, and extension homemakers. I also led an exercise class three times a week. While living in St. Albans I continued my monthly writers' meetings and once a week I joined with my friends, Jo, Louise and Pearl to play Mah-Jong or Crazy Canasta. We called ourselves the "Four Leaf Clover" and on the wall of each of our apartments hung a four leaf clover made of brass. I loved my cozy apartment. I had many friends and the Lord blessed me with good health.

On the thirtieth of December, 1989 I had the surprise of my life. My birthday is December 26 but long in advance, Agnes began asking for addresses and phone numbers of some of my old and new friends. I suspected something was up. Maybe they were planning a little party for me. But never did I dream that an event such as happened was in the works. When I stepped through the door of the "Chilton House," a fine local restaurant, I was swamped by greetings and hugs from a hoard of friends as soft music played in the background. The hall was richly decorated with Christmas trimmings and the aroma of fresh pine filled the air. Long tables of finger food, petit fours, and fresh baked bread and rolls lined one wall along with freshly brewed coffee and fruit punch. On a special table was placed a huge, decorated birthday cake with the word "Eighty" written in script. Hellmut assisted me in blowing out the candles. Off to the side Agnes had prepared a table featuring photographs of my early life in China, along with an old photo album of my family in Germany. This display attracted many of my friends.

My family had secretly plotted this event weeks in advance and prepared a carefully written script. The stage was set and a special chair was reserved for me. Ed served as master of ceremonies as each member of my family related some personal experience we had shared together. Some were comical. Some sad. All of them touched my heart. Many of the incidents I had long forgotten but shortly after they began telling their stories, the memory of those particular incidents brought tears to my eyes. A friend, Tom Griffith video-taped the occasion, as well as Bob McAteer who professionally edited and titled the film "Erna" and presented the tape to me later.

Another surprise awaited me. Near the door was a table piled high with beautifully wrapped gifts. And Agnes further surprised me with a beautiful photograph album filled with birthday cards and letters. On the outside of the album was an inscribed brass plaque marking this occasion. What a beautiful day this was! It was the most memorable day of my life and my Agnes and my family and friends will never know how grateful I was.

I would like to include in my book a tribute, with a thankful heart, to the United States of America, a country in which this family has achieved much.

Epilogue

In 1951 I set foot on American soil with three children and $5 in my pocket. William entered this country several weeks earlier with not much more money than I had. Within a year we had saved $900 and bought an old Singer sewing machine worth $25. That was all I owned when I went to see Mr. Monroe of the Whitney Bank to borrow $1,000, and yet I got it! One month later we had Scheel's Quality Pastry Shop. "Quality not quantity" was our motto. This was only possible in the United States — a great country with a big heart.

My children, Konrad, Agnes and Hellmut are all doing well. Konrad has a Ph.D. in Physiology and was with the University of Texas Health Science Center in Fort Worth, Texas. His oldest daughter, Monica, is a medical doctor and Erica, his youngest, is a successful physical therapist.

Agnes is a registered nurse. Her husband Ed was an Organizational Change Internal Consultant with Union Carbide Corp. They have retired to Long Beach, N.C. where they built a beautiful house. Their daughter, Heidi Miller worked for several years as an elementary school teacher and then married and raised her three children, Jordan, Ethan and Hannah in Teay's Valley, West Virginia. Agnes and Ed's son, Edward earned his Masters degree in Business Administration. He was a Marketing Manager with Sarah Lee in Winston Salem, N.C. at the time of publication.

Hellmut lives in Crofton, Maryland with his wife, Ceferina. He has degrees in Chemical Engineering and Systems Engineering. He became a Principal with a large technical and management consulting firm. His son, Christian, has a Masters Degree in Instructional Systems Design and worked for AT&T. His other son, Brian, has a degree in Finance and worked in Software Sales.

My children all worked for their education as we were not financially able to help them. I am proud of them.

In 1995 I moved to Southport, North Carolina, not far from Ed's and Agnes' home in Long Beach. In 1997 I was still healthy, except for failing eyesight, and at age eighty-seven I led an exercise class for senior citizens of about thirty people. I enjoy the Carolina coast and hopefully this will be the end of moving to new living locations for me.

The United States is a country of great opportunity. God bless America! Yet, even in the United States, the willingness to work with all of our strength and dedication did not assure my family's happiness and success. I am convinced that only the grace of God gave me the strength to survive in my life's most difficult trials.

From the book of James:

"Consider it pure joy, my brothers, whenever you face trials of many kinds, because you know that the testing of your faith develops perseverance. Perseverance must finish its work so that you may be mature and complete, not lacking anything. James 1: 2-4"

I finish my story at the age of eighty-seven, certainly mature in age at least. I also consider myself complete and lacking nothing of real significance. Indeed, with God's help, I had the strength to persevere during the difficult times. I now have pure joy. For this I will be eternally grateful. Writing this book has been like living my life all over again. I've enjoyed the rewards of a broader view of life and gained a better understanding of people in need. I know today that my hardships have contributed to making me a stronger person.

Acknowledgments

I could never have accomplished such a task without the help and encouragement of the St. Albans, West Virginia Writer's Group who listened and critiqued my work. Hazel Lincoln, a member of the group typed and edited my writing. As we turned out the pages, Hazel laughed and cried with me through the ups and downs of my life. The Writer's Group encouraged me to continue to add descriptive detail to the narrative to make the story more readable. Joan McAteer decided to help me and for over six months met with me weekly. She interviewed me extensively and caused me to remember countless details which she then added to the manuscript on her computer. The selfless gift of her time improved the script to the extent that I was starting to believe that the book would actually be published some day. Of course my children also encouraged me. When I was disheartened they urged me on. More than once after I had written about the "down" times of my life I dreamed of those experiences that night and woke up screaming. Ed and Agnes raced downstairs to see what was the matter. "Mutti!" they cried, "What's wrong? We heard you scream. Why are you crying?"

I explained I had been dreaming about the Japanese bombing Nanking and said, "I'm sorry I woke you."

"We understand, Mutti," said Agnes. Agnes sat with me for a while.

These nightmares occurred several times during my writing.

The more I wrote the more I remembered and added to my first draft. Through the critiquing of the whole Writer's Group I was urged to bring in more details concerning people and places. Also to add more dialogue. Gil Brooks and John Souter were especially encouraging and helpful in this endeavor. Tom Moore, an author, provided research on China and advised me on writing a more descriptive narrative. I was surprised that during the writing process certain events came alive in my memory. Once while writing I could hear the shrill sound of sirens, the roar of approaching bombers, people screaming and bombs exploding. These memories often lingered for some time. Once I became so unnerved I called my neighbor and asked if she would come and have a cup of coffee with me. I needed to talk. Finally the stress caused me to set aside the work for a number of years.

In 1996 after I had moved to Southport, North Carolina my son-in-law, Ed Kivett, Jr., decided to help me to revive the goal of publishing my book. Ed, who was then retired, spent about a year working with me to rewrite parts of the book, embellishing details and rearranging some of the material. By 1998 the material was ready to be published. Many attempts to find a publisher in the past had been unsuccessful but we "persevered" and completed the task. Without Ed's support I would not have continued. I am indebted to him.

I also thank Mr. Wolfgang Furstenau of Long Beach, North Carolina, for his detailed review and helpful comments.

The expert computer graphics work and text input by Mr. Chris Howard of Innovative Ideas in Southport, North Carolina greatly enhanced the quality of this book.